P9-CEG-046

My
MacBook®

Lion Edition

John Ray

800 East 96th Street,
Indianapolis, Indiana 46240 USA

My MacBook® (Lion Edition)

Copyright © 2012 by Pearson Education

All rights reserved. No part of this book shall be reproduced, stored in a retrieval system, or transmitted by any means, electronic, mechanical, photocopying, recording, or otherwise, without written permission from the publisher. No patent liability is assumed with respect to the use of the information contained herein. Although every precaution has been taken in the preparation of this book, the publisher and author assume no responsibility for errors or omissions. Nor is any liability assumed for damages resulting from the use of the information contained herein.

ISBN-13: 978-0-7897-4832-4

ISBN-10: 0-7897-4832-0

Library of Congress Cataloging-in-Publication data is on file.

First Printing: September 2011

Trademarks

All terms mentioned in this book that are known to be trademarks or service marks have been appropriately capitalized. Que Publishing cannot attest to the accuracy of this information. Use of a term in this book should not be regarded as affecting the validity of any trademark or service mark.

Warning and Disclaimer

Every effort has been made to make this book as complete and as accurate as possible, but no warranty or fitness is implied. The information provided is on an "as is" basis. The author and the publisher shall have neither liability nor responsibility to any person or entity with respect to any loss or damages arising from the information contained in this book.

Bulk Sales

Que Publishing offers excellent discounts on this book when ordered in quantity for bulk purchases or special sales. For more information, please contact

U.S. Corporate and Government Sales
1-800-382-3419
corpsales@pearsontechgroup.com

For sales outside of the U.S., please contact

International Sales
international@pearson.com

EDITOR-IN-CHIEF
Greg Wiegand

ACQUISITIONS/
DEVELOPMENT EDITOR
Laura Norman

MANAGING EDITOR
Kristy Hart

PROJECT EDITOR
Anne Goebel

SENIOR INDEXER
Cheryl Lenser

PROOFREADER
Kathy Ruiz

TECHNICAL EDITOR
Paul Sihvonen-Binder

PUBLISHING
COORDINATOR
Cindy Teeters

BOOK DESIGNER
Anne Jones

COMPOSITOR
Nonie Ratcliff

Contents at a Glance

Table of Contents

About the Author

John Ray is a life-long fan of Apple's products; he has been an avid Mac user since its inception in 1984. He relies on Mac OS X both at work and at home because it is a robust, flexible platform for programming, networking, and design. Over the past 14 years, John has written books on Mac OS X, iPhone development, Adobe Creative Suite, Linux, networking, and computer security. He currently manages the application development team in the Office of Sponsored Programs at The Ohio State University. He lives with his long-time girlfriend, their dogs, a collection of vintage arcade games, and an assortment of tech toys.

Dedication

Over the years, I've dedicated books to family, pets, readers, favorite colors, seasonings, and even words. All of these are still important to me, and worthy of dedications, but so is cheese. Therefore, this book is dedicated to pepperjack cheese. You are yummy.

Acknowledgments

Many thanks to the group at Que Publishing—Laura Norman and Paul Sihvonen-Binder—for understanding the difficulties of working with beta operating systems and keeping things on track. Special thanks to Nonie Ratcliff for working with hundreds of images and turning them into a layout that works with the text.

Thanks go to my friends and family for dusting me off occasionally while I typed and took screenshots. I promise to shower soon.

We Want to Hear from You!

As the reader of this book, *you* are our most important critic and commentator. We value your opinion and want to know what we're doing right, what we could do better, what areas you'd like to see us publish in, and any other words of wisdom you're willing to pass our way.

As an associate publisher for Que Publishing, I welcome your comments. You can email or write me directly to let me know what you did or didn't like about this book—as well as what we can do to make our books better.

Please note that I cannot help you with technical problems related to the topic of this book. We do have a User Services group, however, where I will forward specific technical questions related to the book.

When you write, please be sure to include this book's title and author as well as your name, email address, and phone number. I will carefully review your comments and share them with the author and editors who worked on the book.

Email: feedback@quepublishing.com

Mail: Greg Wiegand
            Editor-in-Chief
            Que Publishing
            800 East 96th Street
            Indianapolis, IN 46240 USA

Reader Services

Visit our website and register this book at informit.com/register for convenient access to any updates, downloads, or errata that might be available for this book.

Prologue

This book explains how to use and configure your MacBook and Lion to create your ideal working environment. Even though you're working with the most intuitive hardware and software platform available, there are still tips and tricks to discover.

Let's take a few minutes to review the hardware capabilities of your system and the prerequisites necessary to successfully use this book.

Getting to Know the MacBook Hardware

There are currently three different models of the MacBook available— MacBook Pro, MacBook Air, and MacBook. Each model includes a wide array of ports and plugs for connecting to other computers, handheld devices, and peripherals such as printers and external displays. I refer to these hardware options by name throughout the book, so it's a good idea to familiarize yourself with them now.

- **Ethernet**—Ethernet provides high-speed wired network connections. Ethernet offers greater speeds and reliability than wireless service. Your MacBook supports a very fast version of Ethernet—Gigabit Ethernet—that makes it a first-class citizen on any home or corporate network.

- **FireWire 800**—FireWire 800 is a fast peripheral connection standard that is frequently used to connect external storage and video devices.

- **Mini DisplayPort**—The DisplayPort enables you to connect external monitors to your MacBook. Although few monitors support the DisplayPort standard, from Apple you can get adapters for connecting to both VGA and DVI interface standards.

- **Thunderbolt**—The highest speed interconnect available on a personal computer, Thunderbolt allows monitors, storage units, and other devices to be daisy-chained together.

- **USB 2.0**—Universal Serial Bus is a popular peripheral connection standard for everything from mice to scanners to hard drives.

- **SD Card Slot**—SD (Secure Digital) RAM cards are a popular flash RAM format used in many digital cameras. Using the built-in SD RAM slot, you can create a bootable system "disk" that can be used to start your computer in an emergency.

- **Audio In**—A connection for an external microphone.

- **Audio Out**—An output for headphones, speakers, or a home theater/amplifier system.

- **802.11n**—The fastest standard currently available for consumer wireless network connections. Your MacBook's wireless hardware can connect to any standards-based wireless access point for fast, long-range Internet access.

- **Bluetooth**—Bluetooth is used for connecting peripheral devices wirelessly to your Mac. Unlike 802.11n, Bluetooth has a more limited range, but it is easier to configure and doesn't require a specialized base station to use.

- **SuperDrive**—An optical drive that can be used to write CDs and DVDs.

- **Express Card**—An expansion card for portable computers, 17" MacBook Pros can take advantage of this flexible standard.

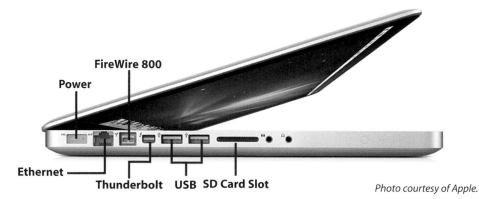

Photo courtesy of Apple.

So, what does your computer have? Apple's MacBook lineup changes throughout the year, so your features will depend on the model and the date it was made. Be sure to consult your owner's manual for a definitive description of what is included in your system.

The Built-In Battery

Looking for a way to remove your battery? Apple eliminated user-serviceable batteries from the MacBook line. This means that you now get a higher-capacity battery with a longer run-time, but, in the event of a failure, you can't replace it yourself.

To replace the battery, you need to visit your local Apple store or registered service center. The battery can be replaced in the store, while you wait, for approximately $130.

Special Keyboard Keys

Take a look across the top of your keyboard. Notice that even though there are "F" (function) designations on the keys, there are also little icons. The keys marked with icons provide system-wide control over important Lion features.

- **F1, F2**—Dim and brighten the display, respectively
- **F3**—Starts Exposé and displays all application windows
- **F4**—Opens the Snow Leopard Dashboard
- **F7, F8, F9**—Rewind, Play, and Fast Forward during media playback
- **F10, F11, F12**—Mute, Decrease, and Increase Volume

The Eject key is located in the farthest-right corner of the keyboard and is used to eject any media in your MacBook's SuperDrive.

Accessing the Function Keys

If you are using an application that requires you to press a Function key, hold down the Fn button in the lower-left corner of the keyboard and then push the required function key.

What You Need to Know

If you're holding this book in your hand, you can see that it contains a few hundred pages packed with information about using your MacBook with Lion. You might also notice books dedicated to the same topic and sitting on the same shelf at the bookstore that include a thousand pages or more! So what's the difference?

My MacBook doesn't cover the basics of using a computer; you already know how to drag windows around the screen and move files by dragging them from folder to folder. If you're switching from Windows, however, you might encounter a few unique features of Mac OS X. Review these features in the next few sections.

The Menu Bar

The menu bar is universally accessible across all running applications and contains a combination of the Apple menu, which is used for accessing common system functions; the active application's menus; and menu items, which are global utilities for controlling and monitoring system functions.

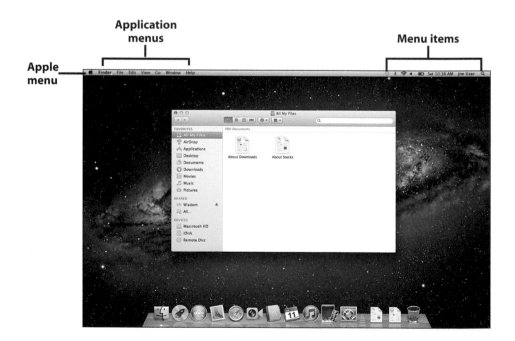

The Dock

The Lion Dock is the starting point for many of your actions when using the MacBook. Part application launcher, part file manager, and part window manager, the Dock gives you quick access to your most frequently used applications and documents without requiring that you navigate the Finder to find things on your hard drive.

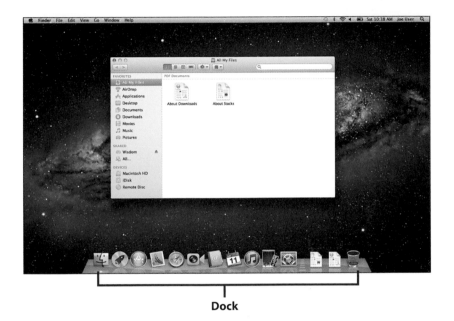

Dock

The Finder

In Windows, Explorer provides many of your file-management needs. In Mac OS X, you work with files within an ever-present application called Finder. The Finder is started as soon as you log into your computer and continues to run until you log out.

To switch to the Finder at any time, you click the blue smiling icon at the left end of the Dock.

Finder ——

System Preferences

Many features that this book explains how to configure require you to access the Lion System Preferences. The System Preferences application (accessible from the Dock or the Apple menu) is the central hub for system configuration. Everything from setting your password to choosing a screen saver can be found in the System Preferences application.

System Preferences

Window Controls

Lion provides up to four controls at the top of each window. On the left: close, minimize, and resize. The close control shuts the window; minimize slides the window off the screen and into the Dock; and resize changes the size of the window to best fit the content being displayed.

On the right side of the window is the fullscreen control. Clicking the fullscreen control switches an app to fullscreen if available. You might not expect it, but fullscreen applications on Lion can take on a completely different appearance from their windowed selves.

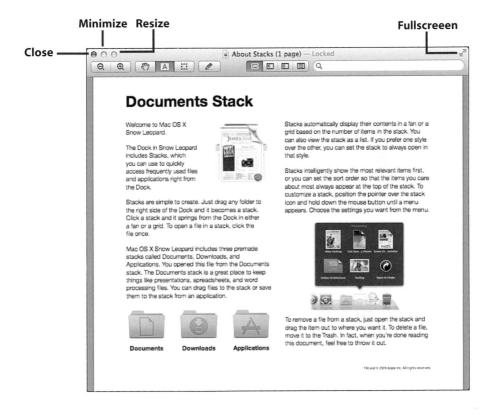

Contextual Menus

If you're new to Mac OS X, you might find it hard to believe that, yes, the Mac has a "right-click" menu in its operating system and it's been there for a long time! Contextual menus can be invoked by right-clicking using a multi-button mouse, Control-clicking with your trackpad, or click in the lower-right corner of the trackpad.

Contextual menus are rarely *required* in any application, but they can give you quick access to features that might otherwise take more clicks.

GESTURES

Although your MacBook trackpad does not have two buttons, you can open a contextual menu by clicking in the lower-right corner of the track-pad. This is made possible by the use of *gestures*, our last primary differentiating feature.

>>> Go Further

Gestures

Gestures are motions that you can make on your trackpad to control your computer. In Lion, gestures are used heavily to navigate between applications and access special features. Gestures can help you navigate web pages, resize images, and much more (such as launching Mission Control, seen here)— with just your fingertips. In fact, without gestures, you'll likely miss out on all Lion has to offer.

Windows Compatibility

If you have a MacBook, you have a powerful Intel-based computer in your hands—a computer that is completely capable of natively running the Windows operating system. The goal of this book is to make you comfortable using your MacBook with Lion, but I'd be remiss in my authoring duties if I didn't mention the options available for running Windows on your hardware.

Boot Camp

Boot Camp is included with Lion and gives you the ability to install and boot Windows directly on your MacBook. Quite simply, when you do this your Mac *becomes* a Windows computer. Switching between Lion and Windows requires a reboot, so this option is best if you need to work in Windows for extended periods of time.

Apple's Boot Camp Assistant (found in the Utilities folder within the Applications folder) guides you through the process of partitioning your MacBook for Windows and burning a CD of drivers for windows, and configuring your system to boot into Windows or Mac OS X.

Boot Camp can be installed at any time as long as there is enough room (about 5GB) for a Windows installation.

Virtualization

Another solution to the Windows-compatibility conundrum is the use of virtualization software. Through virtualization, you can run Windows at near-native speeds at the same time you run Lion. Some virtualization solutions even go so far as to mix Mac and Windows applications on the same screen, blurring the lines of operating systems.

Unlike Boot Camp, virtualization runs operating systems simultaneously. Virtualization requires more resources and has lower performance than a Boot Camp solution, but it is more convenient for running an occasional application or game.

There are three options you should consider for virtualizing Windows on your MacBook:

1. **VMWare Fusion** (www.vmware.com)—A stable solution from a leader in virtualization software. VMWare Fusion is rock solid and fully compatible with a wide range of virtual "appliances" available for VMWare on Windows.

2. **Parallels Desktop** (www.parallels.com)—Parallels Desktop has the widest range of features available of any virtualization solution for Mac OS X, including near seamless integration with Snow Leopard.

3. **VirtualBox** (www.virtualbox.org)—Free virtualization software that offers many of the same features of VMWare and Parallels. VirtualBox is not as polished as the commercial solutions, but it's well supported and has excellent performance.

Other Operating Systems

Virtualization isn't limited to running Windows. You can also run other operating systems, such as Linux and Solaris, using any of these solutions. In fact, if you have enough memory, you can run two, three, or more operating systems simultaneously!

Use the sidebar to quickly access locations, files, and searches on your MacBook.

Navigate and customize your workspace in the Finder.

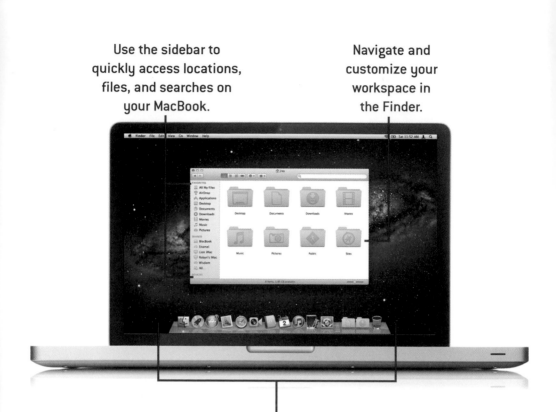

The Dock serves as a launching point for common applications and documents.

In this chapter, you'll learn how to make the most of your MacBook's limited screen space.

- → Organizing files using the Dock
- → Navigating folders within the Dock's Grid view mode
- → Customizing the Finder Sidebar and Toolbar
- → Viewing the contents of files with Quick Look
- → Searching for files and information with Spotlight

Managing Your MacBook Desktop

Introduction

The MacBook portable family has a range of screen sizes all with perfectly respectable high resolutions. Unfortunately, we've become accustomed to desktop systems with multiple monitors and huge HD displays that just aren't feasible for a computer on-the-go.

To help you make the most of the screen space you have, you can take advantage of a variety of time- and space-saving tools built into Lion that will help keep your desktop tidy and make working with files and applications fun and efficient. You'll see that, when it comes to the MacBook screen, size isn't everything!

Organizing in the Dock

The Lion Dock serves as application launcher, filer, and process manager. It enables you to launch applications and documents with a single click, place documents in folders, and even navigate the contents of folders without using the Finder. It also displays running applications so you can easily switch between them. Configuring your Dock to suit your working style and habits can be a big time saver because you don't have to dig through folders within folders just to find a single file.

The Dock is divided into two parts—applications, and files and folders. Applications are on the left of the faint broken line; files and folders are on the right (or top/bottom, if the Dock is oriented vertically).

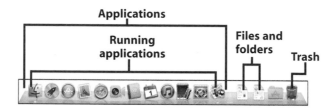

Adding and Removing Items from the Dock

Adding files and folders to the Dock is a simple process of dragging and dropping.

1. Use the Finder to locate the icon you wish to add to the Dock.

2. Drag the item from the Finder window to the appropriate side of the Dock. As you drag the icon into the Dock, the existing icons will move to make room for the addition. Release your mouse when you're happy with the new location.

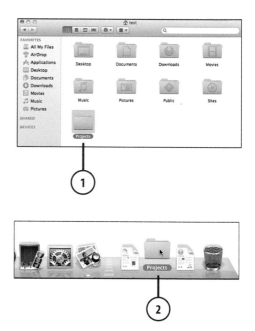

3. You can rearrange Dock items at any time by dragging them to another position in the Dock.

4. To remove an icon from the Dock, click and drag the icon out of the Dock.

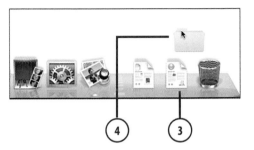

Keep Your Apps Handy

If you start an application and decide you want to keep it in the Dock, click and hold the icon of the running application, then choose Options, Keep In Dock from the menu that appears.

Using Folders and Stacks in the Dock

Folders that are added to the Dock behave differently from files or applications. When you click a folder residing on the Dock, the contents of the folder are displayed above it in one of three different styles—a Fan, Grid, or List. Additionally, the folder icons themselves can be shown as a simple folder or a stack of files, with your most recent file at the top.

Configuring Folders and Stacks

You can dramatically change the behavior of folders and stacks in the Dock by using the configuration options.

1. After adding a folder to the Dock, Control-click on the folder to open the menu to configure its behavior.

2. Choose to display as a Folder or Stack to customize the appearance of the icon on the Dock.

3. Choose Fan, Grid, List, or Automatic to set how the content will be displayed when you click the icon in the Dock. The Automatic setting will choose the best option based on the number of items in the folder.

4. Finally, to customize the sorting of the displayed items, choose an option from the Sort-by menu.

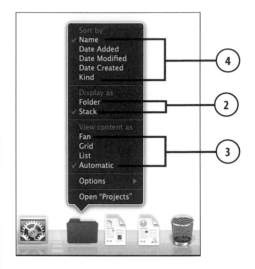

Navigating Files and Folders in Grid Mode

In Lion, the Folder Grid mode offers the most functionality for navigating your files. You can navigate through a scrolling list of files, and you can open additional folders.

1. Click a Folder in the Dock that has been configured to Grid mode. A grid "bubble" appears above the folder icon.

2. Scroll through the available files, if needed.

3. To navigate into a folder, click the folder's icon.

4. The Grid refreshes to show the contents of the folder.

5. Click the back arrow in the upper-left corner to return to the previous "parent" folder.

6. Click "Open in Finder" if you wish to open the current folder as a window in the Finder.

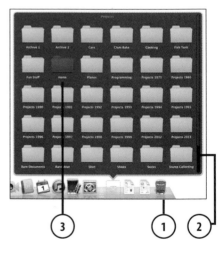

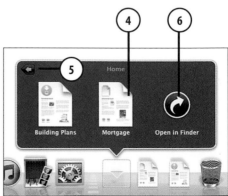

Customizing the Dock's Appearance

The Dock helps keeps your desktop nice and tidy by giving you a place to put your commonly used files and folders, but it also takes up a bit of screen space. You can easily customize the Dock's appearance to make it as unobtrusive as possible.

1. Open the System Preferences panel, and click the Dock icon.

2. Use the Size slider to change the size of the Dock.

3. Click the Magnification checkbox. Use the corresponding slider to set the magnification of the icons as you mouse over them in the Dock.

4. Use the radio buttons to control the position of the Dock on the screen.

5. To control the way windows animate to and from the Dock, click the Minimize Windows Using dropdown to choose between the Genie and Scale effects.

6. Check the Minimize Windows into Application Icon checkbox to help conserve space in the Dock by putting minimized windows into their applications' Dock icons.

7. By default, application icons "bounce" in the Dock while they're opening. Uncheck the "Animate Opening Applications" checkbox to disable this behavior.

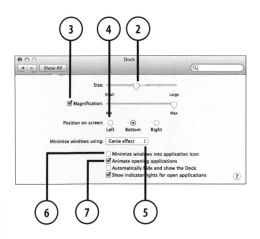

8. Click Automatically Hide and Show the Dock if you'd like the ssDock to disappear altogether when you're not using it.

9. Check Show indicator lights for open applications if you'd like a dot to appear under applications that are running.

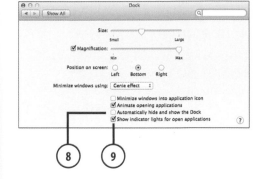

Hiding the Dock

To quickly hide the Dock, press ⌘+Option+D. You can also easily toggle the position and magnification of the Dock using the Dock submenu from the Apple menu.

Customizing Finder Windows

Like the Dock, Finder windows provide an opportunity to configure shortcuts to information that are accessible via a single click. The Finder sidebar and toolbar can be customized with your own files as well as default system shortcuts.

Configuring the Sidebar's System Shortcuts

To change the Sidebar's default shortcuts, you'll need to use the Finder preferences.

1. Open the Finder using its icon in the Dock and choose Finder, Preferences.

2. Click the Sidebar icon at the top of the Preferences window.

3. Use the checkboxes beside the Favorites, Shared, and Devices to configure which folders, network computers, and connected hardware and should be displayed.

4. Close the Finder preferences window.

Manually Modifying the Sidebar

In addition to the predefined shortcuts, you can easily add your own icons to the Sidebar.

1. To add an icon to the Sidebar, first make sure the item's icon is visible in a Finder window.

2. Drag the icon to the Favorites area in the sidebar.

3. A blue line appears to show where the item will be placed. Release your mouse button to add the item to the list.

4. The icon appears in the sidebar.

5. Rearrange the icons in the sidebar by clicking and dragging them up and down.

6. Remove existing sidebar entries by right-clicking (or control-clicking) their icons and choosing Remove from Sidebar.

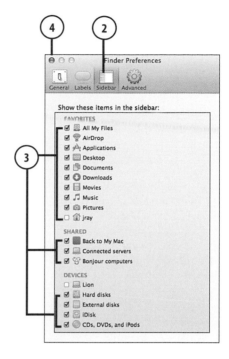

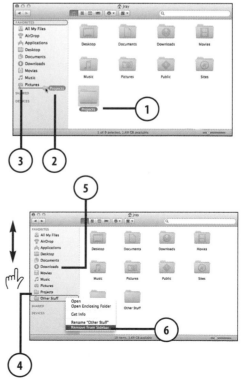

Modifying the Finder Toolbar

Like the Sidebar, the Finder window's toolbar can hold shortcuts to files, folders, and applications.

1. Open the Finder.

2. Drag the icon you wish to add into the toolbar. The other interface elements shift to make room for the new addition.

3. To move an icon to a new location on the toolbar, hold the ⌘ key down, then click and drag. Drag the icon off of the toolbar to remove it altogether.

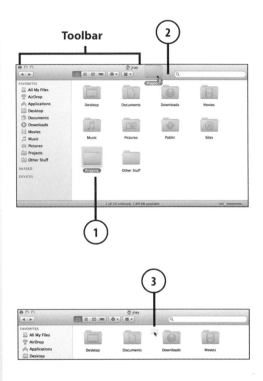

Toolbar

Dragging Allowed!

Toolbar and Sidebar items can serve as drag destinations as well as clickable shortcuts. For example, to file a document in a folder, you can drag it to a folder in the sidebar. To save a document to a file server, you can drag it onto a shared drive, and so on.

Arranging and Grouping Files

You'll notice that this book doesn't take a bunch of time to tell you about how to sort files, open folders, and all the typical things you do on a computer. Why? Because they work exactly the way you'd expect on a modern operating system. That said, Lion introduces some interesting ways of looking at files that you might not be aware of.

Using All My Files

If you've ever wanted to view all the files you have, the All My Files group will help you out. This feature displays, quite literally, *all* your files in your personal MacBook account. To view your files, follow these steps:

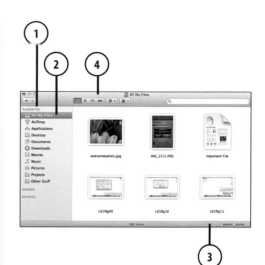

1. Make sure the Favorites section of the Finder sidebar is expanded.

2. Click the All My Files icon, or choose Go, All My Files from the menubar.

3. All the files that belong to you are shown in the Finder window.

4. Use the view icons to change between icon, list, column, and coverflow views, respectively.

Granted, this isn't the most exciting feature in the world, but, when coupled with the Arrange By feature, it becomes far more interesting.

Arranging a Finder View

You're probably used to clicking a column heading and sorting files by name, date, modified, or other attributes. This is expanded in Lion with the Arrange By feature. Using Arrange By, you can view your files arranged by more "human" categories, such as the files you've opened today, in the last week, and so on.

Follow these steps to arrange any finder window, including the All My Files view:

1. Open the finder view you wish to arrange.

2. Use the Arrange By menu to select a category for grouping your files.

3. Different groups are separated by horizontal lines.

4. When in icon view mode, swipe left or right on the trackpad to scroll through a coverflow-like view of the icons within a grouping.

5. Click the Show All link to turn off the coverflow scrolling and show all the items within the window.

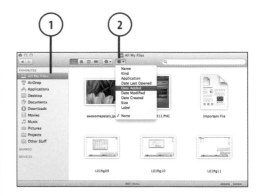

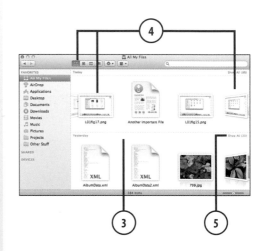

Making Arrangements

To set a default arrangement (among other things) for a folder, choose View, Show View Options from the menubar when viewing the folder.

Previewing Document Contents with Quick Look

Launching applications takes time and resources. Frequently, when we want to open a file, all we really want is to see the contents of the file. Using Lion's equivalent of X-Ray vision, called Quick Look, we can view many of our documents without the need to open an application.

Viewing a File with Quick Look

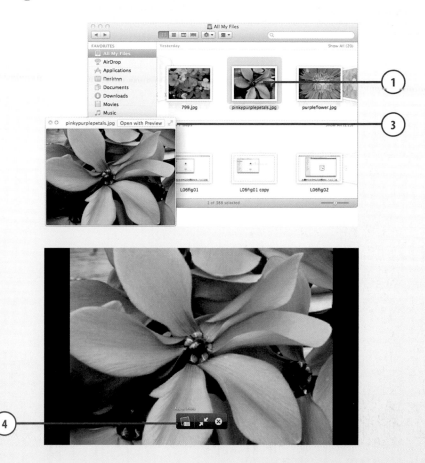

Using Quick Look doesn't require anything more than your mouse and a press of the spacebar.

1. Select a file from the Finder or Desktop by clicking once, but don't open it!

2. Press the spacebar to open Quick Look.

3. Click the double arrows to expand Quick Look to fullscreen.

4. Some files might show additional controls above the preview or when in fullscreen mode. An image, for example, includes a button to open in the Preview application, or, when in fullscreen mode, add the file to iPhoto.

5. Press the spacebar again to exit Quick Look.

Instant Slideshows!

If you start Quick Look on multiple files, you can run a slideshow. The fullscreen Quick Look window includes play, forward, and backward arrows to start and control the slideshow. You can also use an index sheet icon (four squares) to show previews of all the files in a single Quick Look window (also available in windowed mode).

Quick Look even works on music and video files, enabling you to play back media without opening a dedicated application.

Previewing Files Using Finder Icons

The new Lion Finder includes Quick Look-like capability for some files just by mousing over them.

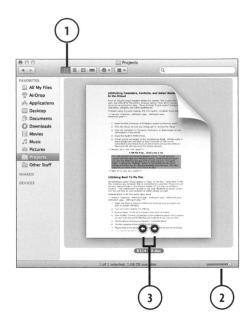

1. To preview a file using icons in Lion, make sure you're in icon view mode.

2. If you're viewing an image or document file with detailed content, use the window's zoom slider to zoom in on what you want to review.

3. Mouse over the file, and use the controls that appear to navigate the contents of the file. As with Quick Look, even media files can be played in this manner.

Using Instant-Access Utilities in the Dashboard

Sometimes it is handy to be able to access information and simple utilities without moving your windows around or digging through your Applications folder to find what you need. For simple tasks, you can to use a Dashboard widget.

The Dashboard is an overlay of useful tools, called widgets, which you can call up and dismiss with a single keystroke. Widgets that you add to the Dashboard persist between reboots, so when you've configured your Dashboard the way you like it, it's there to stay!

Activating the Dashboard

The Lion Dashboard appears and disappears with a keystroke or a click.

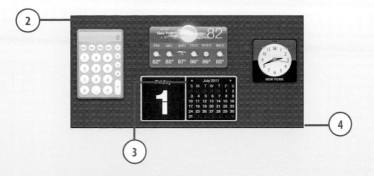

1. To activate the Dashboard, press the Dashboard key on your keyboard, open the Dashboard application in the Applications folder, or, even easier, swipe with four finders to the right across your trackpad.

2. The desktop will slide out of the way and display a default set of Dashboard widgets displays.

3. You can now interact with any of the widgets, including dragging them around to rearrange them, just as you would with normal applications.

4. Exit Dashboard by pressing the Dashboard key on your keyboard, clicking the arrow in the lower-right of the Dashboard, or swiping with four fingers to the left.

Tweaking Your Shortcuts

To configure additional shortcuts to the Dashboard, you can visit the Mission Control system preference panel. This will be discussed further in Chapter 2, "Making the Most of Your MacBook's Screen Space."

It's Not All Good

SEEING THROUGH IT

In previous versions of Mac OS X, the Dashboard was layered on top of your desktop. This meant that you could still see information behind the widgets—something that can be pretty helpful when using a calculator, for example. If you want this behavior to return, uncheck Show Dashboard as a Space in the Mission Control preference panel. This will revert the Dashboard to its previous appearance.

Adding and Removing Dashboard Widgets

One of the best things about widgets is that you can keep adding them to your screen, and they'll always be there until you choose to remove them.

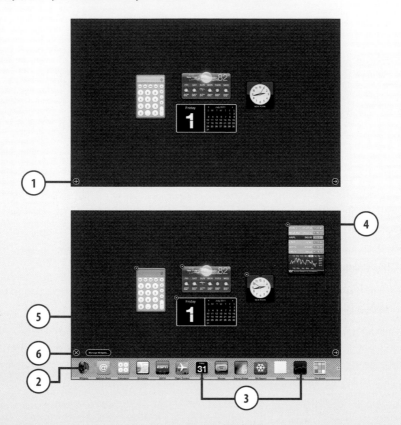

1. To add (or remove) a widget in the Dashboard, start the Dashboard and then click the + (or the –) icon in the lower-left corner.

2. A horizontally scrolling list of widgets appears. Use the arrows on both sides of the list to scroll to the left or right.

3. To add a widget to your desktop, drag it from the list onto your screen. You can drag the widget around to position it as you'd like.

4. To remove a widget, click the X icon in the widget's upper-left corner.

5. To disable a widget so that it can no longer be used, click the Manage Widgets button. In the window that appears, uncheck the checkbox beside the widget.

6. When you've finished adding or removing widgets, click the X icon at the bottom-left corner of the screen to close the list.

Configuring Dashboard Widgets

Widgets are unique applications that each behave differently, but, in general, you configure them one of two ways.

1. Some widgets, when you add them to your screen, automatically prompt you with the information they are expecting. Other widgets must be configured in order to show the proper results.

2. Mouse over a widget you wish to configure. A small "i" appears in the corner of the widget. Click the "i" icon.

3. The widget flips over, revealing the configuration details.

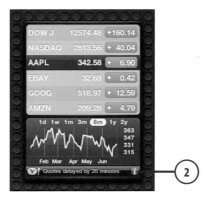

Manage Your Widgets and Get More Widgets!

When adding a widget to your screen, you'll notice a Manage Widgets button in the Dashboard. This opens yet another widget where you can disable existing widgets. Or click More Widgets to launch Safari and download new widgets. To find new widgets outside of the Dashboard, visit www.apple.com/downloads/dashboard/Widgets to download a file in your Downloads folder. You can install them by double-clicking their icons.

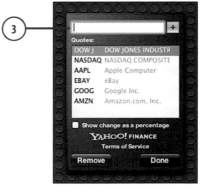

Finding Information with Spotlight

When the Finder's file organization features can't help you find what you want, Lion's amazing Spotlight search system will make it simple. Spotlight can search across files, email messages, even the built-in dictionary to find information!

Searching for Files and Information

Spotlight searches can be started at any time, without needing to launch any additional applications.

1. To start a search, press ⌘+Space, or click the magnifying glass icon in the upper-right corner of your screen. A search field appears.

2. Begin typing.

3. As you type, files, images, folders, and even definitions that match your terms will be displayed in a list.

4. Hover your mouse over a result to see a preview.

5. Click a matched item in the list to open the item.

Customizing Spotlight Searching

Spotlight searches can turn up tons of information. More, perhaps, than you'd like. To choose exactly what you want to display, you need to configure the Spotlight System Preferences panel.

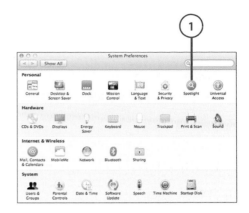

1. Open the Spotlight System Preferences panel.

2. Within the Search Results panel, check items you want to be returned as part of the search results. Uncheck the items you want to exclude.

3. To restrict what volumes are searched, click the Privacy button. You can choose to have Spotlight ignore specific folders or disks.

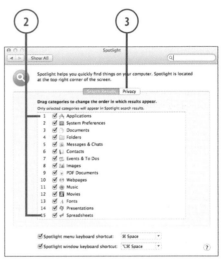

4. Click the + button to choose a folder or disk that you don't want to be searchable. Alternatively, drag folders directly from the Finder into the Privacy list.

5. Use the checkboxes to change how Spotlight is started or disable keyboard shortcuts altogether.

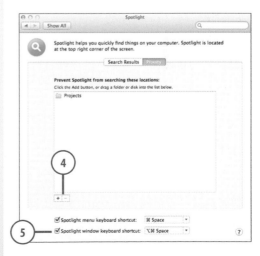

Saving Searches as Smart Folders in the Finder

Spotlight Searches for files can be saved and reused in the form of Smart Folders. If you'd like to create a search that shows all your image files, regardless of where they are stored, for example, you can create and save a Show All Images search.

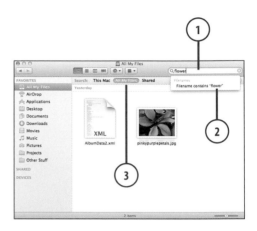

1. Use a Finder window's search field to type the name or content of a file you want to find.

2. Choose whether the search should be just for the file name. The default is to include file content.

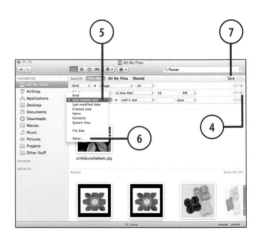

3. Adjust whether you want to search your entire MacBook (indicated by the words "This Mac") or just the folder you're currently in.

4. Use the + and – buttons below the search field to add or subtract additional search criteria lines.

5. Use the pop-up menu at the start of each search line to configure search attributes such as file Kind or Size.

6. To add even more search criteria, choose Other. A window listing all the available search attributes displays. Choose an attribute and click Okay.

7. When you're satisfied with your search, click the Save button.

8. You are prompted for a name for the search and where it should be saved.

9. Click Add To Sidebar.

10. Click Save.

11. If you choose to add the search to your sidebar, it is accessible immediately from your Finder window. Otherwise you need to navigate to the saved location and double-click the search's Smart Folder icon to run it again.

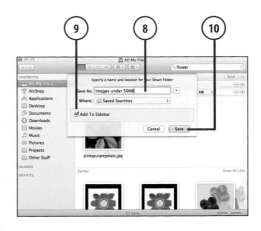

Less Is More

After you've configured a few search criteria beyond the text for the file name or file content, you can erase the search text and Lion includes all of the files that match your other criteria.

Navigate Desktop spaces
and Fullscreen applications.

Create new spaces to
make room for your work.

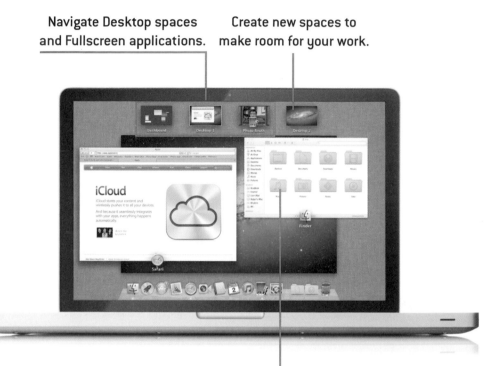

View active applications and
windows in Mission Control.

In this chapter, you'll learn how to take control of your applications and windows.

- → Find your way around Mission Control
- → Manage applications and windows
- → Create new spaces
- → Launch applications with Launchpad
- → Create application groups in Launchpad
- → Uninstall applications through Launchpad

Making the Most of Your MacBook's Screen Space

Introduction

As applications become more complex, so does the task of managing them. Software is installed everywhere, windows are spread out over your desktop, and just trying to find your way through the maze of information overload can be nightmarish. Lion attempts to bring the madness under control by way of Mission Control.

Mission Control, combined with features like full-screen apps, Spaces, and Launchpad, makes it easy to navigate even the most cluttered and convoluted workspace. The biggest problem? Many of these features are hidden until you invoke them! In this chapter, you'll learn how to do just that!

Swimming in a Sea of Application Windows with Mission Control

One of the big benefits of modern operating systems is that they allow you to run multiple applications at once. Unfortunately, our screen real-estate isn't growing as quickly as the amount of "stuff" we can have on our screen at the same time. To help manage the ever-expanding collection of windows that we need to work within, Apple provides Mission Control as part of OS X Lion. Mission Control helps you view your running apps, the windows they have open, and even expand the amount of desktop real estate you have available.

Opening and Closing Mission Control

To manage Mission Control and access its features, follow these instructions:

1. Slide three fingers up the Trackpad or press the Mission Control key (F3) on your keyboard. Mission Control opens. Spaces appear on the top; the current space is in the center of the screen.

2. Slide three fingers down. Mission Control closes.

In Mission Control terms, a "space" is a single screenful of information. It can be your Dashboard screen, your typical desktop, a fullscreen app, or even additional desktop views that you create.

Docking Mission Control

If you'd prefer to start Mission Control by clicking in the Dock, you can add the Mission Control icon (found in your Applications folder).

Navigating Applications and Windows

When you start Mission Control, your current space (probably your desktop, if you're starting Mission Control for the first time) is front and center, along with representations of each app running in the space and its windows.

To switch between applications and their windows, do the following:

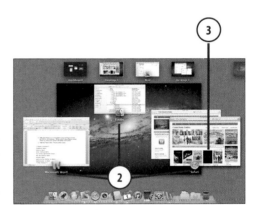

1. Start Mission Control.

2. Click an application icon to exit Mission Control and bring the application to the front.

3. Click a window to exit Mission Control and bring the chosen window to the front.

4. To preview the contents of a window, position your pointer over the window, then press the spacebar. Press the spacebar again to hide the preview.

Creating and Populating a New Space

Your MacBook screen does a fine job of holding two or three apps running simultaneous—but how about 10? 15? Unless you have additional monitors connected, you're going to be digging through dozens of windows. With Mission Control, however, you can create new desktop spaces dedicated to whatever applications you'd like.

1. Start Mission Control.

2. Click in the upper right-hand corner of the screen, and a + graphic will appear.

3. A new space is created and a thumbnail of its contents is added to the top of Mission Control.

4. Drag application icons or even individual windows from the current space to the thumbnail of the new space.

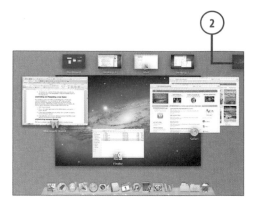

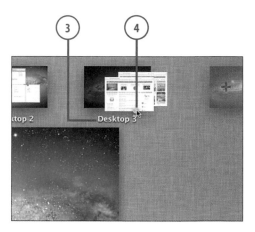

Switching Between Spaces

After you've created a new space, you can switch to it via Mission Control or a Trackpad gesture:

1. Start Mission Control.

2. Click the space thumbnail you wish to display, or swipe left or right with three fingers to move between spaces.

3. Click on the background to exit Mission control.

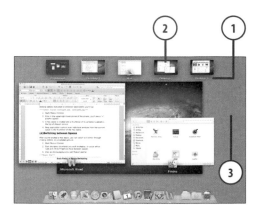

Even Faster Space Switching

The fastest way to switch between Mission Control spaces is without even starting Mission Control. Swipe left or right with three fingers at *any time* to move between spaces on your MacBook.

Closing a Space

It's so easy to create spaces, you might find yourself with some extras that you need to get rid of. To close out a space, follow these steps:

1. Start Mission Control.

2. Position your cursor over a space.

3. After a few seconds an X appears in the upper-left corner of the space thumbnail. Click the X.

4. The space closes and any windows within it move back to the primary desktop space.

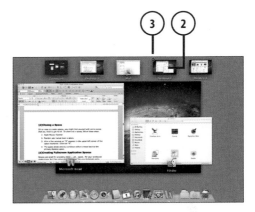

Creating Fullscreen Application Spaces

Spaces are great for providing more…um…space for your windowed applications, but they also serve as a "container" for your fullscreen apps. Rather than a fullscreen application eating up one of your desktop spaces, it automatically creates a new dedicated space when it starts and removes it when it stops.

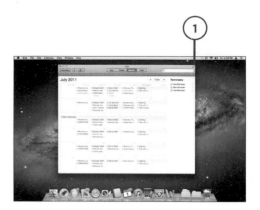

1. Click the double-arrow icon to put an application in fullscreen mode.

2. A new space is created and is visible in Mission Control.

3. Switch to and from the space exactly as you would any other. When you're done using the fullscreen app, either quit or exit fullscreen mode. The space is automatically removed from Mission Control.

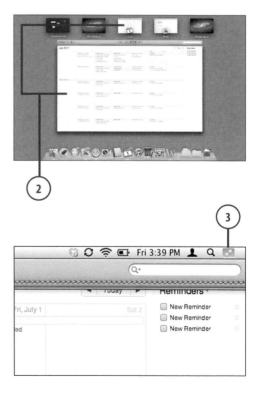

Choosing Between Application Windows

When you just need to navigate your windows, the Mission Control Application windows option comes in handy. Using this, you can show all your application windows, or just the windows for a specific program, with a single click.

1. To display all the windows open within an application, click and hold on an active application's icon in the dock and choose Show All Windows. Alternatively, press Ctrl+down-arrow.

2. The screen refreshes to show miniature versions of your windows. Minimized windows appear in the bottom portion of the display; active windows appear at the top.

3. If you want, press the Tab key to switch between active applications, limiting the miniaturized windows to the highlighted application.

4. Click a window to select it and move it to the front.

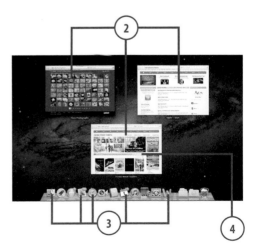

Showing the Desktop

Sometimes you need quick access to the files on your desktop and rearranging windows (or using the Finder's Hide menu) isn't very efficient. Mission Control's Show Desktop feature comes in handy here:

1. To clear all the windows off the screen so that you can temporarily work with the desktop, press F11.

2. You can now work within the desktop with no obstructions.

3. Press F11 again to return the windows to their original positions.

If Only Real Life Were So Easy...

To quickly drop a file from the Finder into another application (such as an attachment into an email message), you can start dragging a file while the Desktop is cleared, press F11 to return the windows to the screen, and then finish dragging and dropping the file into an application.

Configuring Mission Control Features and Shortcuts

If you have a specific way of working and want to customize how Mission Control or any of its features is activated, just follow these steps:

1. Open the System Preferences application, and click the Mission Control panel icon.

2. If you'd like Dashboard to appear on top of your current space rather than in its own space, uncheck Show Dashboard as a space.

3. Uncheck Automatically rearrange spaces based on use if you prefer that Lion keep your spaces in the same order you add them, regardless of your usage patterns.

4. In most cases, leave When Switching to an Application, Switch to a Space with Open Windows for the Application checkbox checked. This indicates that if you switch to an application (using the Dock, or ⌘+Tab), you will automatically switch to the space that contains its open windows.

5. At the bottom of the panel, use the pop-up menus to configure keyboard and mouse button combinations to invoke the Mission Control features and Dashboard.

6. To trigger these features by moving the mouse to the screen corners, click the Hot Corners button.

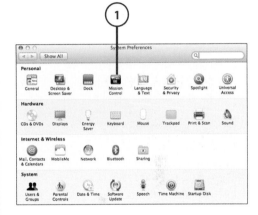

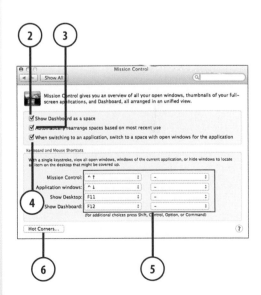

7. Use the pop-up menus beside each screen corner to choose between the different options. After you've made a selection, just move the mouse into that corner to invoke the feature.

8. Click OK when finished.

9. Close the system preferences.

Remember Your Gestures!

As you know, you control Mission Control through gestures, and these aren't set in stone! Use the Trackpad system preference panel to configure the gestures used by Mission Control.

Managing and Launching Applications with Launchpad

While Mission Control helps you find your way through your windows, Lion's Launchpad eliminates the need to open them! Launchpad brings iOS application management to your Mac. Instead of digging through folders to launch an application, you simply start Launchpad and all your installed apps are visible, in one place. No digging required.

Starting Launchpad

Like Mission Control, Apple wants to keep Launchpad at the ready. Unlike other applications, it takes no time to start and can be invoked through a gesture:

1. Open Launchpad by performing a pinching gesture with your thumb and three fingers. Alternatively, click the Launchpad icon in the dock or in the Applications folder.

2. The Launchpad appears, blurring out your background.

3. Reverse the pinching gesture, or click on the background to exit Launchpad.

Navigating Launchpad

If you've used an iPad or an iPhone, you immediately know how to navigate Launchpad. If you haven't, don't worry—it takes about a minute to learn everything you'll need to know.

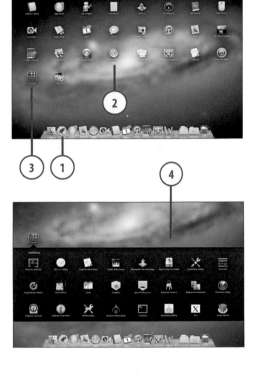

1. Open Launchpad to access your applications.

2. Click an application icon to launch it.

3. Click a folder icon to open it.

4. Click outside the folder to close it.

5. There can be multiple pages of icons, represented by the dots at the center bottom of the screen.

6. Move between pages by swiping left or right with your fingers, clicking the dots, or clicking and dragging left or right.

Rearranging Icons

The Launchpad display is completely customizable. To rearrange the icons on your screen, follow these instructions:

1. Open Launchpad.

2. Click and drag the icon to a new location, even a new page. Release the mouse to place the icon.

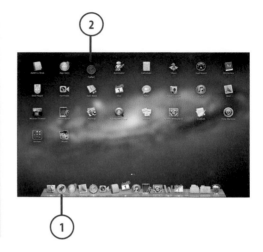

It's Not All Good

A LION DISGUISED AS AN IPHONE

Launchpad suffers from a bit of an identity crisis. It follows the same "click and hold to enter icon wiggle mode"—just like iOS. This behavior, however, isn't necessary for rearranging or even deleting icons as it is in iOS. Whether you use it is up to you and completely superficial. You can even make the icons wiggle manually by pressing and holding the Option key on your keyboard.

Creating New Folders

Unlike folders in the finder, Launchpad folders are created "on the fly" and automatically disappear when all of their contents are removed. To create a folder in Launchpad, follow these steps:

1. Open Launchpad.

2. Drag an icon on top of another icon that you wish to group it with.

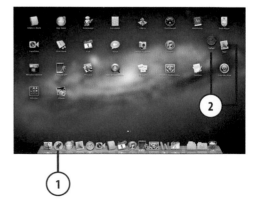

3. A new folder is created, opened, and the icons are added.

4. Click the title of the folder to rename it.

5. Click on the background outside the folder to close it.

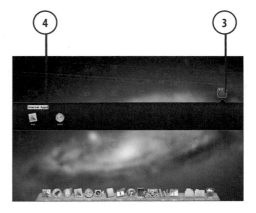

The Folder That Wasn't There

Folders you create or delete in Launchpad do not alter your filesystem. They are purely logical groupings and do not affect the location of your actual files.

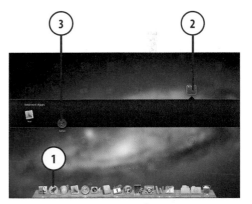

Deleting Folders

To remove a folder from Launchpad, use these instructions:

1. Open Launchpad.

2. Click the folder that you wish to remove.

3. The folder opens.

4. Drag each item out of the folder.

5. When you reach the last item, the folder vanishes automatically.

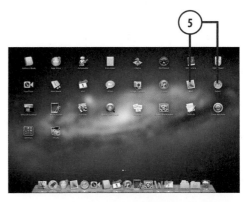

Deleting Applications

In addition to providing a quick way to access your applications, Launchpad also offers an easy way to uninstall applications you've installed from the Mac App Store. (See Chapter 8, "Installing and Managing Software on Your MacBook," for details.)

1. Open Launchpad.

2. Drag an application you wish to uninstall to the trash. Alternatively, click and hold on the icon until an X appears in the upper-left, and click the X.

3. You are prompted to confirm the deletion.

4. Click Delete.

5. The application is uninstalled from your system. You can reinstall through the App Store if needed.

Are you sure you want to delete the application "Navicat for SQL Server Lite"?

Cancel   Delete

It's Not All Good

THE NOT-SO-UNIVERSAL UNINSTALLER

You can only use Launchpad for uninstalling applications you've added through the Mac App Store. To remove other apps, you'll need to revert to the old school method of using an uninstaller (if one came with the application) or manually dragging the application files to the trash.

Configure and control your
MacBook network interfaces
in the Network System
Preferences panel.

Use the Wi-Fi
status menu to find
and join wireless
networks.

In this chapter, you'll learn how to get your MacBook online including tasks like:

3

→ Connecting to wired networks
→ Connecting to secure wireless networks
→ Configuring network address, DNS, and routing information
→ Verifying network connections
→ Tethering to an iPhone
→ Using WWAN cards
→ Creating VPN connections
→ Managing multiple connections with Locations

Connecting Your MacBook to a Network

Introduction

Being connected to a network gives you access to information, files, and services such as email or the web. Your MacBook can keep you connected whenever and wherever you are—from connecting to home and corporate networks to using cellular data cards and iPhone tethering, if there's a network present, you can access it!

In this chapter, we explore the connection options available to you on your MacBook.

Connecting to a Wired Network

The most common type of network connection in the business world is a wired Ethernet connection. The cables used to connect to the network look like oversized phone connectors and, as luck has it, plug directly into your MacBook's Ethernet port. (MacBook Air owners will need to buy Apple's USB Ethernet adapter.) The MacBook supports gigabit Ethernet, making it capable of exchanging information at extremely high speeds.

It's Not All Good

There aren't many things that upset a network administrator more than a person who attempts to guess at the proper configuration of his computer when attaching it to a network. An improperly configured computer can potentially disrupt an entire network, so please make sure you have all of the information you need from your administrator or ISP before attempting the things in this chapter!

Making an Ethernet (Wired) Connection

On a network that is set up to automatically configure your computer using DHCP, the most complicated thing you need to do is plug in the network cable!

1. Open the System Preferences panel and click the Network icon.

2. The network preference panel displays. All of the activate network interfaces are listed here. Red dots indicate that no connection is present on the interface.

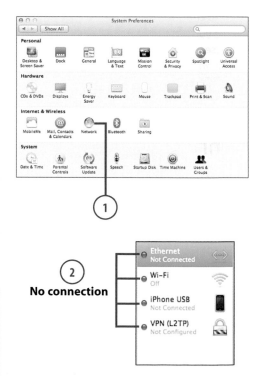

No connection

3. Plug the network cable into the left side of your MacBook.

4. After a few seconds, the interface should update, showing a green dot for an active connection. The pane to the right of the interfaces displays the information that your computer is using to communicate online.

4 **Active Connection**

Ethernet Connected	Status: **Connected**
Wi-Fi Off	Ethernet is currently active and has the IP address 10.0.1.107.
iPhone USB Not Connected	Configure IPv4: Using DHCP
VPN (L2TP) Not Configured	IP Address: 10.0.1.107
	Subnet Mask: 255.255.255.0
	Router: 10.0.1.1
	DNS Server: 10.0.1.240, 8.8.8.8
	Search Domains: poisontooth.com

Things Not Working?

If your network connection is showing a yellow dot, you might have to configure your settings manually, or, if you're using a DSL connection, you might have to use PPPoE to make your connection. If this is the case, skip ahead to "Manually Configuring Network Settings."

If, however, you see a red dot, you need to check your cable or the device you're plugging into because your Macintosh can't detect *any* type of network.

Connecting to a Wireless Network

You have a MacBook, presumably because you love the portability and flexibility to compute whenever and wherever you like. What goes better with a computer that you can carry around than a wireless network? Using the built-in AirPort wireless card in your computer, you can connect to almost any type of wireless network.

>>> Go Further

WHAT TYPE OF WIRELESS NETWORKS CAN MY MACBOOK USE?

The latest MacBooks can make use of 802.11n, 802.11a, 802.11b, and 802.11g networks! This represents the full range of consumer and business wireless networking standards. Your MacBook is also capable of talking to a wide range of 802.1x authentication protocols and encryption methods. Set up is usually automatic, so you won't need to know the specifics unless your administrator tells you otherwise.

To learn more about wireless security, read http://en.wikipedia.org/wiki/Wireless_security.

Making a Wireless Connection

Apple makes life easy. Your MacBook comes ready (and able) to connect to wireless networks with a minimal amount of fuss.

Finding and Connecting to a Network

By default, your MacBook's WiFi (wireless) card is active and searching for networks that it can connect to.

1. If your MacBook finds an available network, it prompts you to make a connection.

Find and join a Wi-Fi network.
Choose the Wi-Fi network you want to join from the list below.

Enamel
Guest
WiggleTooth

Join Other   Cancel   Join

2. Choose the network name to connect to. Note that the network signal strength and security are denoted by icons to the right of the name. If a lock is present, the network requires authentication. This is covered in "Authenticating on a Wireless Network" later in this chapter.

3. Click Join to connect to the selected network.

4. If you've been given the specific name of a network (called an SSID) by a network administrator and it doesn't appear in the available networks list, click the Join Other button to enter the name and attempt to find the network.

Find and join a Wi-Fi network.

Choose the Wi-Fi network you want to join from the list below.

Enamel
Guest
WiggleTooth

(?) Join Other   Cancel   Join

Things Not Working?

If you've successfully connected to a wireless network, but it doesn't seem to work, you may need to configure the network settings manually. Keep in mind, you need to get those settings from your wireless network administrator.

If this is the case, skip ahead to the "Manually Configuring Network Settings" task.

Manually Choosing a Wireless Connection

If you want to manually choose a wireless network connection, you can use the Wi-Fi menu in your menu bar.

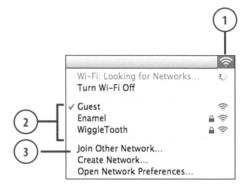

1. The Wi-Fi menu displays a list of all of the available wireless access points, their signal strengths, and their security requirements.

2. Choose the network name to which you wish to connect from the list. If you're connecting to a network that shows a lock icon, it requires authentication. This topic is covered in "Authenticating on a Wireless Network" later in this chapter.

3. If you want to connect to a network using only its name, choose Join Other Network to enter the name and attempt the connection.

Alternate Wi-Fi Configuration

If you'd prefer to manage all your network connection information in one place, you can access these same options by opening the Network System Preference panel and selecting the Wi-Fi interface.

You can also use the Show Wi-Fi Status in menu bar checkbox to remove or add (if it's missing) the Wi-Fi status menu item.

Authenticating on a Wireless Network

When your MacBook connects to an open (unsecured) network, it works immediately. If you're connecting to a network that is secure, however, you need to authenticate, which means you need to provide a password or other identifying information. This requirement is usually denoted by a lock icon in the Network panel.

1. If you attempt to connect to a network that has a security requirement, you are prompted for a password.

2. Enter the password (or other information, depending on the security settings).

3. Click Show Password if you'd like to see the password instead of dots while you type.

4. To make sure that the network can be used again in the future without requiring that you retype the password, check the Remember This Network button.

5. Click Join to finish and authenticate to the network.

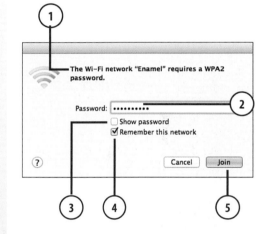

Disabling (and Enabling) Wireless Networking

Not everyone *wants* to have wireless networking always enabled. It can drain your battery faster and potentially open you up to network attacks on poorly secured wireless networks. Disabling the Wi-Fi network interface, and re-enabling it, is just a menu option away.

1. To disable the Wi-Fi card, choose Turn Wi-Fi Off from the Wi-Fi status menu.

2. The Wi-Fi menu updates to an outline of the usual multiline symbol. The Wi-Fi hardware is now powered down.

3. To re-enable the Wi-Fi card, choose Turn Wi-Fi On from the Wi-Fi status menu.

Manually Configuring Network Settings

Network connections, when automatically configured, seem to work almost like magic. Your computer finds a signal (wired or wireless), makes a connection, and everything just "works." Behind the scenes, however, there are a handful of network settings that make this happen. If a network doesn't support auto-configuration via DHCP, you need to make these settings manually.

What to Collect Before Proceeding

Your network administrator needs to provide the following settings in order to successfully manually set up your network:

- **IP Address**—A numerical address that uniquely identifies your computer.

- **Subnet Mask**—A value that helps your computer determine what network it is on.

- **Router**—The address of a device that moves network traffic between other local computers and remote networks (such as the Internet).

- **DNS**—The address of a device providing domain name lookups to your network. This service translates human-readable names (such as www.apple.com) into IP addresses and vice-versa.

- **Proxy Settings**—A device that sends and receives network traffic on your behalf, acting as a middleman for services.

Configuring TCP/IP and Proxy Settings

To manually change your TCP/IP and Proxy settings, follow these simple steps:

1. Open System Preferences and click the Network panel icon.

2. The network panel opens, showing all the available interfaces. Click the interface you wish to configure (usually Ethernet or Wi-Fi).

3. Click the Advanced button to view the full manual interface for network settings.

4. The Advanced configuration screen appears. Click TCP/IP in the button bar to access the common TCP/IP network settings.

5. Use the Configure IPv4 drop-down menu to change your settings to be configured Manually.

6. Enter the IP address, Subnet Mask, and Router, as provided by your network administrator.

7. Click DNS in the button bar to change your domain name server settings.

8. Click the + button below the DNS Servers list to add a new server to the list. Your ISP or network administrator usually provides at least two addresses to use; be sure to type it exactly as provided. (Use the – button to remove unused DNS Servers. Search Domains are not required unless specified by your administrator.)

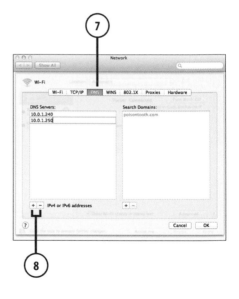

9. If your network requires the use of a proxy, click the Proxies button in the button bar. If not, skip ahead to Step 13.

10. Click the checkboxes beside the protocols that you want to configure.

11. Click the protocol names to configure each proxy. Setup fields appear to the right of the protocol list.

12. Enter the proxy information as provided by your network administrator.

13. Click OK to exit advanced setup.

14. Click Apply to activate and begin using your new network settings.

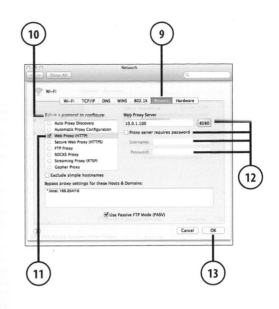

Switching to Automatic Configuration

To revert back to the default "automatic" configuration of a network interface, you need to select Using DHCP from the Configure IPv4 drop-down menu.

Activating PPPoE for DSL Connections

In some cases, most typically when using a DSL modem, you need to activate PPPoE (Point-to-Point Protocol over Ethernet) in order to make a connection.

1. Open System Preferences and click the Network panel icon.

2. Select your active Ethernet Interface.

3. Choose Create PPPoE Service from the Configure IPv4 drop-down menu.

4. Choose a name for the connection. (The default, PPPoE, is fine.)

5. Click Done.

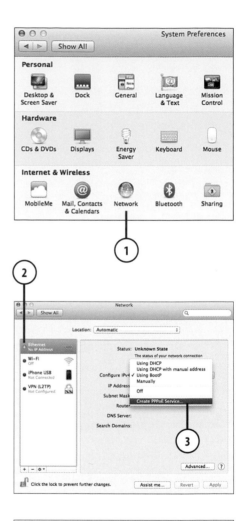

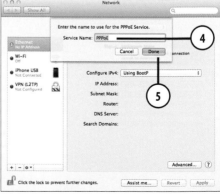

6. Enter the PPPoE information as provided by your ISP. Choose to remember the password if desired.

7. Click the Show PPPoE Status in Menu Bar checkbox to add a convenient menu option for connecting and disconnecting to the service.

8. Click the Advanced button.

9. Click PPP to open a variety of options for configuring your connection.

10. To help maintain a stable connection, check Connect Automatically When Needed and uncheck the Disconnect checkboxes if desired.

11. If required by your ISP, configure the TCP/IP settings manually as described in the "Configuring TCP/IP and Proxy Settings" task.

12. Click OK to close the Advanced settings.

13. Click Connect to begin using the PPPoE interface you've configured.

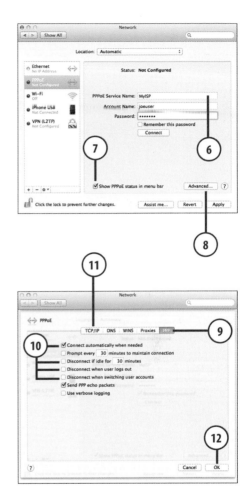

Making Mobile Connections with the iPhone and Cellular Data Cards

If you're one of the millions of people with an iPhone or a cellular data card, also called a wireless wide area network (WWAN) network access card, chances are that you can use it (with the proper plan!) to access the Internet using your MacBook wherever you are. This process is called *tethering* and can be performed either wirelessly via Wi-Fi, Bluetooth, or through a direct (USB) connection to your MacBook.

Tethering Wirelessly to an iPhone Using Wi-Fi

To access the Internet wirelessly using your iPhone's data services, you first need to subscribe to a tethering plan through AT&T or Verizon. Once your plan is ready, you have several options for how to connect your phone to your MacBook. If you have an iPhone 4 or newer, you can create a Wi-Fi hotspot to quickly get your MacBook and other Wi-Fi-ready devices online.

Enable tethering on the iPhone by following these steps:

1. Open the Settings application.

2. Choose Personal Hotspot.

3. Enter a password you want to use to connect to your iPhone hotspot in the Wi-Fi Password field on the iPhone.

4. Turn Personal Hotspot ON using the switch in the iPhone interface.

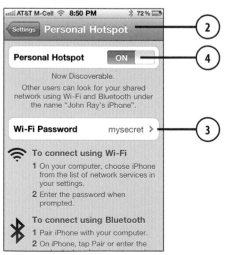

5. After a few seconds, your Wi-Fi hotspot will be ready—it will be named using the name set for your iPhone. Follow the instructions described in "Making a Wireless Connection" earlier in this chapter to connect to the Wi-Fi hotspot.

Tethering Wirelessly to an iPhone Using Bluetooth

Another Internet access method is via Bluetooth. You will need to use this (or USB tethering), if you have an iPhone 3GS. Enable Bluetooth tethering by completing these actions:

1. Open the Settings application.

2. Choose Personal Hotspot.

3. Turn Personal Hotspot ON using the switch in the iPhone interface.

4. Open the System Preferences application on your MacBook, and click the Bluetooth icon.

5. Make sure that Bluetooth is turned on.

6. Click the Show Bluetooth Status in the Menu Bar checkbox. This provides a convenient place for you to disconnect and connect from the network through your iPhone.

7. Click the Set up New Device or + button to set up a new device. You need to "pair" your iPhone to your computer to use the iPhone's Internet service. (Pairing is covered in depth in Chapter 10, "Connecting Devices to Your MacBook.")

8. The Bluetooth Setup Assistant launches and searches for devices.

9. After a few seconds, the Bluetooth Setup Assistant displays an entry for your iPhone.

10. Make sure your iPhone is selected in the list and then click Continue.

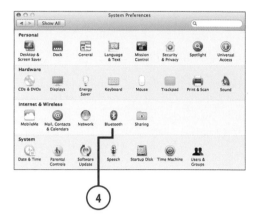

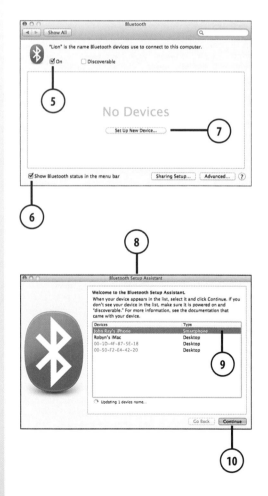

11. The Setup Assistant provides a PIN and, simultaneously, you are prompted on your iPhone.

12. Confirm the PIN and tap the Pair button on the iPhone screen. The iPhone-specific setup is now complete.

13. The Setup Assistant on your MacBook shows that setup was successful. Click the Quit button.

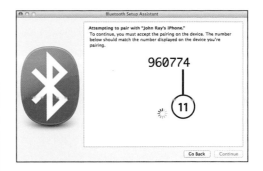

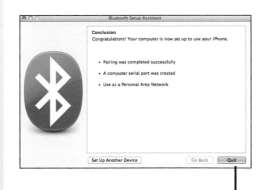

14. Open the System Preferences and click the Network Preferences button.

15. Select the Bluetooth PAN interface.

16. Click Connect to begin using your iPhone to access the Internet using your MacBook's network.

Tethering with USB to an iPhone

If you find your iPhone low on power or are having signal strength problems with Bluetooth, you might want to use a USB connection to charge your phone and access the Internet simultaneously.

1. To tether to your iPhone via USB, make sure that iPhone Internet tethering is active (as described in "Tethering Wirelessly to an iPhone").

2. Using an Apple iPhone cable, connect the iPhone to one of your MacBook's unused USB ports.

3. Open the System Preferences and click the Network icon.

4. IPhone USB appears In the lIst of network interfaces. Click to select it.

5. Click Apply to connect and begin using the iPhone's Internet connection on your computer.

6. To disconnect, unplug your iPhone.

Using Cellular Data Cards

If you don't have an iPhone, you might want to use a cellular data card (WWAN card) to connect your MacBook to the Internet. There are a wide variety of WWAN cards that work out of the box on Snow Leopard.

Finding a Supported Data Card

To see a list of the cards that Apple officially supports, read the knowledge base article at http://support.apple.com/kb/HT1122.

Refer to your cellular provider for information on the fees and data limits associated with its WWAN cards.

Configuring a WWAN Card for Use with Your MacBook

Using a supported WWAN card is easy, as long as the card has been properly provisioned by your service provider!

1. Plug the WWAN card into your computer.

2. Open the Network System Preference panel.

3. The Network Preference panel opens, showing the new device. Make sure it is selected in the interface list.

4. Configure the settings using the information provided by your ISP. In most cases, you won't need to do *anything*.

5. Click the Show WWAN Status in Menu Bar button to display a menu item for the card.

6. Choose to connect automatically, if desired.

7. If you have been given specific network settings instructions by your ISP, click the Advanced button and enter the options as described in "Manually Configuring Network Settings."

8. Click Connect to begin using your WWAN card.

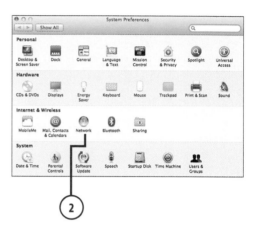

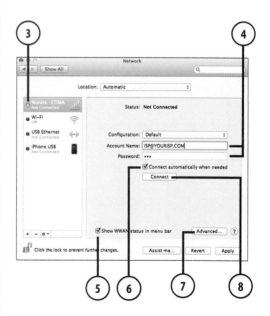

Managing Your WWAN Connection

If you chose to add the WWAN status to your menu bar as described in the previous section, you can use it to monitor and manage your connection.

1. The WWAN menu bar displays the signal strength of your device.

2. Use the Connect and Disconnect options under the menu to connect or disconnect from the Internet.

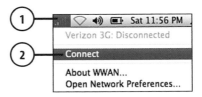

Creating Virtual Private Network Connections

With the MacBook, you have many different ways to connect to networks wherever you are. Many companies, however, only give you access to certain resources when you're connected directly to their networks. This puts a small crimp on the idea of "working on the go."

To get around the access problem, many organizations provide VPN, or Virtual Private Network, servers. Using a VPN server, your MacBook can use its current network connection (wireless, wired, through an iPhone, or using a WWAN card) to securely connect to your company's network. You are able to access all of the same resources that you see when you're sitting in your office chair.

Creating a VPN Connection

Snow Leopard supports three types of VPN connections—L2TP, PPTP, and Cisco IPSec. You need to find out from your network administrator which option is right for you, along with the settings you need to make the connection.

1. Create a new VPN connection by opening the System Preferences and clicking the Network icon.

2. Click the + button at the bottom of the interfaces pane.

3. Choose VPN as the interface.

4. Set the VPN type to the type specified by your network administrator.

5. Enter a meaningful name for the VPN service, such as "Work VPN."

6. Click Create.

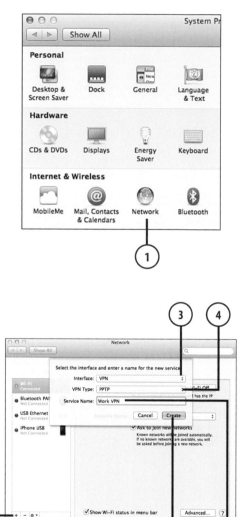

7. A new VPN interface is created and added to the list of network interfaces. Make sure the VPN interface is highlighted.

8. Configuration options appear on the right side of the network preference panel. Enter the server address and account information provided by your network administrator.

9. Click the Show VPN Status in Menu Bar item. This adds a menu item to the menu bar so you can quickly connect and disconnect from a VPN.

10. Click the Authentication Settings button.

11. You are prompted for a method of authentication. Enter a password or choose one of the other available options as directed by your network administrator

12. Click OK.

13. If you have been given specific network settings by your network administrator, click the Advanced button and enter the options as described in "Manually Configuring Network Settings."

14. Click the Connect button to connect to the VPN.

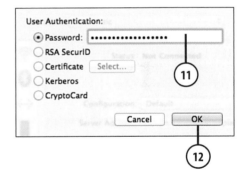

Managing Your VPN Connection

If you've chosen to show the VPN status in your menu bar, you can use the menu item to quickly connect and disconnect at any time. In addition, you can show the amount of time you've been connected, in case connection charges apply.

Configuring VPN on Demand

VPNs, like cookies, are a "sometimes" thing. If you don't need to have a VPN connection active, you shouldn't because it slows down your computer and eats up resources on the VPN server itself. Snow Leopard provides a simple way to automatically connect to your VPN when you need it. If, for example, you try to access an intranet website, Snow Leopard detects what you're doing and connects to your VPN server automatically.

1. To configure VPN on Demand service, open the System Preferences and click the Network icon.

2. Highlight your VPN interface in the interface list.

3. Click the Advanced button.

4. Click VPN on Demand in the button bar.

5. Click the + button to add a domain that triggers your VPN connection. (If you enter a domain you no longer want, remove it with the – button.)

6. Type the domain into the field that appears (for example, "intranet. mycompanydomain.net").

7. If multiple configurations have been created (see the next section), you can choose a specific configuration to trigger when making the connection.

8. Click OK to finish setting up VPN on Demand.

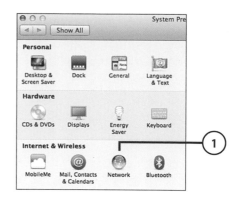

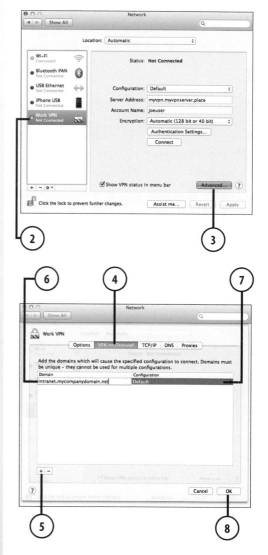

Managing Multiple Connections with Locations and Configurations

If you have a MacBook, chances are you're not one to sit still. One day you might be connecting from a beach in Maui, and the next, from a coffee shop in Columbus, Ohio. To help accommodate your mobile lifestyle, Apple provides two mechanisms for managing network connections: configurations and locations.

For interfaces such as VPNs, WWAN modems, or other devices that might have multiple different "versions" of their settings, you can create configurations. A configuration holds information such as the server you're connecting to and your specific network settings.

Creating Configurations

To create a configuration, do the following:

1. To create a configuration (if supported by your network interface), first open the system preferences and click the Network icon.

2. Click the interface for which you want to create a new configuration.

3. Using the Configuration popup menu, choose Add Configuration.

4. Enter a name for the configuration.

5. Click Create. You may now configure the network interface as described in the chapter.

6. Your new settings are stored and accessible under the configuration name you provided so that you can easily switch from one to another. (You can also remove or rename configurations under this menu.)

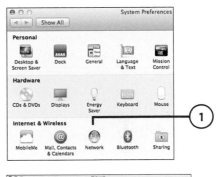

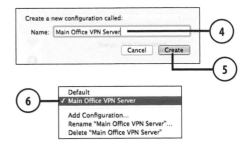

Adding and Using Locations

Locations are like configurations on steroids. Lots of steroids. Using locations, you can create entirely new sets of network interfaces and options and switch between them easily.

1. Open the System Preferences and click the Network icon.

2. The default location of Automatic is set at the top of the network panel.

3. Choose Edit Locations from the Location drop-down menu.

4. A dialog box that lists any configured locations displays.

5. Click the + button to add an entry for a new location. (Use – to remove locations you no longer want.)

6. Type a name to describe the location, such as "Coffee Shop."

7. Click Done.

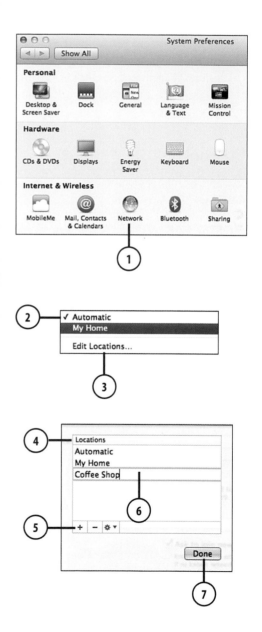

8. All your network settings are now set to their defaults for the new location. All VPN connections and other interfaces are gone. You are, in effect, starting fresh with configuring your MacBook network setup.

9. Configure your network settings as described in this chapter.

10. After you've completed your setup, you can switch between locations using the Location drop-down menu within the System Preferences Network panel. Remember that you can return to your original network settings by choosing the location named "Automatic."

Seeking Automated Network Assistance

The Snow Leopard operating system provides a few automated tools to help you configure and diagnose your MacBook's network settings. Be aware that the automated tools might not be able to fully set up your connection, and if you have complicated network configurations, you might want to manage the settings manually anyway. Let's review what you need to do to use these tools.

Launching Diagnostics

To launch the diagnostics system, follow these steps:

1. Open the System Preferences Network panel and click the Network icon.

2. Click the Assist Me button at the bottom of the window.

3. Click Diagnostics in the dialog box that displays.

4. Choose the Network interface to run diagnostics on. If you've configured locations, you are first prompted to choose your location.

5. Click Continue.

6. Review the results and follow the onscreen instructions.

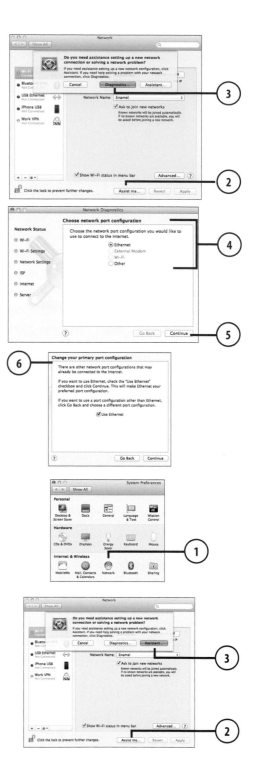

Launching the Setup Assistant

To launch the setup assistant, follow these steps:

1. Open the System Preferences Network panel and click the Network icon.

2. Click the Assist Me button at the bottom of the window.

3. Click Assistant in the dialog box that appears.

4. Provide a location where you will be using the network connection. This process creates a new location, as described in the previous "Using Locations" section.

5. Click Continue.

6. Choose the type of connection you are making.

7. Click Continue.

8. Follow the onscreen instructions to let Snow Leopard attempt to configure your network settings for you.

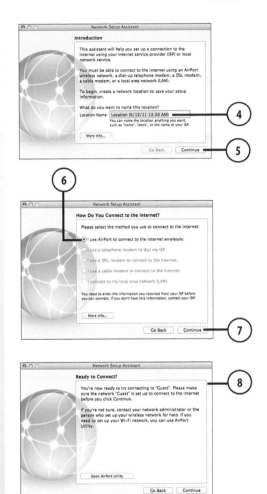

It's Not All Good

DON'T DISCOUNT YOUR ADMIN!

It is impossible for me to stress this enough: Your network administrator or ISP is your best resource for correcting network problems. Using Snow Leopard's assistant tools is not a silver bullet; if you don't have the information required to make a network connection (IP address, and so on), it won't "just work"!

Read your email and the latest news in the Mail application.

Browse the web and keep track of your favorite articles in Safari.

Chat with friends and family via FaceTime.

In this chapter, you'll learn how to use your MacBook to access Online Services, including:

→ Connecting to email accounts
→ Accessing Microsoft Exchange Servers
→ Using threading and spam-filtering features
→ Configuring instant messaging in iChat
→ Conducting video and audio chats
→ Sending text messages to mobile devices
→ Browsing the Web using Safari 5.x
→ Creating web clippings
→ Using Safari Extensions

Communicating Online with Your MacBook

Introduction

The Internet has de-shackled us from our desks. We can communicate instantly with family, friends, and colleagues no matter where we are in the world as long we can access an Internet connection. Your MacBook comes with everything you need to keep in touch when you're on the road or kicked back on your couch.

In this chapter, you learn how to use some of the unique features of the Lion's Mail, Web, and Instant/Video Messaging applications. Even if you're working in a Microsoft-centric environment, you'll find that your MacBook's tools are up to the job.

Getting Started with Accounts

For all the fun and information the Internet has brought us, it has also created a mess in terms of managing all the accounts we use to communicate online. If you're like many people, you have multiple email accounts—possibly one through iCloud, one from work, and one through your ISP. You have accounts for chatting with instant messenger. You have accounts for sharing contacts and calendars. In other words, you've got tons of different usernames and passwords that all need to be configured in different applications, just so you can be connected.

In Lion, Apple has recognized the problem of account overload and worked to consolidate all your online account management in a single centralized preference panel—Mail, Contacts, and Calendars. Here you can set up email, instant messenger, iCloud, Exchange, iCal, and other account types—without needing to figure out where they're managed in your individual applications.

I'll be showing the use of this panel as needed in the chapters, but let's take a very brief look at how you'll interact with this tool on your MacBook.

Adding an Account

To add an account for an online service (email, contacts, calendars, iCloud, Exchange, etc.), follow these steps:

1. Open the Mail, Contacts, and Calendars System Preference Panel.

2. Make sure the Add Account item is highlighted on the left.

3. Choose an online service that you want to configure by clicking its name on the right.

4. Click Other to choose from a list of additional service types.

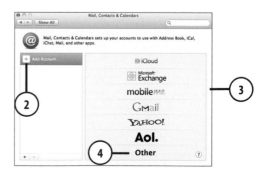

5. Fill in the requested information in the setup wizard that appears.

6. The completed account is listed in the preference panel.

7. Close System Preferences when finished.

It's Not All Good

EXPLORATION IS REWARDED!

While the Mail, Contacts, and Calendars panel is a great place for establishing new accounts and performing high-level configuration, you may still find yourself needing to dig for various esoteric settings within your individual Internet applications.

Using Mail

The first thing that many of us do when we have an Internet connection is check our email. Email is now a way to exchange rich media—such as photos, files, and movies—in addition to a way to exchange written messages. The email application, Mail (found in the Applications folder by clicking the Mail icon), is provided with your MacBook. With Mail, you can connect to a variety of different mail servers, including Microsoft Exchange, with only a few clicks of your mouse.

Things You Need Before Setting up an Email Connection

As with the networking information in the last chapter, configuring your email account isn't a matter of guessing. Apple's Mail application can automatically set up several popular email services (such as Google and Yahoo), but if you're connecting to a corporate email server, you should collect as much information as possible from your email system administrator or ISP before proceeding. This includes your email address, password, email server, email server type (POP, IMAP, or Exchange), and SMTP server:

- **Incoming Mail Server**—The server that you connect to when retrieving your email.
- **Incoming Mail Server Type**—The type of server that you're connecting to. Apple's Mail application supports Exchange, IMAP, and POP servers.
- **Outgoing (SMTP) Server**—The server that sends your messages.
- **Authentication**—Typically, a user name and password required to retrieve or send messages.

Adding an Email Account (Simple)

If you have an email account that Lion recognizes, configuration couldn't be easier—you just need your email address, name, and password to make a connection. Lion attempts to identify and configure your account. If for some reason it fails, you can continue with an advanced manual configuration (see the next task).

1. Open the Mail, Contacts, and Calendars System Preference Panel.

2. Make sure the Add Account item is highlighted on the left.

3. Choose an email service that you want to configure by clicking its name on the right.

4. The Add Account window displays. Type your name (as you want it to appear in outgoing messages), email address, and password for the account.

5. Click Set Up.

6. Lion attempts to automatically configure your account. If additional features are determined to be available from the email provider, they are listed in the window. Choose which services you want to use by checking/unchecking the checkboxes.

7. Click Add Account to finish adding the account.

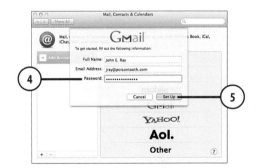

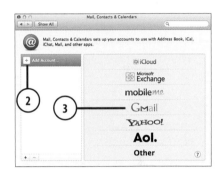

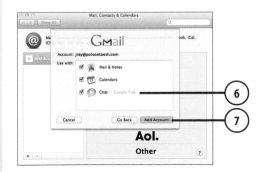

8. If it's successful, the newly config- ured email account appears in the account list. If the setup fails, can- cel setup and skip ahead to the next section, "Adding an Email Account (Advanced)."

9. Clicking the account name in the list displays the account details on the right. You can edit these val- ues if you want to change your display name or the name of your account.

10. You can now close System Preferences and begin using your account in Mail.

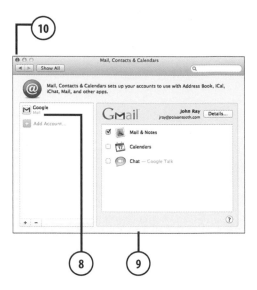

Adding an Email Account (Advanced)

Email accounts that aren't immedi- ately recognized by Lion require more information to be entered before they can be used. This is the case for some ISP email accounts, corporate, and educational systems. Be sure you have all the information listed previously under the "Things You Need Before Setting Up an Email Connection."

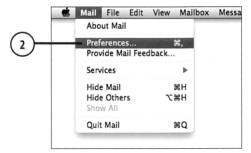

1. Open the Mail application from the Dock or Applications folder.

2. Choose Preferences from the Mail menu.

3. Click the Accounts button within the Mail preferences window.

4. Click + to add a new account.

5. Provide the basic account information when prompted and click Continue.

6. When Mail cannot automatically configure the account, it displays a new dialog to collect information about your incoming mail server.

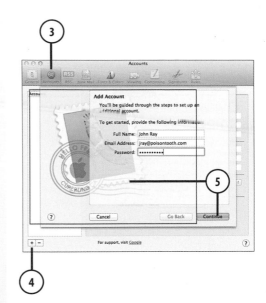

7. Enter the account information provided by your system administrator or ISP (the incoming mail server, username, and password). Use the description field to name the account with something meaningful that helps you differentiate it from other accounts.

8. If you are setting up an Exchange account, click the Address Book Contacts and iCal Calendars checkboxes if you would like your MacBook to have access to your Exchange-based address book and calendars directly within Address Book and iCal (discussed in Chapter 5, "Managing Contacts and Appointments").

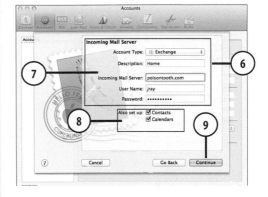

9. Click Continue. Mail automatically tests the information you've provided. If a failure occurs, recheck your information. After it is correct, click Continue again.

10. Mail displays the security settings for your incoming mail server. Typically, you are prompted for whether or not to use Secure Sockets Layer. If it's available, this option is recommended.

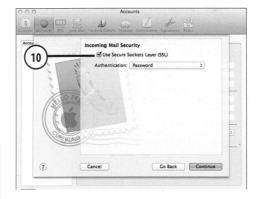

11. Use the Authentication dropdown menu to choose how you authenticate with the server. Typically you choose password (some complex configurations might use more advanced authentication methods).

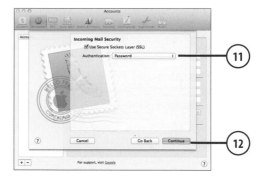

12. Click Continue.

13. Mail displays the outgoing mail server settings, known as the SMTP server settings. You should enter the information provided by your system administrator or ISP, or choose an existing outgoing server from the Outgoing Mail server dropdown menu. Again, use the description field to provide a meaningful name for the mail server.

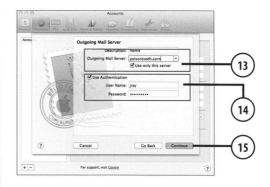

14. If your outgoing mail server requires authentication (many do!), click the Use Authentication checkbox and then provide a user name and password.

15. Click Continue.

16. Now you are prompted for whether or not to use Secure Sockets Layer for outgoing mail, as well as the authentication type. (Again, you would typically choose Password here.)

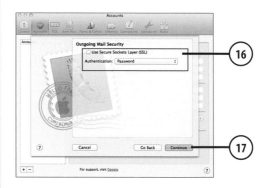

17. Click Continue to review your final settings. If an error occurs, check your settings, or click Continue to proceed with the settings you provided.

18. Make sure the Take Account Online checkbox is selected so that you can begin using your account.

19. Click Create to finish setting up the account.

Troubleshooting Your Connection

To troubleshoot your account settings, from within Mail choose Window, Connection Doctor. Your MacBook tests all your email account settings and shows you exactly where any errors are occurring.

Multiple Email Addresses, One Account

It isn't uncommon for one email account to have multiple addresses associated with it. I might have a single account with addresses, such as *mymacbook@ placeforstuff.com* or *johnray@me.com*, which I want to appear when I send a message. To configure multiple addresses for a single account, Open Mail's preferences, click Accounts, and then click the account you want to add an alias to. Enter the alias email addresses, separated by commas, in the Email Address field in the account details. The email addresses are then available in a popup menu when you compose a new message.

Finding Your Way Around Mail

After your email account is configured, Mail connects and retrieves your messages. The Mail application workspace is split into three columns, from left to right: mailboxes, a message list, and message content.

On the left, the mailbox list shows different mailboxes (or folders) for categorizing your messages. To review the messages in one of your mailboxes (such as Inbox), click the mailbox. The message list, to the immediate right of the mailboxes, refreshes to show all of the email within the mailbox, including a several-line preview of the contents. Any message that you click in the Message list is displayed in the message content area on the right.

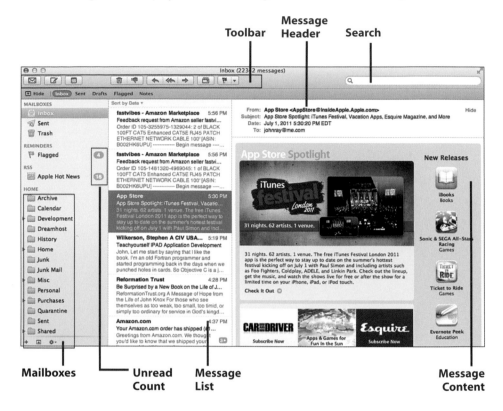

Mailboxes   Unread   Message   Message
                  Count   List   Content

Now that you know the basics of finding your way around Mail, let's take a look at the common tasks you should familiarize yourself with.

Out with the New, In with the Old

If you've been using Apple Mail for the past decade, you'll recognize that Lion's Mail layout is a dramatic departure from previous versions. If you'd prefer to live in the past, you can change to the older style layout by checking the Use classic layout option found within the Viewing section of the Mail preferences (Mail, Preferences).

Reading Email

Reading messages is typically a matter of finding a message in the message list, clicking it, and reading. Even so, you can improve the experience by taking advantage of several tools built into Mail.

Sorting Mail

In previous versions of mail, it used to be that you'd click a column heading and "poof," your mail was sorted. In Lion's Mail application, however, the message list doesn't have columns, so you'll need to follow this approach:

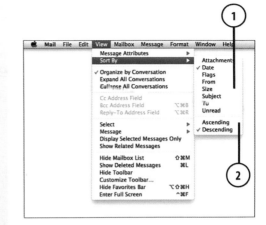

1. Choose View, Sort By, and a message attribute to use as your sorting criteria.

2. Choose View, Sort By, and Ascending or Descending to set the order of your sorting preferences.

Viewing Additional Attributes

Much as you can set the mail attributes you want to use for sorting, you can also set the attributes displayed in the message list. Use the View, Message List menu to set which attributes will be visible in the message list items.

Previewing Attachments

In Chapter 1, "Managing Your MacBook Desktop," you learned about the Quick Look system for previewing files in the Finder. In Mail, if your message contains an attachment, you can also use the Quick Look system.

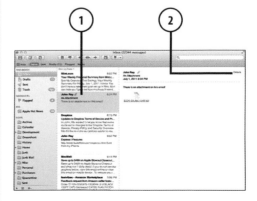

1. Choose a message with an attachment—represented by a paperclip in the message list.

2. Click the Details link at the top of the message content to show buttons for saving and viewing Attachments.

3. Click the Quick Look button at the top of the message content area.

4. A Quick Look window appears, displaying the selected content.

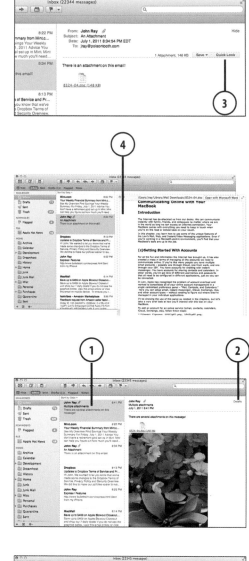

Saving Attachments

You can easily save one or more attachments to your MacBook's hard drive, and even add images to iPhoto, directly from Mail.

1. Choose a message with an attachment—represented by a paperclip in the message list.

2. Click the Details link at the top of the message content to show buttons for saving and viewing Attachments.

3. Click the Save button at the top of the message content area.

4. A menu appears, enabling you to Save All, choose an individual file to save, or, if applicable, add the file to iPhoto.

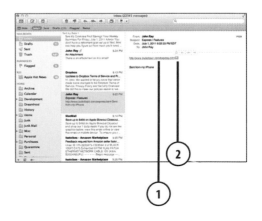

>>> Go Further

WORKING WITH ATTACHMENTS

If you prefer a more Finder-like approach to dealing with attachments, you can also work with attached files as icons. Scroll through your email and you'll see the attached files represented as icons in the message (usually at the bottom). You can drag these icons to your desktop (or anywhere you'd like to store them). You can also click an icon to immediately open it in a compatible Lion application.

Viewing Web Pages within an Email

Have you ever gotten a link to a webpage in email and wanted to view it without having to launch Safari? In Lion, you can. To preview a web link directly in Mail, follow these steps:

1. Position your cursor over the link within the message content, but do not click!

2. A small downward-pointing arrow appears to the right of the link. Click it.

3. A popover window appears displaying the web page.

4. Click Open in Safari to open the full page in your web browser.

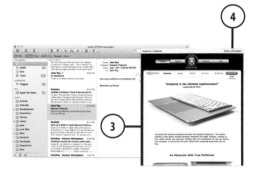

Using Data Detectors

The icon that appears at the end of a web link in mail (and the subsequent preview of the page) is an example of a Lion "Data Detector" in action. You may notice other icons beside dates, addresses, phone numbers, and so on. Clicking these icons will do similar helpful actions, such as setting appointments, adding information to a contact, or tracking shipments.

Organizing with Email Conversations

Email conversations can grow quite lengthy with back-and-forth replies. To help keep long conversations under control, Lion's Mail, by default, collapses your conversations into a single entry in your message list. You can expand the entry to show the individual messages whenever you need to see one.

1. Conversations are denoted by a number within an entry in the message list.

2. Click the message list entry to show all the messages in the conversation within the content area.

3. Messages are numbered at the top to show the order in which they were received.

4. To focus on a single message, click the arrow beside the number in the message list to show a list of individual senders and dates.

5. Click the individual name/date to show only that message.

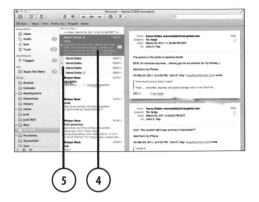

⑤ ④

It's Not All Good

SILENCE THE CONVERSATION!

Many people find the conversation view to be disorienting in Mail. If you're one of those people, you can turn it off entirely by choosing Organize by Conversation from Mail's View Menu.

Managing Spam Filtering

Mail can learn (with some help) which messages in your inbox are spam and then filter similar messages so you don't have to see them. To manage your spam filtering, follow these steps:

1. Choose Mail, Preferences from the menu bar.

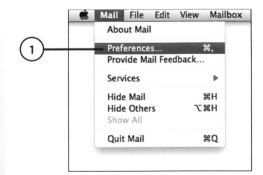

2. Click the Junk Mail toolbar icon.

3. Click Enable Junk Mail Filtering to turn on spam filtering. You can disable it by unchecking this box at any time.

4. Choose where Mail should file spam messages. Moving messages to the Junk mailbox is a good choice.

5. To help prevent getting false positives, use the spam exemptions to identify types of messages that you don't consider to be spam.

6. If your ISP offers spam filtering (and you trust it), make sure the Trust Junk Mail Headers in Messages option is set.

7. Close the Mail Preferences.

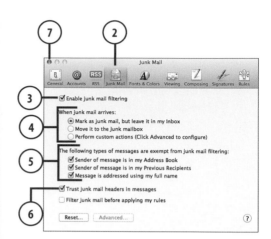

Classifying Spam

If you receive spam mail, select it and click the Junk icon (thumbs down) in the Mail toolbar. This classifies messages as spam. When new messages recognized as spam come in, they are automatically placed in the Junk folder. If *good* mail is accidentally classified as spam, use the thumbs up icon in the toolbar to tell Mail it made a mistake.

Changing How Often Mail Is Retrieved

You can force Mail to retrieve messages using the Get Mail toolbar button, but to change the frequency with which it forces a check you need to access the preferences.

1. Choose Mail, Preferences from the menu bar.

2. Click the General icon in the Preferences Toolbar.

3. Use the Check for New Messages pop-up menu to set how frequently Mail looks for new messages.

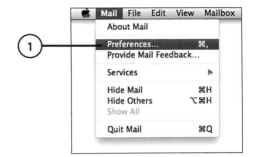

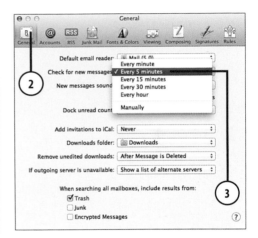

Composing Email

Email today is a bit more than just typing a message—it can include sending photos, files, or even professionally designed invitations and announcements. Lion's Mail on your MacBook enables you to do all of these things.

Let's take a look at what you can do beyond simple text.

Sending Messages with Attachments

Mail can attach virtually any type of file to your messages with ease. Follow these steps to add Windows-compatible attachments to a mail message.

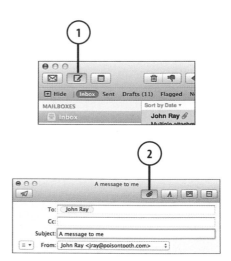

1. Start a new message by clicking the new message icon (pencil and paper) in the Mail toolbar.

2. Click the Attach icon (paperclip) in the New Message window.

3. Choose the files or folders to send from the file chooser dialog. Select multiples by holding down the ⌘ key and clicking.

4. Check the Send Windows-Friendly Attachments checkbox to ensure that anyone (regardless of their platform choice) can open the attachments.

5. Click Choose File to add the attachments.

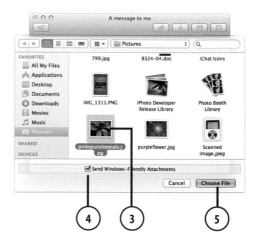

6. Compose the message as normal and then click the send icon (paper airplane).

Attaching Pictures from iPhoto

To quickly attach photos from iPhoto, click the Photo Browser button to open a small window that shows your iPhoto galleries. Choose your photos and drag them into the message to attach them!

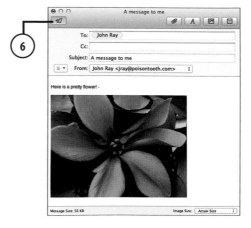

Using Stationery Templates

If you'd like to send an invitation or a fancy greeting, you can make use of prebuilt templates, called "Stationery," that come with Lion's Mail application. Stationery is available whenever you're composing a message:

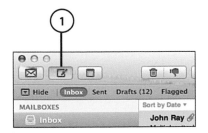

1. Start a new message by clicking the new message icon (pencil and paper) in the Mail toolbar.

2. Click the Show Stationery icon (paper with dots) in the New Message toolbar.

3. Choose a category of templates on the left side of the Stationery bar.

4. Click the thumbnail of the template you want to apply.

5. Click to edit the text within the template.

6. If the template contains images, replace them by dragging photo files from the Finder onto the template image (or use the Photo Browser button to locate an image).

7. Click the send icon (paper airplane) when you are finished with the message.

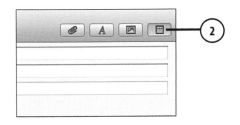

Changing Templates

After you change the content of a template, you can choose another template and your changes will be maintained as much as possible.

Creating Signatures

When you send a lot of email, you probably get a bit tired of typing the same
thing at the end of each message—your
name, email, and other contact information. To add this information automatically to the end of each message you
write, create a signature.

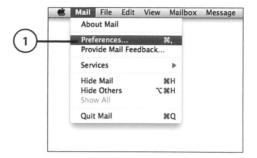

1. Choose Mail, Preferences from the
   menu bar.

2. Click the Signatures icon in the
   preferences toolbar.

3. Choose an account that the signature should be used with, or choose
   All Signatures to not associate the
   signature with a specific account.

4. Click + to add a new signature.

5. Type a name for the signature.

6. Enter the text for the signature in
   the space to the right.

7. Click Always Match My Default
   Message Font so that the signature
   always matches the font you're
   using.

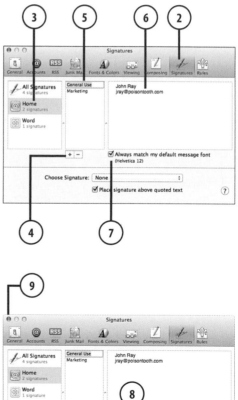

8. If you're adding the signature to an
   account, use the signature popup
   menu to choose which signature is
   displayed when you write a message. You can also choose a signature using the Choose Signature
   pop-up menu in the message com-
   position window.

9. Close the Mail Preferences window.

Adding a vCard

To attach your personal information to
your signature as a virtual business card,
you can drag a card out of your Address
Panel (Window, Address Panel) into the
signature.

Managing Your Email

Email can be overwhelming, especially if you have several different accounts and dozens of incoming messages each day. To help you cope with the incoming mail, you can create mailboxes in which to file or copy messages. You can also set up smart mailboxes that automatically display messages that match certain criteria.

Creating Mailboxes

To create a new mailbox, follow these steps:

1. Click the + button at the bottom of the Mailbox list.

2. Choose New Mailbox.

3. Using the Location pop-up menu, choose where the mailbox should be stored. You see all of your existing Mailboxes in the menu, as well as On My Mac. Choosing an existing location creates the new mailbox inside of that location.

4. Enter a name for the new mailbox and then click OK.

5. The new mailbox is created and displayed in the Mailbox list.

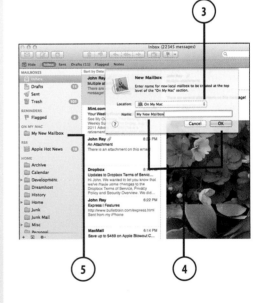

Make Room for Your Mail

Since the mailbox display eats up a bunch of room on your screen, Apple has made it simple to hide and show the mailbox column using the Hide/Show button in the upper-left corner of the Mail window. In addition, you can quickly change between your Inbox, Sent, Drafts, and Flagged folders using the links directly in the Mail toolbar.

Deleting and Renaming Mailboxes

If you find yourself with extra mailboxes or mailboxes that are no longer serving their original purposes, you can delete or rename them.

1. Select the mailbox you want to change in your mailbox list.

2. Click the Action icon (the gear) at the bottom of the mailbox list.

3. Choose Delete Mailbox or Rename Mailbox as needed. Any messages stored in a mailbox being deleted are also deleted.

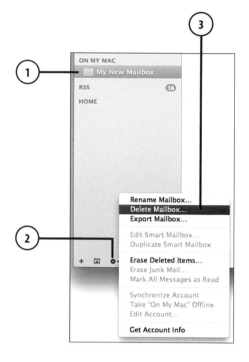

Nesting Folders

Even though you chose where to put your mailbox when it was first created, you can move it within your mailbox hierarchy easily. Mailboxes can be moved inside of other mailboxes by clicking and dragging their folder icons into (or out of) another mailbox.

Filing Messages in Mailboxes

Mailboxes are only useful if you file your messages in them. You can either copy or move messages one at a time or en masse to a mailbox. This can be done either manually, as described here, or automatically using Smart Mailboxes or Email Rules, discussed in the tasks following this one.

1. Select a message by clicking it in the message list. You can select a contiguous range of messages by holding down Shift and clicking another message, or select several scattered messages by holding down ⌘ and clicking multiple messages.

2. Move the messages to a mailbox by dragging them onto the desired mailbox. To copy—rather than move—the messages, hold down the Option key while you're dragging the messages. The messages are moved (or copied) to the other mailbox.

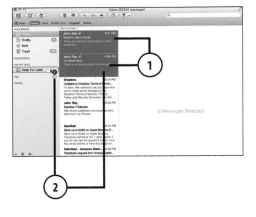

Filing without Dragging

If you have a large number of mailboxes, or just find the process of dragging to the mailbox list to be cumbersome, you can select the messages, then use Move To or Copy To from the Messages menu to file the email without any dragging required.

Automatic Email Organization with Smart Mailboxes

Much as Smart Folders in the Finder can help you keep track of files that share certain attributes, Smart Mailboxes can do the same for your email. Using information such as the sender, recipient, and even attachment names, you can group messages together in a Smart Mailbox, regardless of what mailbox, or even what email account, they're associated with.

1. To create a new Smart Mailbox, click the + button at the bottom of the Mailbox list and choose New Smart Mailbox.

2. Type a name for the mailbox.

3. Choose whether the mailbox should match any or all conditions.

4. Configure your search criteria. Use the first pop-up menu to choose a message attribute (such as Subject), the second to choose a comparison, and the field (where applicable) to provide the value that you are comparing against.

5. Use the + and – buttons to add or remove additional criteria.

6. To include messages from the Trash mailbox or Sent mailbox, click the appropriate Include Messages checkboxes.

7. Click OK when you're finished configuring the Smart Mailbox.

8. The new mailbox is created and displayed in the SMART MAILBOXES section within the Mailbox list.

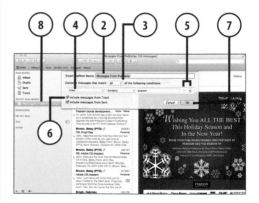

Nesting Smart Mailboxes

Smart Mailboxes can't be arranged hierarchically inside one another as normal mailboxes can. To create a hierarchy of smart mailboxes, you must create a Smart Mailbox Folder (Mailbox, New Smart Mailbox Folder). This special folder will be added to the SMART MAILBOXES section and can be used to organize any Smart Mailboxes you create.

Searching for Messages

Mail makes it easy to quickly search all of your email for particular content, and to turn that search into a Smart Mailbox for future reference. To search your mail, follow these steps:

1. Type the text you are looking for into the search field in the upper-right corner.

2. Potential search options appear in a dropdown list for matched people, mailboxes, subjects, and message content. Choose what best matches what you want to find.

3. Click the mailbox where the search should be performed.

4. The results appear in the message list.

5. Click Save to save the search as a Smart Mailbox. (See steps 2-8 of the "Automatic Email Organization with Smart Mailboxes" task.)

6. Alternatively, click the X button in the search field to clear the search results.

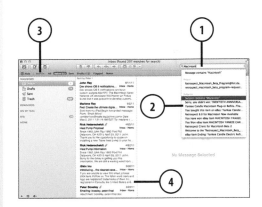

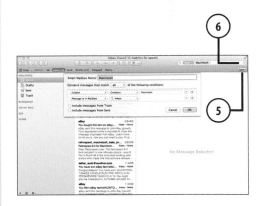

Writing Email Rules

If you'd prefer to have messages filed to actual mailboxes rather than Smart Mailboxes, you can write email rules. Email rules can file messages, highlight messages in the message list, and even forward them to another account. To write a rule, follow these steps:

1. Choose Mail, Preferences from the menu bar.

2. Click the Rules icon in the Preferences toolbar.

3. Click Add Rule.

4. Enter a description for the rule so that you can identify it later.

5. Use the Any pop-up menu to choose where any or all rules must evaluate as "true" in order for the rule's actions to be carried out.

6. Configure the conditions under which the rule executes. The first pop-up menu chooses what is evaluated, the second the comparison to be made, and field is the value that should be used in the comparison.

7. Use + or − to add or remove additional conditions.

8. Configure the actions that are performed when the conditions are met.

9. Use + or − to add or remove actions.

10. Click OK to save the rule. Close the Mail Preferences.

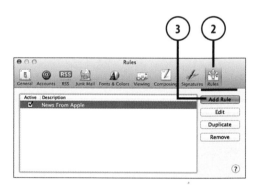

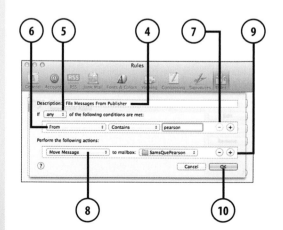

Using RSS Feeds in Mail

Mail isn't just an email reader; it's also an RSS reader that can display news feeds from your favorite websites. These are visible under the RSS section in the mailbox list. When an RSS feed is selected, its contents are displayed in the message list area. Choosing one of the feed items shows a summary in the message content area—just like when you're reading email.

Adding RSS Feeds to Mail

You can add new feeds to Mail and read summaries of your favorite news sites directly in Mail:

1. Click the + button at the bottom of the Mailbox list.

2. Choose Add RSS Feeds.

3. Click Browse Feeds in Safari Bookmarks to add previously bookmarked feeds.

4. Add a feed directly using its URL by clicking the Specify URL for a Feed button. Enter the URL in the field that appears.

5. Click Add to finish.

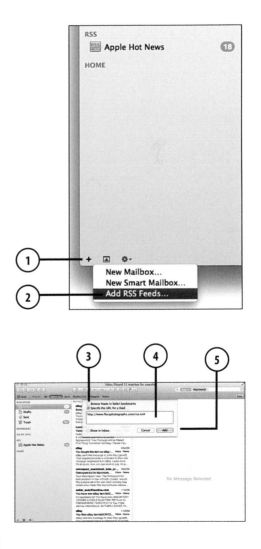

Changing RSS Preferences

If you want to change how frequently your news feeds are refreshed in Mail, you need to access the RSS preferences.

1. Choose Mail, Preferences from the menu.

2. Click the RSS icon in the Preferences toolbar.

3. Use the Default RSS Reader to verify that Mail is set as your preferred RSS reader.

4. Choose a frequency with which to check for updates.

5. Configure how often Mail removes items from the RSS feeds it receives.

6. Close the Preferences to save your settings.

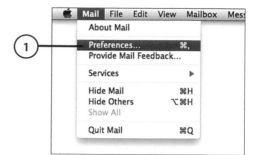

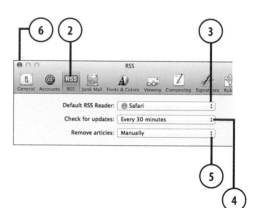

CHOOSE YOUR RSS READER

If using Mail to read and manage your RSS feeds seems awkward, never fear. The Safari web browser is also a full-fledged RSS reader and any RSS feed can be viewed and bookmarked just by entering its URL—the same as viewing a web page.

>>> Go Further

Instant Messaging with iChat

When email isn't conversational enough, instant messaging can take over. Your MacBook comes with a first-rate instant messaging application called iChat (found in the Applications folder). iChat can be used for text messaging, audio conferencing, video conferencing, and even screen sharing. If you have an iCloud, GoogleTalk, Jabber, or AIM (AOL Instant Messenger) account, you're ready to go.

Adding an Account to iChat

As with Mail, before you can use iChat, you need to set up an account. You need to know your account type, username, and password before continuing.

1. Open the Mail, Contacts, and Calendars System Preference Panel.

2. Make sure the Add Account item is highlighted on the left.

3. Choose the online service that provides your IM account by click-ing its name on the right. If your service only provides IM and not mail or calendaring, click Other to directly configure an iChat account.

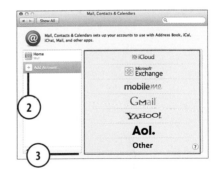

4. If you chose Other, select Add an iChat account.

5. Click Create.

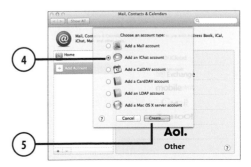

6. Fill in the requested information in the setup wizard that appears.

7. Click Create.

8. The account is displayed in the panel.

9. Close the System Preferences window by clicking the red button in the upper-left corner.

Multiple IM Accounts? No Problem!

Adding multiple IM accounts to iChat is no problem. The iChat buddy list window will combine your buddy lists into a single consolidated list. You can log in and out of the different services using the availability controls for each account (they are stacked on top of each other) as described in the "Logging Into (and Out of) Your Account" task.

Logging Into (and Out of) Your Account

When iChat has an account configured, you're ready to start iChat and begin chatting immediately. The first time you start iChat, your buddy list window appears and you are logged in. In fact, you are automatically logged in each time iChat starts. To manually log out of or into iChat, you simply need to set your status.

1. Start iChat from your Applications folder.

2. Click the status message below your name at the top of the iChat window. If you have multiple accounts set up, each one is represented by a line with separate status settings for that account.

3. To keep your status in sync between accounts, make sure Use Same Status for All Accounts is checked.

4. Choose Offline to Log out.

5. Choose any other status to log back into your IM account.

6. Choose Invisible to log in but hide your availability from other people.

Adding an iChat Status Menu
To add an iChat status menu to your menu bar, open the iChat Preferences and click Show Status in Menu Bar within the General settings. This gives you the ability to log in and out of your account when iChat isn't running.

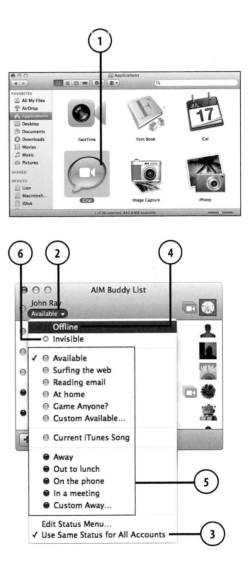

Configuring Your iChat Identity

Setting up an account in iChat gets you online, but you should customize your identity to better represent your online presence. With iChat, it's simple to set custom status messages and pictures to reflect your current mood.

Setting the iChat Picture

Because your MacBook has a camera built-in, you can swap your iChat picture whenever you'd like. Just smile and click, and instantly your buddies are seeing a new image.

1. Click the picture in the upper-right corner of the iChat buddy list.

2. Choose from a previous picture, or click Edit Picture to choose a new picture.

3. Click the Camera icon to take a new picture.

4. Alternatively, click Choose to choose a picture from your computer.

5. Set cropping and size for the picture by dragging it within the Buddy Picture window and adjusting the zoom slider.

6. Apply effects, if desired, using the Effects button.

7. Click Set to start using the new picture.

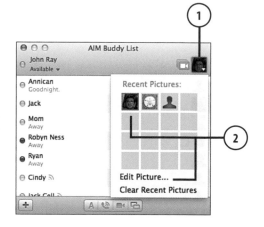

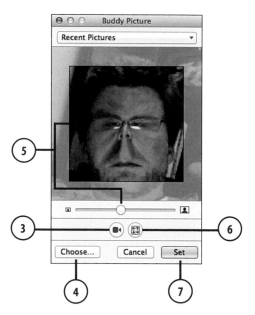

Configuring Custom Status Messages

Your status message can convey your state of mind, ask a question, or present some other information to your buddies. To configure a new status message, follow these steps:

1. Click the status popup menu.

2. Choose Edit Status Menu.

3. Click + or – under the Available or Away lists to add or remove status messages.

4. Click OK to save your status message settings.

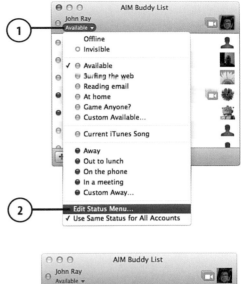

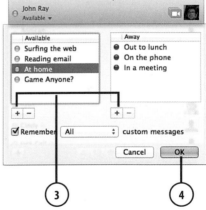

Managing Your Buddy List

Almost everything you do in iChat starts with your "buddy list." The iChat buddy list contains all the people that you want to chat with (and possibly some you don't). With each buddy is a display of his status (Away, Available, Idle, and so on) and an icon to indicate his chat capability.

The buddy list displays the people you can communicate with.

Cross-Platform Video Conferencing
iChat can carry out cross-platform A/V chats with Windows users using AIM, Google Talk, or Yahoo!.

Adding Buddies

In order to initiate a chat with someone, you must first add them to your buddy list.

1. Click the + button at the bottom of the buddy list. Choose Add Buddy.

2. If you have an address card for the person you want to add, click the disclosure arrow in the lower-right corner of the window to display your address book and then find and click the person's name.

3. Enter the screen name of your buddy in the Account Name field.

4. Enter a first and last name for your addition, and a group if any are available. Think of groups as a "folder" for your buddy.

5. Click Add.

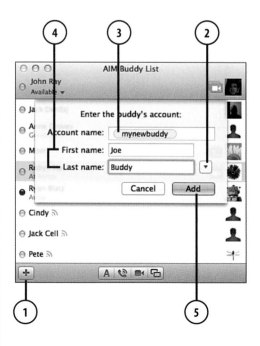

Adding Groups

As your buddy list grows, you might want to consider organizing them into groups, such as friends, family, coworkers, and so on. Adding new groups is similar to adding new buddies.

1. Make sure View, Use Groups is selected in the iChat menu bar.

2. Click the + button at the bottom of the buddy list.

3. Choose Add Group.

4. Enter a name for the new group.

5. Click Add.

6. Drag buddies within the buddy list into the group where you want them to appear.

___

Recent Buddies

By default, a group called Recent Buddies is added to your buddy list. This group contains all of the new contacts that you've communicated with recently. You can disable this group within the iChat account settings.

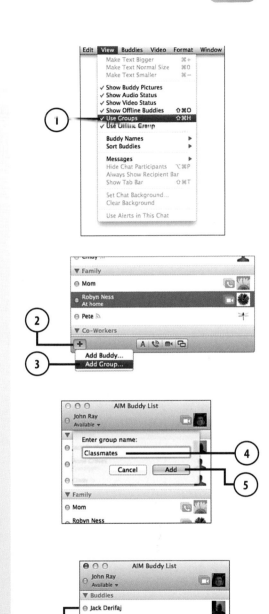

Communicating with Your Buddies

As mentioned previously, iChat supports a number of different communications methods including text, audio, and video. iChat theater even makes it possible to share visual media from your MacBook across a chat session. You might, for example, review an upcoming presentation with colleagues to fine-tune the content, or present a slideshow of a vacation to friends and family.

Responding to an Incoming Chat Request

After you've configured iChat and given out your screen name to your buddies, chances are you'll start getting a few messages. To respond to an incoming chat request, follow these steps:

1. iChat displays the first message (or a request for an audio or video chat) in a white chat bubble.

2. Click the bubble to show the chat window.

3. Click Accept to begin chatting, or Decline to ignore the request.

4. If you don't know the individual or don't want to hear from them, click Block.

5. When you're finished chatting, close the chat window.

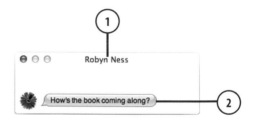

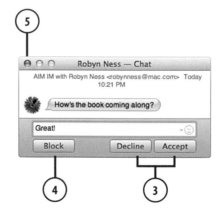

Neither Seen nor Heard

If you receive a video or audio chat request, you will have the option of choosing Text Reply if you'd prefer to type, rather than be seen or heard.

Starting a Text Chat

To initiate a text chat with one or more buddies, follow these steps:

1. Select one or more individuals in your buddy list. Shift-click to select multiple people.

2. Click the A button at the bottom of the iChat window.

3. A chat window that shows all the participants displays.

4. Type an invitation message and wait for responses!

Double-Click to Chat

If you've ever used a chat program before, you're probably familiar with the double-click-a-buddy-to-chat paradigm. This also works in iChat.

Consolidate or Separate Your iChat Sessions

If you have more than one active text chat, iChat will automatically consolidate them into a single window. You can switch between chat sessions by clicking your chat partner's name on the left side of the window. To move a chat to a completely separate window, simply drag the user's name out of the chat list and it becomes its own standalone chat window.

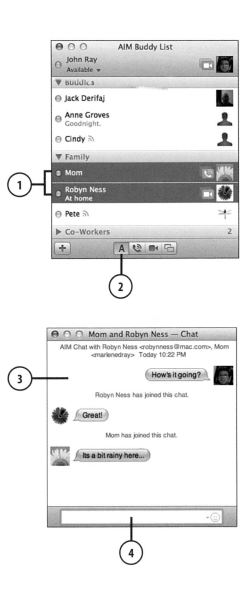

Starting an Audio or Video Chat

A/V chats require significantly more bandwidth than text chats. iChat automatically senses the capabilities of your machine and Internet connection and that of your buddies and does not allow chats unless it thinks they will be successful. You can chat with up to 3 other people via video and 10 via audio, depending on your connection and assuming they have microphone or camera-enabled systems.

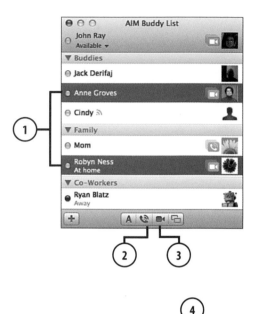

1. Select the individuals that you want to include in an audio or video chat. The icons by each buddy's name indicate the chat capabilities.

2. Click the telephone icon to initiate an audio chat.

3. Click the video icon to start a video chat.

4. A chat window appears displaying the participants as they join.

5. Click the + button to add additional members to the chat.

6. Toggle mute on the chat by clicking the microphone.

7. When conducting a video chat, click Effects to apply real-time video effects to your onscreen image.

8. Click the double arrows during a video chat to expand the video to full screen.

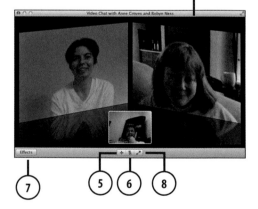

Be Heard with a Headset

If you find yourself using video or audio chat frequently, you might want to invest in a microphone or headset. To change the iChat microphone and set up a headset, open the Audio/Video section of the iChat preferences.

Sending SMS Messages via iChat

iChat can be used to communicate with a buddy via SMS (text messaging to a mobile phone) just as if the buddy was logged into iChat. To start a text messaging session, you need to know the mobile phone number or have it stored in Address Book.

1. Choose File, New SMS from the iChat menu bar.

2. Enter the phone number you want to send a message to.

3. Choose the instant messaging account that should get the response.

4. Click Chat.

5. Begin typing in the new chat window. Your messages are automatically sent to the recipient's mobile phone.

Texting from iChat

If your buddy already has a mobile phone number stored in their address book, you can initiate an SMS session with them by right-clicking (or Control-clicking) their name and choosing Send SMS.

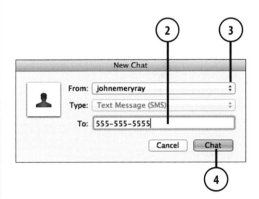

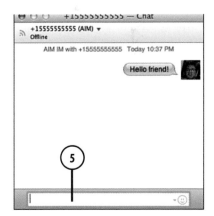

Sharing Files, Photos, and Your Screen

In addition to being a great communications tool, iChat can serve as a collaboration platform or even a way to interact on the same desktop. If you've ever found yourself in the position of having to talk through a document at long distance or troubleshoot technical problems remotely, you'll appreciate the additional functionality built into iChat.

Presenting Files, Photos, and Webpages in iChat Theater

Using iChat Theater, you can share the content that you've created on your MacBook—photos, videos, and even webpages. These items can be shared with any buddy whose connection supports video chats.

1. Initiate a video chat with the individuals with whom you want to share a file.

2. Click the + button in the video chat window and then choose Share a File with iChat Theater to share an individual file, or Share iPhoto with iChat Theater to share an iPhoto album.

3. Choose the file, album, or webpage you want to share.

4. Click the Share button.

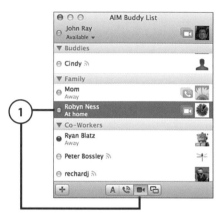

5. After the sharing session begins, use the onscreen controls to move through the presentation. Text and PDF files display page controls, video files include typical video controls, and so on.

6. Click the X button in the upper-right corner of the shared file's display to stop sharing and return to the video chat.

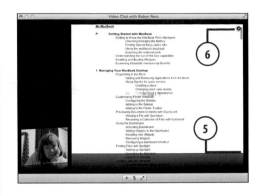

Transferring Files over iChat

iChat provides a very convenient mechanism for sending files to your buddies. You can send individual files, or even entire folders, just by dragging them into iChat.

1. Find the file or folder that you want to share.

2. To transfer to an online buddy who you aren't currently chatting with, drag the file to their name in your buddy list.

3. To transfer a file within an active chat session, drag the file to the chat window. Files such as images are displayed inline in the chat and can be previewed without opening the file.

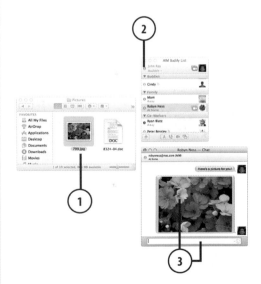

Confirming File Transfers

If someone attempts to transfer a file to you over iChat, you are prompted whether or not to accept the download. By default, all transferred files are saved in the Downloads directory.

Starting a Screen Sharing Session

A unique Mac-only feature of iChat is the ability to share someone else's screen. Using this tool, you can control the other person's computer as if you were sitting directly in front of it.

1. Choose the buddy that you want to share screens with.

2. Click the Screen Sharing button.

3. Choose whether you want to request access to your buddy's screen or if you want to share your screen.

4. After the request is accepted, you (or your buddy) have access to the remote screen. You can interact with the desktop as if you were sitting in front of the computer.

5. Click the miniaturized version of the screen to switch between viewing the local screen and the remote screen.

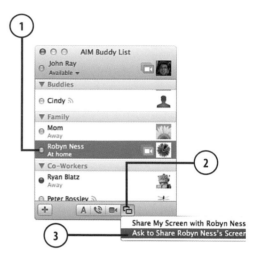

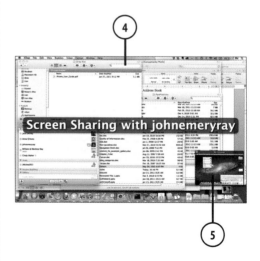

Screen Sharing with johnemeryray

Remote Support via iChat
When screens are being shared, iChat also starts a simultaneous audio chat, which makes it easy for you to talk through issues with the remote party.

Video Calls with FaceTime

The question I get when I ask someone to sign up for FaceTime is "Isn't iChat enough?" And I've wondered myself why Apple has introduced a new video chatting tool without simply integrating it into iChat. While I suspect that ultimately an integrated communications tool *will* appear, for now, consider FaceTime to be similar to a phone. Unlike iChat, which needs to be running, FaceTime will start automatically if someone places a FaceTime call, and it will simultaneously ring on as many Macs, iPhones, and iPads as you'd like.

FaceTime also requires zero configuration beyond providing an email address that your friends can "call."

Setting Up FaceTime

The first time FaceTime starts, you need to provide it with an Apple ID that will be used for registration. After the initial ID is provided, you can associate as many email addresses as you'd like with a given install. Follow these steps to add FaceTime addresses:

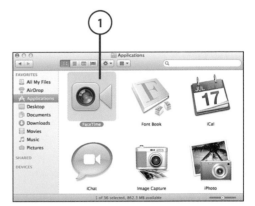

1. Open FaceTime from the dock or from the Applications folder.

2. Enter your Apple ID and password.

3. If you do not have an ID, click Create New Account to walk through an ID creation wizard.

4. Click Sign In.

5. Provide the primary email address you want to use for FaceTime.

6. Click Next.

7. FaceTime logs in, and you're ready for calls.

Placing FaceTime Calls

To place a call with FaceTime, you need to have the address or phone number of a FaceTime-compatible contact in your address book. In other words, make sure your family and friends have an iOS device or a Mac and have configured FaceTime. You also need to be sure you've stored their contact information in your address book. (See Chapter 5 for more information.)

Placing Calls from the Contacts List

Once you've got yourself a few equipped friends, follow these steps to call them over FaceTime:

1. Click the Contacts button at the bottom of the FaceTime window.

2. Browse through your contacts. When you find the person you want to call, click their name.

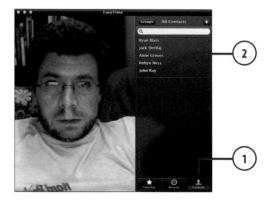

3. The contact information for your friend is displayed.

4. Click the phone number or email address you want to call.

5. If you want to call the person frequently, click the Add to Favorites button to add a shortcut for future use.

6. If the call is connected, you'll be able to see and talk to the other person. Otherwise, skip to step 9.

7. Use the button at the bottom-left corner of the window to mute the call, or the bottom-right to go fullscreen.

8. Click End to hang up when you are finished talking.

9. If the call does not connect, you'll be given the options of cancelling the call or calling back (redial).

See Your Surroundings

By default, the FaceTime camera takes a portrait image. If you'd like to see more of your surroundings, you can rotate to a landscape mode by choosing Video, Use Landscape (⌘+R) from the menubar.

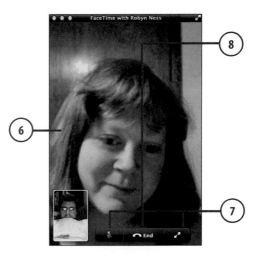

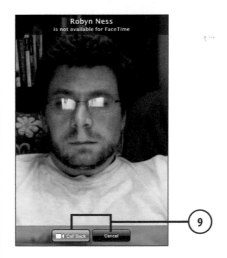

Placing Calls from the Favorites List

To place a call to someone you've marked as a favorite, complete these steps:

1. Click the Favorites button at the bottom-right corner of the FaceTime window.

2. Click a name in the Favorites list to place a call.

3. Click the arrow at the end of a favorite to open that individual's contact information.

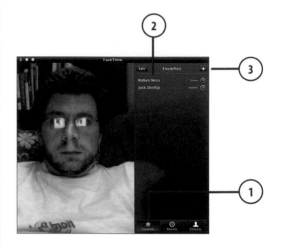

Receiving a FaceTime call

If you've ever received a call on an iPhone, you'll be right at home receiving FaceTime calls on your MacBook:

1. When there is an incoming call, FaceTime automatically starts with no user intervention.

2. Click Decline to ignore the call.

3. Click Accept to begin talking.

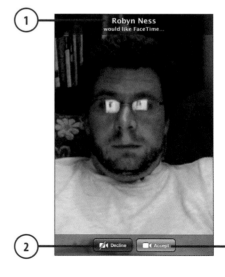

Accessing Your Call List

FaceTime keeps a list of all incoming and outgoing calls, even if you aren't around your computer when a call comes, so you can check to see who it was later.

1. Click the Recents button at the bottom-right corner of the FaceTime window.

2. Click All to show all incoming and outgoing calls. Missed calls are displayed in red.

3. Click Missed to filter the list to missed incoming calls.

4. Click an entry in one of the lists to place a call.

5. Touch the arrow at the right side of an entry to view that person's address book information.

6. Click Clear to remove the call history.

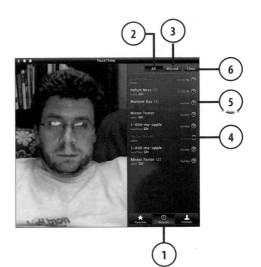

Disabling FaceTime

FaceTime is great, but, like a phone, sometimes you want to just ignore it. If you're having one of those days, you can disable FaceTime on your MacBook so that it won't ring if someone tries to call.

1. Choose Turn FaceTime Off (⌘+K) from the FaceTime menu.

2. FaceTime is now disabled on your MacBook.

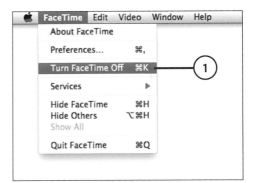

Updating Account Information and FaceTime Addresses

If you've registered several FaceTime accounts and would like them all to ring on your MacBook, you'll need to edit the preferences to list all the email addresses you have. To do this, follow these steps:

1. Open the FaceTime Preferences by choosing FaceTime, Preferences from the menu.

2. Click the Account line if you'd like to change the Apple ID associated with your account.

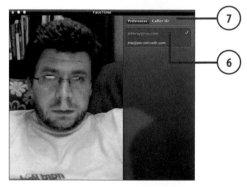

3. Click Add Another Email Account to add an alternative email account. If that address has not been registered with Apple, you'll need to look for an email with a clickable link for verifying your address.

4. Repeat step 3 for as many addresses as you want to use with your FaceTime installation.

5. Click the Caller ID line to display all addresses associated with your FaceTime.

6. Click a line to set that address as your caller ID.

7. Click the Preferences Back button to return to the main preferences.

8. Click Done to finalize your preferences.

Web Browsing in Safari

While similar in many ways to other web browsers, Safari (found in the Applications, Safari folder) offers a few unique features that set it apart.

Safari has seen dramatic improvements over the past few years. With support for Webkit (the engine that forms the foundation for Safari) found in Google Chrome and on the iPhone, HP WebOS, and Android platforms, Safari is quickly becoming a web browsing standard, rather than an exception.

It's Not All Good

BRING YOUR OWN FLASH

If you're browsing with Safari and your webpages seem a bit "bare," it might be because Lion doesn't include Adobe Flash by default. To add the Flash plug-in to your browser, visit http://www.adobe.com/products/flashplayer/ in Safari.

Managing Your Bookmarks, Top Sites, and Reading List

In Safari, there are four primary areas where you can store sites for easy access: the bookmark menu, which appears under the bookmarks menu item; the bookmarks bar, displayed under the URL; the top sites screen, which shows the sites you (or Safari) have identified as being frequently visited; and, new in Lion, the Reading List. The Reading List (denoted by an icon of eyeglasses) holds pages and links that you want to visit at a later time, but aren't planning to keep as a permanent bookmark.

Adding a Bookmark

To add a bookmark to Safari, you need to know what site you want to bookmark, and where the bookmark should be stored:

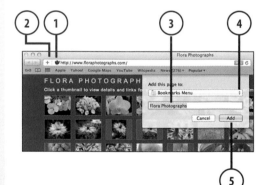

1. Visit the site that you want to bookmark by typing its address into the URL field.

2. Click the + button.

3. Enter a name for the bookmark so you can identify it later.

4. Choose where to file the bookmark (Top Sites, Bookmark Menu, Bookmark Bar, Reading List, or a folder within one of these areas).

5. Click Add.

Previewing Bookmarks

Amassing a huge collection of bookmarks can make it difficult to find what you're looking for. With Safari you can quickly preview the websites in your bookmarks or history.

1. Click the Show Bookmarks button.

2. Choose a collection of bookmarks from the left-hand pane.

3. Select a folder of bookmarks (if any) from the bookmark list.

4. Drag the handle to resize the preview Cover-flow pane so that you can get a clear preview of the pages.

5. Use the scrollbar below the preview area to flip through the sites in the folder.

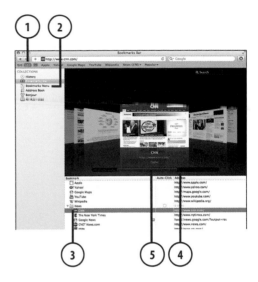

Organizing Bookmarks

After you've added a few bookmarks to the bookmark menu or bookmark bar, you can re-categorize them using these steps:

1. Click the Show Bookmark button.

2. Click the collection with which you want to work.

3. Navigate the folders and individual bookmarks as you would navigate a Finder window.

4. Click and drag bookmarks between folders or collections to organize them.

5. Click the + buttons to add new bookmark collections or folders for additional filing options.

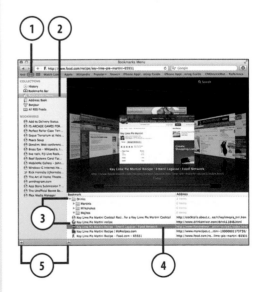

Organizing Top Sites

As you browse, Safari identifies your "top sites." The Top Sites button switches to display previews and marks sites that have updates with a star. Clicking a site opens it in Safari.

To manage the ordering and display of the top sites in Safari, follow these steps:

1. Click the Top Sites button.

2. Click Edit.

3. Click the X button by a site to remove it, or the "pin" button to make sure the site stays on the screen.

4. Rearrange the sites by clicking and dragging their preview images.

5. Add new sites by dragging their URLs into the top sites window.

A History Lesson

When viewing Top Sites, you'll see a History button at the top of the display. Clicking History will take you to a coverflow view of your browsing history.

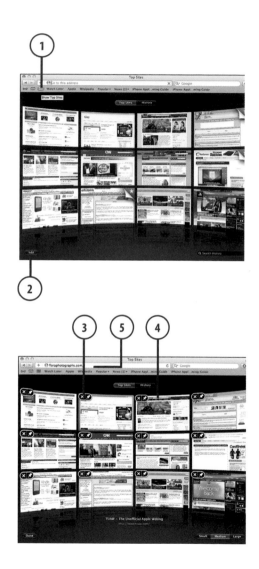

Adding to Your Reading List

The Reading List is a simple feature that holds links and pages until you have a chance to go back and read them. If you have an iCloud account shared between your iOS devices and your Mac, you'll even see the same synced reading list between all of them.

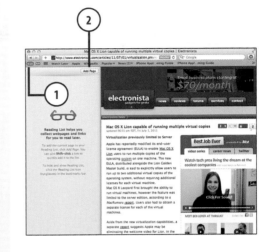

To manage your reading list in Safari, first browse to a webpage that you want to view later, and then do the following:

1. Open the Reading List by Clicking the Reading List Icon.

2. Click Add Page at the top of the Reading List Pane.

3. The page and summary text appear in the list.

4. Click the Reading List icon again to hide the list.

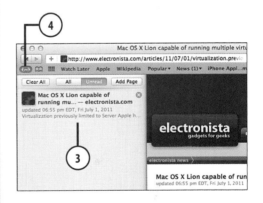

Paneless Reading List Additions

In addition to the steps described here, you can also Shift-click links to add them to the Reading List, or press Shift-⌘-D to add your current page to the list. If you're more of a click and drag person, you can drag individual links to the Reading List pane or to the Reading List icon to add them to the list as well.

Managing Your Reading List

After you add things to your list, you want to read them, right? To manage your list, just follow these steps:

1. Open the Reading List by clicking the Reading List icon.

2. Click All or Unread to limit your view of the list to all pages, or just pages you haven't finished reading.

3. Click a Reading List entry to load the page in Safari.

4. Click the X icon in the upper-right corner of an entry to remove it from the list.

5. Click Clear All to remove all items from the list.

6. Click the Reading List icon again to hide the list when you're finished.

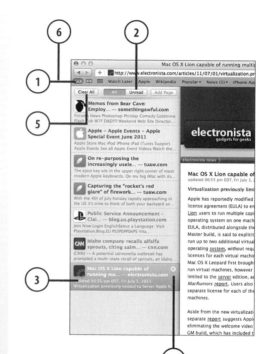

Advanced Browsing Features

Although "web browsing" as a pastime is only a little more than a decade old, it's a skill that it almost seems that we were born with. Little by little, browser developers have been refining the process to add additional features. Safari is no different.

Using Tabbed Browsing

Originally, web browsers created a new window for each page you visited. In Safari, all these windows can be combined under a single window with tabs representing individual websites within that window. To use tabbed browsing in Safari, follow these steps:

1. Choose Safari, Preferences from the menu bar.

2. Click the Tabs Toolbar icon.

3. Check the ⌘-Click Opens a Link in a New Tab option.

4. If you'd like all new windows to open in a new tab, choose Always from the Open Pages in Tabs Instead of Windows dropdown menu.

5. While you're browsing, hold down ⌘ as you click links. The links create a new tab in the Safari browser window. Use the tabs to quickly switch between web pages.

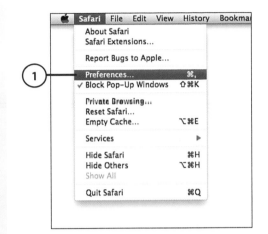

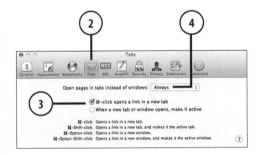

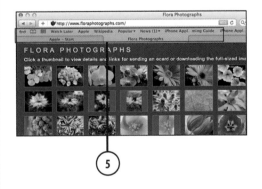

Viewing PDFs Online

In Lion, Apple has included a helpful PDF viewer that makes reviewing PDF documents a breeze. When you click a PDF link, the viewer opens. To control the viewer, follow these steps:

1. Position the cursor near the bottom center of the browser window to show the PDF controls.

2. Click + or – to zoom in and out.

3. Click the Preview icon to open the PDF in the Lion Preview application.

4. Click the Download button to save the PDF to your downloads folder.

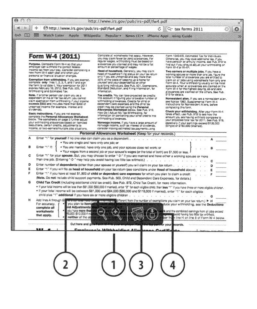

Enabling Private Browsing

If you share a computer with other people, and there's a chance that they might stumble upon something in your web history that you'd prefer they didn't (holiday gift orders, for example), you can enable private browsing.

When private browsing is enabled, no website content is saved to your MacBook—it's as if you were never there:

1. Choose Safari, Private Browsing from the menu bar.

2. Click OK when prompted to verify whether private browsing should be enabled.

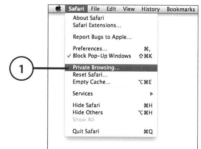

3. You can now use Safari as you would normally, but your session is private.

4. Choose Safari, Private Browsing again to disable private browsing.

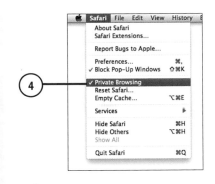

Protecting Yourself Online

Safari offers several tools to help protect you from fraudulent activity online. To ensure that you have the most secure browsing experience possible, complete the following configuration:

1. Choose Safari, Preferences from the menu.

2. Click the Security toolbar icon.

3. Check the checkbox beside Warn When Visiting a Fraudulent Website.

4. Check the checkbox beside Block Pop-up Windows.

5. Click the Privacy toolbar icon.

6. Be sure that the Block cookies option is set to From Third Parties and Advertisers.

7. Choose whether Safari should deny all access to your location information, or to prompt you if a website requests it. Note that some online services can provide valuable customized information using your location.

8. Close the Safari Preferences.

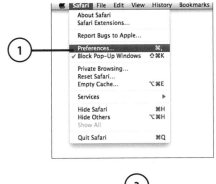

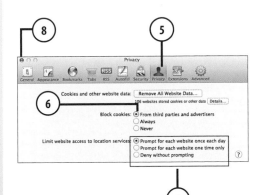

Tip

As a general rule, you should never download files online unless you trust the source. By default, Safari opens files that it has identified as safe. If you would prefer to prevent Safari from opening *any* file it downloads, you can find this option under the General Safari Preferences.

Adding Web Content to the Dashboard

Many of us visit a webpage just to see a tiny piece of content, such as the latest weather report or breaking news. With Safari and Lion's Dashboard, you can create your own widget, called a web clipping, that is accessible directly from your MacBook's dashboard. This gives you instant access to information you like without needing to open Safari. The content even updates automatically as long as you are connected to the Internet.

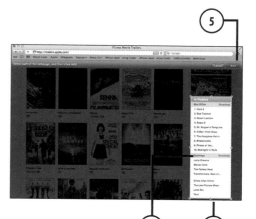

1. Visit the web page with the content you want to add to the dashboard.

2. Choose File, Open in Dashboard.

3. Position the box on the page so that the content you want to capture is highlighted as best possible and then click your mouse.

4. Fine-tune the selected area by dragging it within the Safari window and using the circular handles on the sides to resize it.

5. Click Add when you are satisfied with the results.

6. The Dashboard opens and the new web clipping widget is displayed.

Changing the Clipping Appearance

To customize the web clipping even more, click the i icon in the lower-right corner of the widget in Dashboard. You are given the option of several different borders that can be applied to stylize the clipping.

Extending Safari's Capabilities with Extensions

Safari supports developer-created extensions that can add additional functionality to your browsing experience—such as the ability to quickly access Twitter, eBay, and other services without leaving your current webpage. Safari extensions are supported by the individual developers, so after you install one, you're on your own!

Installing an Extension

Installing extensions doesn't require any more than clicking a link on a website.

To find and install Safari extensions, follow these steps:

1. Choose Safari Extensions from the Safari menu.

2. An Apple website opens listing all registered extensions.

3. Use the website to browse to an extension you are interested in, and then click the Install Now button beside the extension.

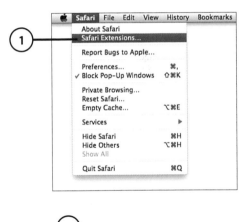

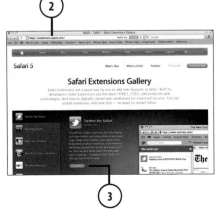

4. After a few seconds, the extension is installed and activated. Depending on how it works, you may see a new button or area added to the Safari toolbar.

5. Follow the author's instructions to use the extension.

Managing Extensions

To manage the extensions that you've installed—including configuring them, if configuration is necessary—use the Safari preferences. Follow these steps to access your extension settings:

1. Open the Safari preferences by choosing Safari, Preferences from the menu.

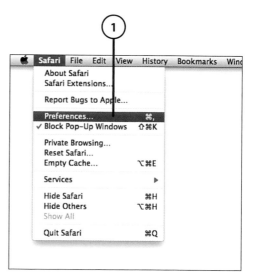

2. Click the Extensions button in the top of the Preferences window.

3. Click an individual extension to view its configuration options.

4. Use the Enable checkbox to enable or disable individual extensions.

5. Click Uninstall to remove the extension entirely.

6. Use the On/Off switch to disable all extensions.

7. Click the Updates button to look for and install updates to any installed extensions.

8. Close the Preferences when finished.

Manage your business and personal
contacts in Address Book.

Use iCal to schedule appointments
and remind you of upcoming events.

In this chapter, you'll learn how to use your MacBook to manage your contacts, calendars, and appointments, including:

→ Adding contacts to Address Book

→ Organizing contacts into groups

→ Connecting to enterprise contact servers

→ Creating calendars in iCal

→ Adding appointments to calendars

→ Inviting contacts to meetings

→ Connecting to network calendar servers

Managing Contacts and Appointments

Introduction

Part of the pleasure of owning a MacBook is that you don't need to sit at a desk to get work done. In a portable workspace, however, you still need to interact with coworkers and manage meetings, appointments, and deadlines.

Lion gives you the tools to organize contacts and tie into enterprise personnel directory systems. It also works with your company's scheduling system to track calendars, meeting invitations, and even to-do items. In this chapter, you learn about Address Book and iCal—your MacBook's personal information management utilities.

Managing Contacts in Address Book

Many of the applications you use on your MacBook send information to, or receive information from, other people. Lion offers a central contact database that you can access in Mail, iCal, iChat, FaceTime, and other programs. Appropriately enough, you manage this database through an application called Address Book (found in the Applications folder).

Address Book acts as a digital rolodex, pulling together personal and business contacts. With it you can connect to enterprise directory servers for accessing centralized company personnel listings. The Address Book application is similar to many other Lion applications, providing a drill-down view from a group list, to a contact list, and, finally, to contact details.

Adding Groups

When you first start Address Book, there is a single pseudo-group available: All Contacts. The group displays any contact available in Address Book. To make the most efficient use of Address Book, you should add groups for the different types of contacts you use—businesses, coworkers, family, friends, doctors, and so on. Like Mail, Address Book can use rules to create Smart Groups.

Emailing to a Group

Contacts groups are more than just organizational tools; they also add functionality to applications that support them. Once you've defined a group, you can use it in Mail as your message recipient, effectively sending the email to everyone in the group!

Creating a Group

To create a new group, decide what you'd like it to be called, then follow these steps:

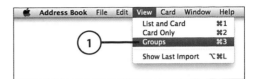

1. Navigate to the Group page by clicking the bookmark with the silhouette of two people, or by choosing View, Groups from the menu bar.

2. Click the + button below the group list.

3. A new "untitled group" is added. Type to change the name of the group.

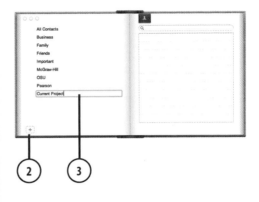

Creating a Smart Group

If you'd like to use search criteria to define your address book groups, you're in luck! Address Book supports Smart Groups, capable of pulling contacts together from multiple different groups, and even network accounts:

1. Click and hold the + button below the group list. Choose New Smart Group from the pop-up menu that appears.

2. Enter a name for the new Smart Group.

3. Use the + and – buttons to add or remove selection criteria.

4. Use the first pop-up menu from the selection lines to choose a contact attribute.

5. Use the second pop-up menu to set a comparison.

6. Enter the value to use in the comparison in the text field at the end of the selection line.

7. Click OK when you're satisfied with your group definition.

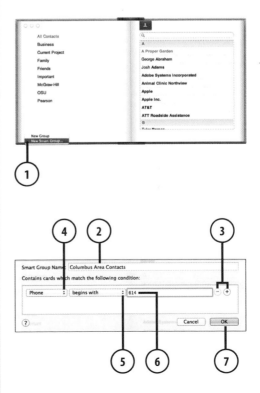

Adding Contacts

The bulk of what you'll do with Address Book is entering contacts. When it comes to people, one size contact does not fit all. For your family, you might want to store email addresses, instant messaging screen names, and birthdays. But for business contacts, you might only be interested in an address and a phone number. Address Book adapts to the information that you want to store.

Creating a New Contact

To create a new contact, gather all the information you have available for the person, then do the following:

1. From the Group page of the address book, double-click the group name that the contact should be added to.

2. The group opens to show members and details. Click the + button below the member names column.

3. A new No Name contact is added, and the empty contact details display.

4. Use the fields in the detail view to enter information for the contact.

5. Click Company to classify the entry as a business rather than a personal contact.

6. Set the context for the card's fields (for example, choose home, work, or cell for a phone number) using the pop-up menu in front of each field.

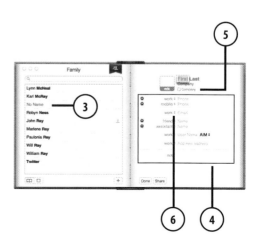

7. If you'd like to store additional information for the contact, choose Card, Add Field from the menu.

8. Click the Done button at the bottom of the contact details to finish editing the contact.

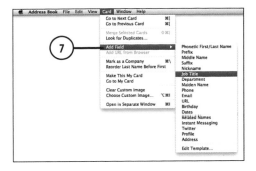

Moving and Editing Contacts

If you find that you've filed your contact in the wrong group, just drag and drop the contact name into another group. You can re-edit contact details at any time by selecting them and clicking the edit button below the details pane.

Setting a Contact Image

Contact images can help you visually identify individuals in your address book and are even displayed in Mail or shown on your iPhone if you sync your phone with Address Book. To set an image for a contact, complete these steps:

1. Find and select the contact that you want to associate with an image.

2. Select Card, Choose Custom Image from the menu bar, or double-click the picture within the card details.

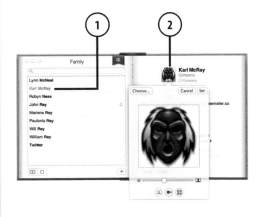

3. Click the Camera icon to take a new picture.

4. Alternatively, click Choose to choose a picture from your computer.

5. Set cropping and size for the picture by dragging it within the image window and adjusting the zoom slider.

6. Apply effects, if desired, using the Effects button.

7. Click Set to finalize the contact's custom image.

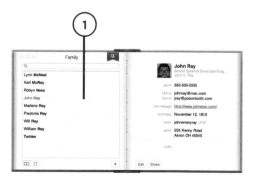

Creating "My" Card

Many system applications and utilities need to identify information about you. To tell Address Book who you are, enter a new contact for yourself, and then follow these steps:

1. Find and select your name in the Address Book

2. Choose Card, Make This My Card from the menu bar.

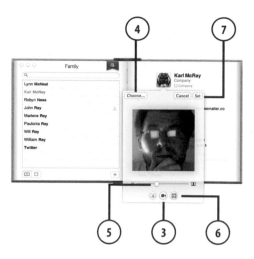

The Importance of Me

You need a functional "My" card to fully use iCal, so be sure to set this if you have any intention of running iCal.

Editing the Contact Template

If you find that you constantly need to add new fields to contacts, you might want to consider modifying the default contact template. Changing the default gives you a starting place for all future contacts.

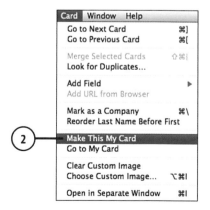

1. Choose Address Book, Preferences from the menu bar.

2. Click the Template icon in the Preferences toolbar.

3. Use the Add Field drop-down menu to add additional fields to the contact template.

4. Click the double arrows to open the pop-up menus in the front of each field to set the context for fields displayed in the template.

5. Close the Address Book preference window when you're finished.

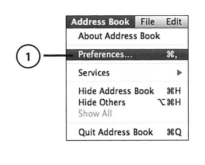

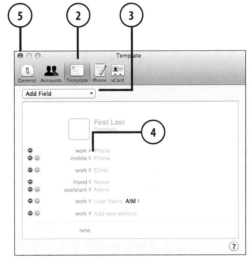

Searching Contacts

When you aren't sure of an exact name, or where you filed a contact, you can quickly search across all of your groups and contact data.

1. Navigate to the Groups page of the address book and highlight the address group to search.

2. Type into the search field in the upper-right corner.

3. As you type, the contact list is filtered to show only matching contacts.

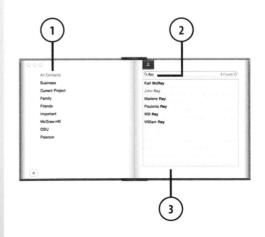

Detecting and Merging Duplicates

Over time you might find that you've created several Address Book entries for a single person. To identify and merge duplicate cards, follow these steps:

1. Choose Card, Look for Duplicates from the menu bar.

2. Address Book analyzes your contacts and presents you with the option to merge identified duplicates.

3. Click Merge to fix the duplicates.

Merging Cards

If you manually identify two or more cards that need to be merged, select the cards, then choose Card, Merge Selected Cards from the Address Book menu bar.

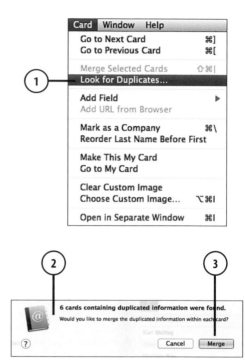

Using Network Contacts

Address Book isn't just limited to keeping information on your MacBook; it can also synchronize with Google, Yahoo contacts and connect to enterprise directory servers, such as Exchange, standard LDAP servers, as well as Apple's iCloud service.

Synchronizing with Google and Yahoo! Contacts

If you have a Google Mail or Yahoo! Account and would like to transfer your contacts to or from these systems, you can easily configure Address Book to automate the process.

1. Choose Address Book, Preferences from the menu bar.

2. Click the Accounts icon in the preference window.

3. Click On My Mac.

4. Choose the Account Information button in the details pane to the right.

5. Click the checkboxes in front of Synchronize with Yahoo!, Synchronize with Google, or both.

6. Enter your Google or Yahoo! Account information, when prompted.

7. Click OK.

8. Close the Address Book preferences window.

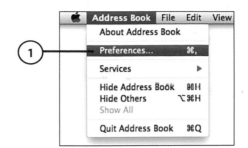

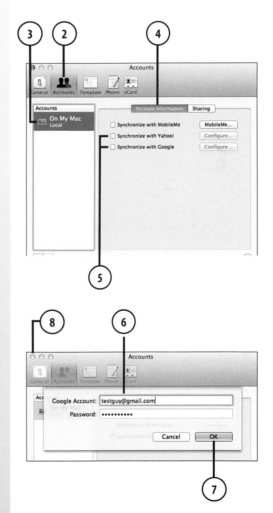

Connecting to Exchange, CardDAV, LDAP, and iCloud Servers

Many organizations provide central enterprise contact directories that you can access via Address Book. Address Book supports several enterprise standards in addition to the Google and Yahoo! Syncing options. Using a central server means that changes and updates are available immediately for everyone who is connected. Like Mail and iChat, you'll want to configure these options through the Mail, Contacts, and Calendars system preference panel:

1. Open the Mail, Contacts, and Calendars panel.

2. Click to highlight Add Account on the left.

3. Choose the service providing contact information from the list on the right.

4. Alternatively, click Other to add LDAP, CardDAV, or Mac OS X Server accounts.

5. The account creation window appears. Use the fields in the window to configure your account information.

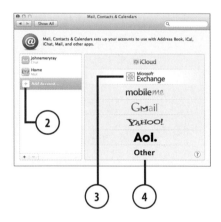

6. Click Continue to walk through the account setup wizard.

7. If you're setting up a service that provides more than just contacts (such as Exchange), you are prompted to automatically set up corresponding email accounts and iCal calendars.

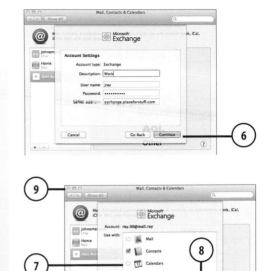

8. Click Add Account to provision the server.

9. Close the System Preferences.

10. The new server appears in the Address Book group list. You can click to select it and search the group.

Exporting vCards from Address Book

vCards are small files that store all the Address Book entries for one or more individuals or organizations. Exporting the vCard enables you to share your contacts with others by sending them as an email attachment to someone else.

To export vCards from Address Book, follow these steps:

1. Highlight one or more entries in the Address Book.

2. Drag from one of the contact names to your desktop.

Importing vCards

To import a vCard, reverse the process. Drag a received vCard into Address Book (or double-click it in the Finder) and it is imported automatically.

Dragging from Name list to Desktop

3. A vCard file is created with all of the exported contacts.

Email Sharing

When viewing the details for a contact, you'll notice a Share button at the bottom of the Address Book window. Clicking this will open a new Mail message with a vCard attachment of the contact you were viewing.

Printing Addresses

For those times when you need to use actual paper for your communications, Address Book provides several useful print options for printing your contacts onto envelopes or labels.

1. Select individual contacts or contact groups to print.

2. Choose File, Print from the menu bar.

3. Click the Hide/Show Details button so the full print dialog window appears.

4. Use the Style pop-up menu to select an output format (Mailing Labels, Envelopes, and so on).

5. Set any of the additional configuration options for the style you've chosen.

6. Click Print to output the contact information in the selected style.

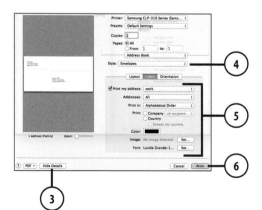

Working with Schedules in iCal

Much of our lives, like it or not, revolve around adhering to a schedule. Calendars, in whatever form we use them, keep us informed of upcoming appointments, holidays, birthdays, and anniversaries. Your MacBook can serve as your scheduling work center. Lion's iCal application (found in the Applications folder) is a fast and well-connected way to keep your life in order.

Unlike applications such as Microsoft Outlook, iCal is an unimposing piece of software that shows you everything you need within a single window.

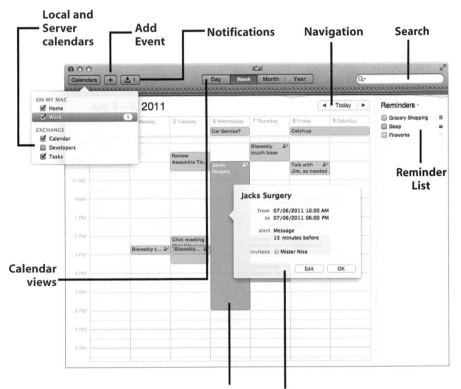

iCal's general operation is similar to other Lion applications you've used. Clicking the Calendar button displays a list of calendars you have access to. Selecting a calendar in the calendar list displays the content of the calendar to the right. Double-clicking a calendar entry shows the details of the entry.

The four buttons at the top (Day, Week, Month, Year) coupled with the View menu control the appearance of the calendars.

Despite its simple styling, iCal works just as well for managing calendars located on your MacBook as it can interacting with Exchange, iCloud, Google, and other standards-based enterprise calendaring systems.

Adding Calendars

The first step in using iCal is to establish the calendars that you use to store your events. iCal comes with two local calendars already created: Home and Work. Use these default calendars or create new calendars depending on how you want to categorize your events.

Creating Local Calendars

Local calendars store their information directly on your MacBook and cannot be viewed from anywhere else:

1. Open the iCal application from the Applications folder.

2. Click the Calendar button to view the list of calendars on your MacBook.

3. Pick File, New Calendar from the main menu bar. You can also right-click (or Control-click) on the list and choose New Calendar from the contextual menu that appears.

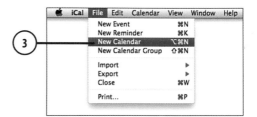

4. A new Untitled calendar is added at the bottom of the calendar list. Type to replace Untitled with whatever name you'd like.

5. Verify that the checkbox next to the calendar is selected so that the calendar entries are visible.

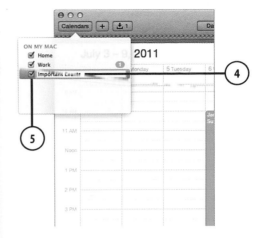

Creating Local or Network Calendars

If you have network calendars connected to iCal, when you add a calendar you are given an option of creating a new calendar on one of the server accounts or On My Mac (locally).

Nesting Local Calendars in Groups

To help organize calendars, you can create groups—similar to folders— that hold local calendars. Groups make it simple to turn several calendars on and off.

1. In iCal, choose File, New Calendar Group, from the menu bar.

2. The calendar list is displayed and a new Group item appears; type to replace the name with the label you'd like.

3. Click and drag one or more existing calendars onto the group name.

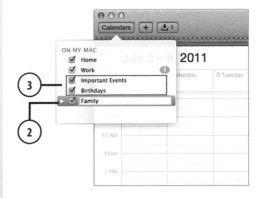

4. Use the arrow in front of the group to expand or collapse the group as needed.

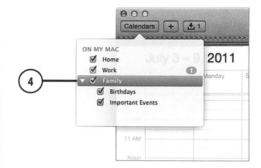

Connecting to Server-based Calendars

Unlike a local calendar, server-based calendars are stored on a central network location rather than on your MacBook. Network calendars can be accessed and modified in iCal on multiple computers. Many businesses use Exchange Server, for example, to provide shared calendars and scheduling. Apple's iCloud service provides free shared calendaring that can be used across your Mac and iOS devices. Another option, Google Calendar, is also free and can be used on virtually any desktop or mobile device.

Things You Need

Most server-hosted calendars are associated, in some way, with an email account. To configure a server-based calendar, you probably only need an email account and password. If you know, however, that your calendar is hosted somewhere else, you should collect the server name in addition to your username and password before proceeding. As you'd expect, calendar services are configured through the Mail, Contacts, and Calendars panel, as you've become accustomed:

1. Open the Mail, Contacts, and Calendars panel.

2. Click to highlight Add Account on the left side.

3. Choose the service providing calendar information from the list on the right.

4. Alternatively, click Other to manually add a CalDAV account.

5. The account creation window appears. Use the fields in the window to configure your account information.

6. Click Continue to step through the account setup wizard.

7. If you're setting up a service that provides more than just calendars (such as Exchange, iCloud, or Gmail), you are prompted to automatically set up corresponding email accounts and contact servers.

8. Click Add Account.

9. Close the System Preferences when finished.

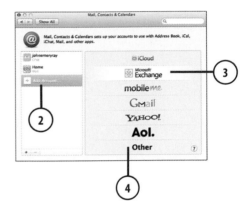

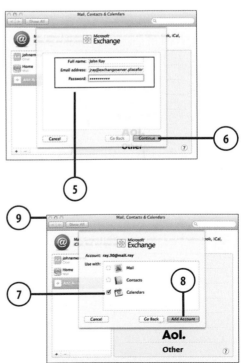

10. The iCal calendar list displays a new section with any calendars that are located on the server.

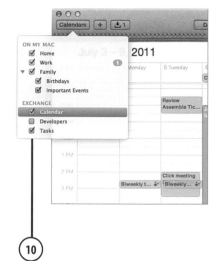

Subscribing to a Public Shared Calendar

Another iCal calendar type is a shared calendar. These read-only Internet-published calendars are available for TV show schedules, holidays, sports team game dates, and other useful information. To subscribe to a shared calendar, copy the URL for the calendar and then follow these steps:

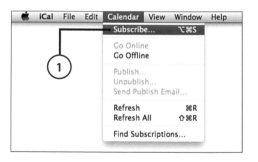

1. Choose Calendar, Subscribe from the iCal menu bar.

2. Enter the URL for the calendar you are subscribing to.

3. Click Subscribe.

4. If prompted, enter a login name and password to access the calendar and click OK.

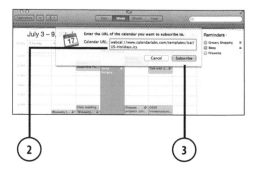

5. Set a name, color, and storage location for the calendar.

6. If there are any embedded Alerts, Attachments, or Reminders in the calendar (this depends entirely on the person making the calendar available), you may want to strip them out. Click the Remove checkboxes to make sure you get only calendar data and no surprises!

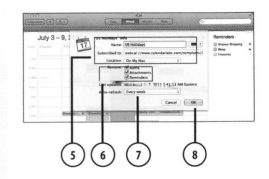

7. To enable the calendar to automatically update, choose an auto-refresh time.

8. Click OK.

9. The subscribed calendar appears in a new section within the calendar list.

Viewing Calendars and Calendar Groups

After you've set up one or more calendars in iCal, you can view their contents. To view a calendar or calendar group in the calendar list, follow these steps.

1. In iCal, click the checkbox in front of the calendar you wish to view.

2. Use the Day, Week, Month, and Year buttons to narrow or expand your calendar view.

3. Use the arrows to move forward or backward by day, week, month, or year depending on the current view.

4. Click Today to jump to today's date.

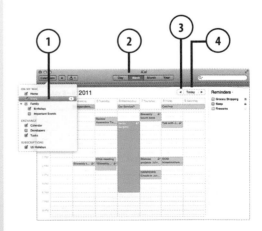

Working with Events

What good is a calendar if you don't have the ability to add events? In iCal, events can be anything you'd like—birthdays, outings, reminders, anything—as long as they are associated with a date. If you'd like to include other people in the event, you can even send out invitations that are compatible with other calendaring systems, such as Exchange.

Creating a New Event

Events can hold a large number of attributes that describe what the events are, when they are, where they are located, and so on. All you need to know to create an event, though, is the date and a name for the event:

1. Navigate to the day on which the event takes place.

2. Switch to day or week view.

3. Click and drag from the start time to the end time to create the event. The default event name, New Event, is highlighted automatically.

4. Type a name for the event, and then click off of the event to save it.

5. Right-click the event box, and choose the calendar that the event should be added to.

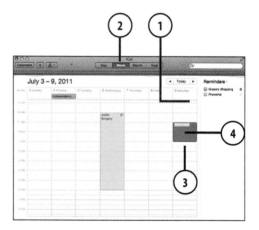

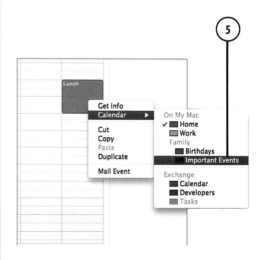

Double-Click to Add

You can add an event in the month view of the calendar by double-clicking a day. This method, however, does not let you define the start and end time initially so you need to edit it later.

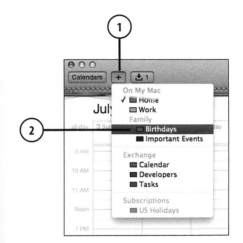

Using the Quick Event Feature

Lion's iCal application also supports a simple way of creating events without any calendar navigation at all. Quick Event provides simple, plain-text entry of new events directly from the iCal toolbar. To use this feature, follow these steps:

1. Click and hold the + icon in the iCal toolbar.

2. Choose the calendar that should hold the new event.

3. In the Quick Event field that appears, type a description of the event, such as "Dinner on November 12th at 6 pm."

4. A new event is added and opened for additional editing.

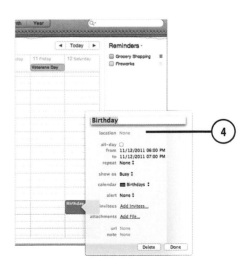

Editing Event Information

To edit the information for an event that you've created, first find the event on the calendar where you added it and then follow these steps.

1. Find and double-click the event you want to edit.

2. Unless you've just added the event, an event summary window appears.

3. Click Edit.

4. The event information window appears.

5. Click any of the available fields to change values such as start or end times, location, alarms (notifications), and so on.

6. Click Done when you are finished editing the event.

Sending Event Invitations

iCal can work directly with Mail to send invitations to your events. When the invitees respond, their attendance status is updated directly in iCal. Use these steps to send invitations to an event.

1. Find and double-click the event you wish to send invitations for.

2. Unless you've just added the event, an event summary window appears.

3. Click Edit.

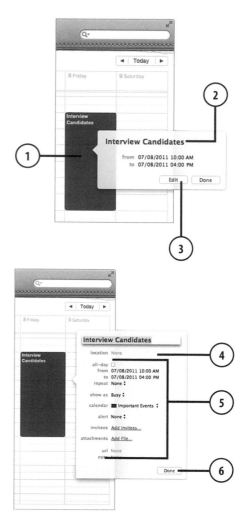

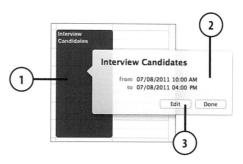

4. The event information window appears.

5. Click the Add Invitees link.

6. Enter email addresses in the field that appears, just as you would in Mail.

7. Click Send to send the invitations.

8. An icon appears in the upper-right corner of the event to show that invitations have been sent. A question mark indicates that responses haven't been received from all invitees.

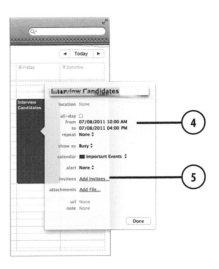

Setting Optional Attendees and Resending Invitations

After you've added an invitee to an event, you can click the name in the event summary or edit screen to show a drop-down menu that enables you to flag the person as an optional attendee or to re-send an invitation.

Checking Availability

If supported by your calendar server (such as Exchange), you can view an individual's availability for events by selecting an event, then choosing Window, Availability Panel from the menu bar.

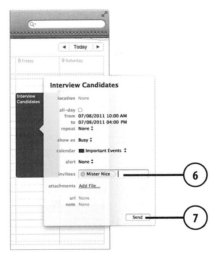

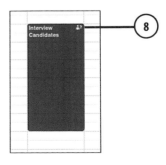

Accepting Invitations

You can easily add to your calendar invitations that you receive. Even though invitations are sent through email, Lion's Mail program works with iCal to automatically transfer the invitations to the iCal Notifications area where you can act on them.

1. When a new invitation arrives, the iCal application icon updates to show the count of invitations in the Dock.

2. The event is shown with a dotted outline in iCal.

3. Click the notification button to show the notification panel in iCal.

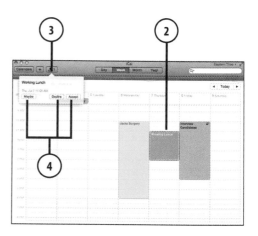

4. Use the Maybe, Decline, and Accept buttons to respond to the invitation.

5. Declined invitations are removed from your calendar, accepted and tentative invitations are added.

Changing Your Event Status

If you change your mind about an event, you can edit it in iCal and change the My Status field to Accept, Maybe, or Decline.

Searching Events

If you're a heavy scheduler, or have dozens of enterprise calendars to manage, sometimes it's useful to be able to quickly search for events, which is a breeze in iCal.

1. Make sure the checkboxes are selected for the calendars and calendar groups you want to search.

2. Choose which fields to include in the search using the drop-down menu in the Search field.

3. Enter your search terms in the Search field.

4. The results of the search are displayed in a pane at the bottom of the iCal window. Click an entry to jump to that event.

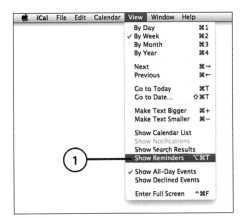

Working with Reminders

In addition to events, iCal offers a simple to do list called Reminders. Combined with events, reminders provide a means of managing projects and other task-oriented or time-sensitive happenings.

Displaying the Reminder List

Your default iCal view does not include Reminder items. To see them, you need to follow these steps:

1. Choose View, Show Reminders from the menu bar.

2. The Reminder list appears.

Adding a Reminder Item

Reminders are added in a way that's similar to how you add calendar events. With the Reminders visible, complete these steps.

1. Double-click the empty space inside the Reminder list.

2. A Reminder is created and the name is highlighted. Type to enter a new name.

3. Use the drop-down menu to the right of the item to set a priority.

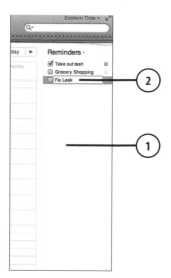

Editing Reminder Details

After creating a new Reminder, you might want to fine-tune the details. Editing the Reminder's details gives you the ability to set an associated calendar, due date, priority, and more.

1. Double-click the name of the Reminder.

2. The Reminder detail window displays.

3. Use the available fields to set alarms, associate the item with a specific calendar, or set a due date.

4. Click the Close button.

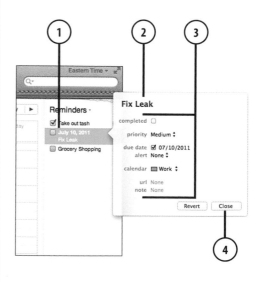

Removing Reminder Items

After you've completed a Reminder, chances are that you don't want to have to think about it any more. To automatically delete or hide Reminders after they've been checked as complete, follow these steps:

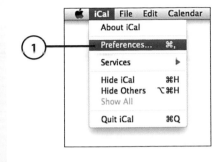

1. Choose iCal, Preferences from the menu bar.

2. Click the Advanced icon in the toolbar.

3. Check the boxes beside Hide Reminders or Delete Reminders and provide the number of days before these rules take effect.

4. Close the iCal preferences.

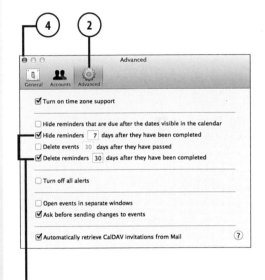

Keeping Things in Order

The Reminder heading is a drop-down menu that gives you options for sorting and grouping Reminders for additional organization control.

Printing Calendars

Despite our best efforts, sometimes we can't take our MacBooks (or even our iPads and iPhones) *everywhere*. When you need your calendar information in paper form, iCal does an amazing job of printing calendar and itinerary views.

1. Choose File, Print from the iCal menu bar.

2. Set the view you want to print.

3. Set a time range for the calendar being printed.

4. Click the checkboxes beside each calendar to print.

5. Select which options should be added to the printed page.

6. Click Continue to start the typical Lion printing process.

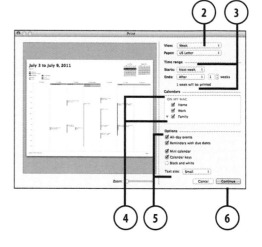

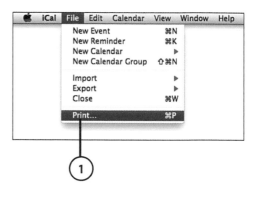

Configure the file, printer, scanner, and Internet sharing in the Sharing System Preferences panel.

Point and click to browse available servers on your network.

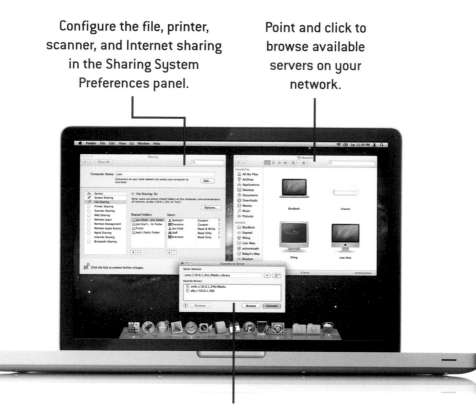

Connect directly to a wide range of servers using their Internet addresses.

In this chapter, you'll learn how to use your MacBook to share and access resources over a network, including

→ Sharing files and folders with Macs Using AirDrop and File Sharing

→ File sharing with Windows 7 computers

→ Setting Share Permissions

→ Sharing and accessing network printers

→ Sharing and accessing flatbed scanners

→ Viewing and sharing your MacBook screen

→ Turning your MacBook into an Internet Access Point

Sharing Devices, Files, and Services on a Network

Introduction

Your MacBook is a self-contained workstation that packs all the power you need into a highly portable package. That doesn't mean, however, that you have to live in a bubble. A MacBook with Lion can share and access a variety of resources with other computers on your network. Files and folders can be shared with other Macs and Windows PCs; printers and scanners can be shared with other Macs; even your screen can be made available to other computers on your network.

To make the most use of the information in this chapter, the assumption is that you've already established a network connection and have connected any printers or scanners to either your MacBook or another Lion-based Macintosh on your network. You might want to refer to Chapter 3, "Connecting Your MacBook to a Network," and Chapter 10, "Connecting Devices to Your MacBook," for more details on networking and peripherals, respectively.

File Sharing on Your MacBook

The most common network activity (beyond email and Web surfing) is file sharing. Your MacBook comes ready to share files using several popular protocols—AFP (Apple Filing Protocol) and SMB (Simple Message Block) are the most popular. AFP, as the name suggests, is for Mac-to-Mac file sharing, and SMB is used primarily in Windows environments. In addition to the protocols for sharing files, you also have different methods for *how* you share them. Traditional file sharing requires that you turn on file sharing, choose what you want to share, tell another person how to connect, and so on. With Lion, your MacBook includes a zero-configuration version of file sharing called AirDrop. AirDrop lets you wirelessly share files with other Mac users who are in your vicinity—with no setup required!

Authenticate to Make Changes!

Many of the settings in this chapter require you to authenticate with Lion before the settings can be made. If you find yourself in a situation where a setting is grayed out, click the padlock icon in the lower-left corner of the window to authenticate and make the necessary change.

Using AirDrop to Wirelessly Share Files and Folders

AirDrop is a fast and easy file-sharing system that lets you send files to another Lion-based Macintosh without any setup—no usernames, no passwords, nothing except a Wi-Fi adapter that is turned on! Unlike traditional file sharing, AirDrop's simplicity does present a few challenges that might make it less than ideal for your particular file-sharing situation. Specifically, AirDrop requires the following:

- All computers sharing files must be using the Lion (or later) operating system.

- All systems must have recent wireless-N Wi-Fi hardware. This has not been formally defined by Apple yet, but 2010 or later MacBooks will work fine.

- Your MacBook will not be able to browse the contents of other computers, only send files.

Sending Files with AirDrop

To use AirDrop, be sure that your Wi-Fi adapter is turned on (see Chapter 3 for details), identify the files that you want to share with another person, and then follow these steps:

1. Open a new Finder window and make sure the Favorites sidebar section is expanded.

2. Click the AirDrop icon to browse for other Lion computers.

3. Other computers are shown using the owner's avatar picture (set in Address Book) as their icon.

4. Drag the files you want to transfer to the icon of another computer.

5. Confirm the transfer by clicking Send when prompted.

6. You will be asked to wait while the remote system confirms the transfer.

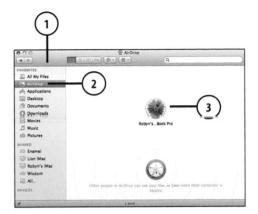

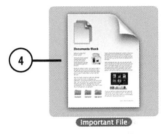

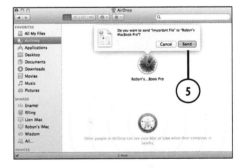

7. The files are copied to the remote system. A blue circle around the receiving computer indicates progress.

8. Close the AirDrop window to stop being visible on the network.

After you've closed the AirDrop window, you can go your merry way. There is no need to disconnect or change your network settings. You're done!

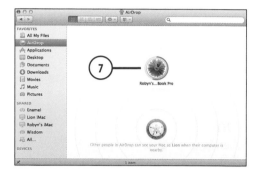

Receiving Files with AirDrop

Receiving files with AirDrop is even easier than sending them. When a nearby Lion user wants to send files to your MacBook, follow these steps:

1. Open a new Finder window and make sure the Favorites sidebar section is expanded.

2. Click the AirDrop icon to become visible to other AirDrop users.

3. When prompted to receive files, click Save or Save and Open to accept the transfer, or Decline to cancel.

4. The files are transferred to your Download folder.

5. Close the AirDrop window to stop being visible on the network.

That's it! Your AirDrop session is automatically ended when the window closes.

Note

AirDrop uses peer-to-peer ad hoc wireless networking which is only supported in recent MacBooks and desktop Macs. While this may seem limiting, this hardware is what makes it possible to communicate with zero configuration and without using a common Wi-Fi access point.

Configuring Traditional File and Folder Sharing

When AirDrop won't do (you need to browse another computer's files or share with Windows/non-Lion Macs), you need to turn to the traditional file sharing features built into Lion. Lion provides consolidated controls for sharing files, regardless of what type of computer you want to share them with. You set up file sharing by first enabling sharing for your MacBook and then choosing the protocols available for accessing the files. Finally, you decide which folders should be shared and who should see them.

Enabling File Sharing

Before your MacBook can make any files or folders available over a network, file sharing must be enabled.

1. In the System Preferences window, click the Sharing icon.

2. Click the checkbox in front of the service labeled File Sharing.

3. The details about your sharing configuration are displayed on the right side of the sharing window.

4. Close the Sharing Preferences panel, or continue configuring other sharing options.

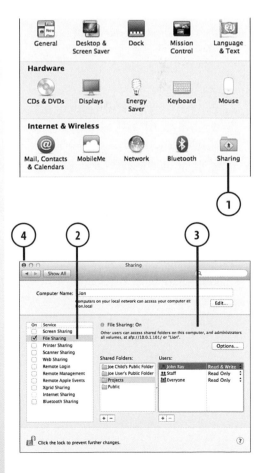

Choosing File Sharing Protocols

Files can be shared over AFP (Mac) or SMB (Windows). If you're working in a Mac-only environment, AFP will be perfect. Mixed environments should use SMB.

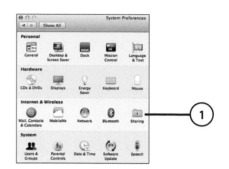

To choose which protocols can be used to access the files on your MacBook, follow these steps:

1. In the System Preferences window, click the Sharing icon.

2. Click the File Sharing service label.

3. Click the Options button to display the available sharing protocols.

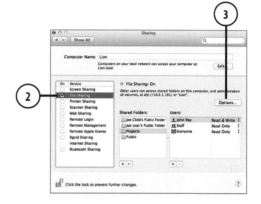

4. Check or uncheck the protocols that you want to use.

5. If you're configuring Windows file sharing (SMB), all accounts are disabled by default. Check the box in front of each user account that should be *allowed* to connect.

6. Enter the password for each account.

7. Click Done.

8. Close the Sharing Preferences, or continue configuring sharing options.

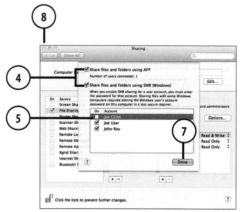

WHAT IS WITH THE ACCOUNT CHECKBOXES AND PASSWORDS FOR WINDOWS FILE SHARING?

The Lion SMB implementation requires that user accounts and passwords be stored in a different format than how they are used natively by Mac OS X. By enabling or disabling accounts for Windows access and the passwords for the accounts, you are creating the user authentication information that the SMB protocol needs to run.

Selecting Folders and Permissions

After enabling file sharing and choosing the protocols that are used, your next step is to pick the folders that can be shared. By default, each user's Public folder is shared and accessible by anyone with an account on your computer. (See Chapter 11, "Securing and Protecting Your MacBook Data," for configuring user accounts.)

1. In the System Preferences window, click the Sharing icon.

2. Click the File Sharing service label.

3. Click the + button under Shared Folders to share a new folder.

4. Find the folder you want to make available and then click the Add button.

5. Close the System Preferences panel, or continue configuring sharing options.

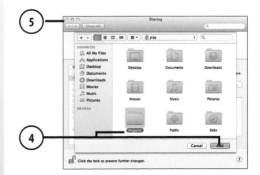

Setting Folder Access Permissions

By default, your user account has full access to anything that you share. The default user group named Staff, and everyone with an account on the computer, have read-only access.

To change who can access a file share, complete the following steps:

1. In the System Preferences window, click the Sharing icon.

2. Click the File Sharing service label.

3. Click the Shared Folder name that you want to modify.

4. Click the + button under the User's list to add a new user (or – to remove access for a selected user).

5. A window for selecting a user displays. Choose the user or group and click Select.

6. Use the pop-up menu to the right of each user in the Users list to choose what the user can do within the shared folder.

7. Close the System Preferences.

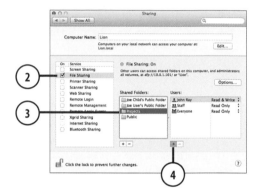

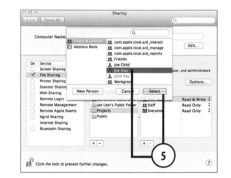

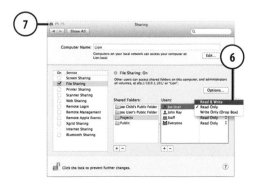

>>> Go Further

WHAT PERMISSIONS CAN BE APPLIED TO A SHARED FOLDER?

Shared folders can have the following permissions set on a per-user or per-group basis:

Read & Write—Grants full access to the folder and files within it. Users can add, edit, and delete items within the folder.

Read Only—Provides access to the files in the folder, but users cannot modify or delete them, nor can they create new files or folders.

Write Only (Drop Box)—Allows users to write to the folder, but not see its contents.

No Access—Available only for the Everyone group; disables access for all user accounts except those explicitly granted access in the permissions.

Accessing Shared Files

Shared files are only useful if you can access them! Your MacBook provides two methods of connecting to shared folders: by browsing for them on your local network and by entering a URL to connect directly to the shared resource.

Browsing and Connecting to Network Shares

Browsing and connecting to a local network share is similar to browsing through the folders located on your MacBook. To browse for available network shares, do the following:

1. Open a new Finder window and make sure the Shared sidebar section is expanded.

2. Click the computer that is sharing the folders and files that you want to access.

3. If you have not logged into the computer before and saved your password, a list of the publicly accessible file shares is displayed in the Finder window.

4. Click the Connect As button on the upper right of the Finder window.

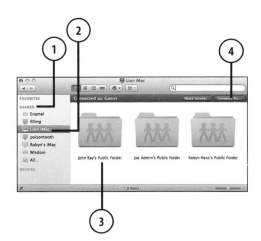

5. Enter the username and password that you have established for accessing files on the server.

6. Click Remember This Password in My Keychain to enable browsing directly to the file shares in the future.

7. Click Connect.

8. The file share list updates to display all the shares that your user account can access.

9. Double-click a share to mount it as a disk and begin using it.

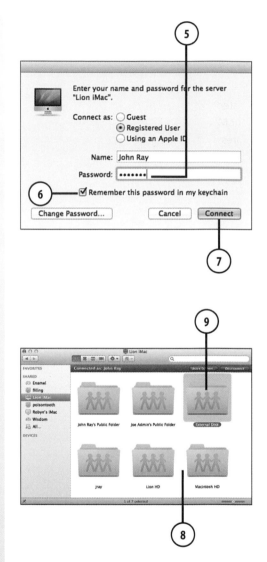

One Password to Rule Them All

You may notice when connecting to other Lion servers that you are given the option of connecting with your Apple ID. This will work if your account has had an Apple ID associated with it on the remote server. This association is made by selecting a user within the Users & Groups system preference panel and then clicking the Set button that is next to the Apple ID field.

Browsing Large Networks

If there are many different computers sharing files on your network, you can browse them in a Finder window rather than the Finder sidebar. To open a Finder window that browses your network, choose Go, Network from the menu bar, or click the All… icon within the Shared section of the Finder sidebar.

Connecting to Remote Shares

Sometimes file shares aren't directly browseable because they're hiding their available shares, or they are located on a different network from your MacBook. To access remote shares by URL, follow these steps:

1. When you create a new file share on your MacBook, Lion provides you with a list of URLs that can be used to access that file share (see Step 3 of "Enabling File Sharing"). You can use these URLs to directly access a file share rather than browsing.

2. Choose Go, Connect to Server from the Finder menu.

3. Enter the URL for the file share in the Server Address field.

4. Click + if you want to add the server to the list of favorite servers.

5. Click Connect to connect to the server and view the available shares.

Tip

Your Windows friends might give you network shares to connect to in the format \\servername\share-name. You can translate this into a "Mac-friendly" URL by adding the prefix smb: and reversing the direction of the slashes—that is, smb://servername/sharename.

Sharing Printers

Sharing a printer is a convenient way to provide printing services to your MacBook without having to connect any physical wires. With Lion, printer sharing just takes a few clicks and then your MacBook can act as if it has a physical printer attached.

Enabling Network Printer Sharing

To share a printer, you must first have the printer connected and configured on another Macintosh (see Chapter 10 for details). After the printer is set up and working, follow these steps to make it available over a local network:

1. In the System Preferences window, click the Sharing icon.

2. Click the checkbox in front of the Printer Sharing service.

3. Within the Printers list, click the checkboxes in front of each printer you want to share. The printers are immediately made available to everyone on your network.

4. Close the System Preferences, or continue setting sharing preferences.

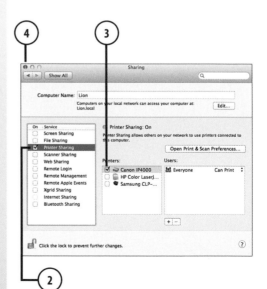

Setting Printer Sharing Permissions

Any shared printer is initially available to anyone with a computer connected to your network. To restrict access to specific user accounts on your computer, do the following:

1. In the System Preferences window, click the Sharing icon.

2. Click the label for the Printer Sharing service.

3. Highlight the name of the shared printer that you want to configure.

4. Click the + button to select a user that can print to your printer. (Use – to remove access for a user you added previously.)

5. A window is displayed to select a user. Choose the user or group and click Select.

Tip

The Everyone group can't be removed from the Users list. To remove access for Everyone, the group must be toggled to No Access.

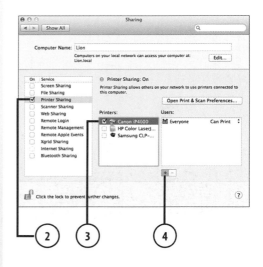

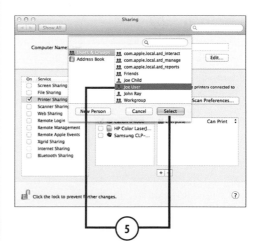

6. Toggle the pop-up menu beside the Everyone group to No Access to keep everyone except the listed individuals from being able to access the printer.

7. Close the System Preferences.

Accessing a Network Printer

To access a printer that is being shared by another Macintosh, first make sure that both computers are on and connected to the same network and then follow these steps:

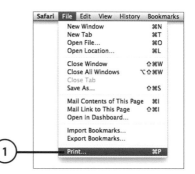

1. Choose File, Print from the menu bar within an application of your choice.

2. The Printer dialog box appears. Click the Printer drop-down menu to see the options.

3. If you haven't used the shared printer before, select the printer from the Nearby Printers section of the drop-down menu.

4. Lion automatically connects your MacBook to the printer and configures it.

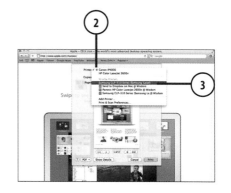

5. Choose the options for the document you are printing, then click Print. The printer behaves exactly as if it is local. The next time you print, the printer will be available directly in your main printer list.

Printing to Protected Printers

If you set up specific user accounts that can access the printer, you are prompted for a username and password the first time you print. You can, at that time, choose to save the printer connection information to your keychain, which eliminates the need to authenticate for subsequent use.

Sharing a Scanner

A unique (and little known) ability of OS X is sharing scanners! With scanner sharing, you can use a scanner that is connected to a desktop system as if it were connected directly to your MacBook. Before proceeding, make sure that you've correctly installed a scanner on a Macintosh on your local network (see Chapter 10 for details).

Tip

If you can start Image Capture or Preview (both are found in the Applications folder) on the Macintosh with the directly connected scanner and create a scan, you're ready to enable sharing.

Enabling Network Scanner Sharing

Scanner sharing is virtually configuration-free! To enable scanner sharing on your Macintosh, follow these steps:

1. In the System Preferences window, click the Sharing icon.

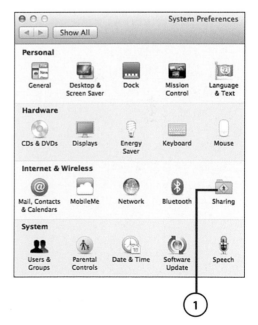

2. Click the checkbox in front of the Scanner Sharing service.

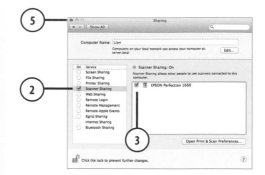

3. Review the list of available scanners and then click the checkboxes in front of each scanner that you want to share.

4. The scanners can now be accessed in Image Capture or Preview from any Macintosh connected to the local network.

5. Close the System Preferences.

Accessing a Shared Scanner

Accessing a shared scanner is just like using a locally connected scanner. Make sure that both the computer sharing the scanner and the scanner are turned on, gather your materials to scan, and then follow along:

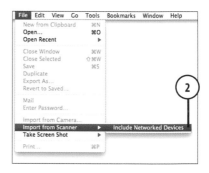

1. Open your preferred Lion scanning utility—Preview or Image Capture (Preview is used here).

2. Choose Import from Scanner, Include Networked Devices from the Preview application's File menu.

3. Again, choose Import from Scanner from the File menu. This time, however, select the name of your scanner from the list of available devices.

4. Proceed with scanning as if the scanner were connected directly to your MacBook.

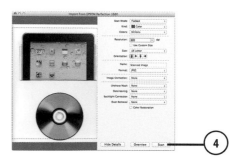

Sharing an Optical Drive

For those using a CD- or DVD-less Macintosh, such as the MacBook Air, you
can use another Macintosh on your network (including another MacBook) to
share a CD or DVD inserted into the other Macintosh's drive. This gives you
the ability to install software and access files even if you don't have a physical
drive connected.

Enabling DVD and CD Sharing

From a Macintosh with CD or DVD
drives available, follow these steps to
turn on optical drive sharing:

1. In the System Preferences window, click the Sharing icon.

2. Click the checkbox in front of the
   DVD or CD Sharing service.

3. Click the Ask Me Before Allowing
   Others to Use My DVD Drive
   checkbox to prompt you when
   other people attempt to access
   your optical drive.

4. Close the System Preferences.

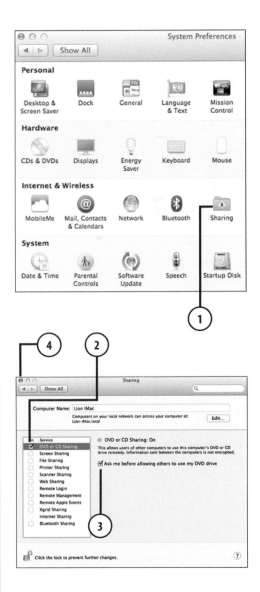

Accessing a Shared Optical Drive

To access a shared optical drive from your DVD-free Mac, do the following:

1. Open a new Finder Window.

2. Make sure the Devices section in the Finder sidebar is expanded.

3. Click the Remote Disc item in the Devices sidebar area.

4. Double-click the computer that is sharing the DVD you want to use.

5. If the DVD is not immediately visible, click Ask to Use to prompt the host computer that you'd like to use its drive.

6. After access has been granted, the available DVD or CD is listed. Double-click the DVD or CD to begin using it.

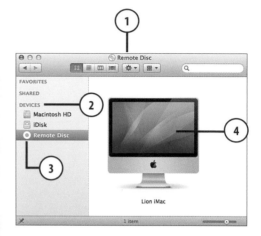

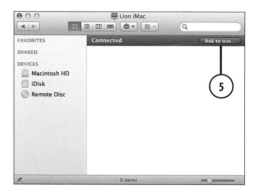

Can I Access a Shared Optical Drive Even If My MacBook Has a DVD Drive?

Yes, but not without a few changes. You'll need to open the Terminal application (found in the Utilities folder in the Applications folder) and then type in the following two lines to enable optical drive sharing:

defaults write com.apple.NetworkBrowser EnableODiskBrowsing -bool true

defaults write com.apple.NetworkBrowser ODSSupported -bool true

Reboot your computer after entering these commands.

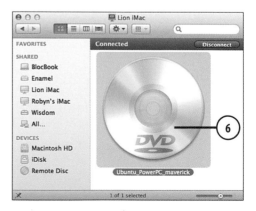

Sharing Your MacBook Screen

Chapter 5, "Managing Contacts and Appointments," includes instructions on how to share your Macintosh's screen using iChat, but there are many instances where you might want to access another Mac's display without having to start a chat.

Built into Lion is a standards-based screen-sharing system. Using screen sharing, you can access your Mac's display from anywhere on your local network or, in some cases, from anywhere in the world. New in Lion is the ability to share a computer's "screen" even if someone else is using the computer. The screen sharing software can now automatically create a virtual screen that you can see and use while the person sitting in front of the computer continues to see their own desktop!

Enabling Screen Sharing

To configure another Mac so that you can access its screen from your MacBook, you initially need direct access to the computer:

1. In the System Preferences window, click the Sharing icon.

2. Click the checkbox in front of the Screen Sharing service.

3. A URL that you can use to connect to your computer is displayed on the right side of the sharing pane.

4. Close the System Preferences, or continue setting sharing preferences.

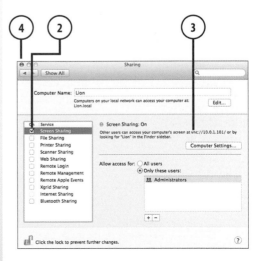

Setting Screen Sharing Permissions

After screen sharing is enabled, choose who can access the display. Initially, only administrative users can view your screen.

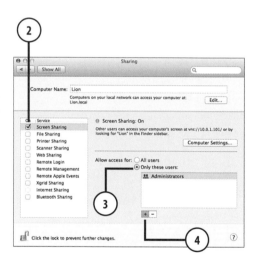

1. In the System Preferences window, click the Sharing icon.

2. Click the Screen Sharing service label.

3. Choose whether All Users on the computer can access its screen, or click Only These Users to restrict access to specific individuals or groups.

4. Use the + button to choose a user or group that should be granted access, or use – to remove a user or group that you had previously added.

5. A window for selecting a user displays. Choose the user or group and click Select.

6. For additional control, click the Computer Settings button.

7. In the dialog box that appears, click Anyone May Request Permission to Control Screen to allow anyone to access the display if the person sitting in front of the computer grants them access.

8. To provide access to your Mac's screen using a standard VNC (Virtual Network Computing) client, click the VNC Viewers May Control Screen with Password checkbox and provide a password that grants access to those users.

9. Click OK.

10. Close the System Preferences.

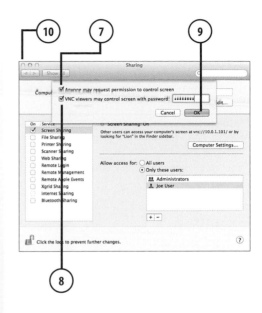

Tip

There are VNC clients available for Windows, Linux, and even platform-independent Java. If you want to access your Mac's screen from another operating system, check out TightVNC (www.tightvnc.com).

Accessing the Screen of a Local Mac

To access the shared screen of a Mac on your local network, make sure that your MacBook is connected to the network and then follow these steps:

1. Open a new Finder window.

2. Make sure the Shared sidebar section heading is expanded.

3. Click the computer whose screen you want to access.

4. Click Share Screen in the upper-right corner of the Finder window.

5. Enter your username and password on the remote system, if prompted.

6. Click Remember This Password in My Keychain to store the password and enable password-less connections in the future.

7. Click Connect to begin using the remote display.

8. If another person is using the computer, you can ask to share the display with them, or connect to a new virtual display. Click whichever approach you prefer.

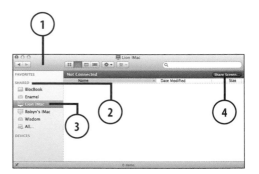

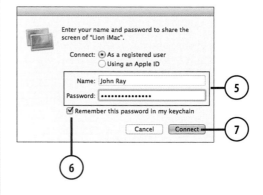

9. The remote display is shown in a window on your MacBook.

10. Switch between controlling and observing with the arrow icon in the toolbar.

11. Use the toolbar icon with four arrows to shrink the display to fit into the window.

12. Click the camera icon in the tool-bar to take a screenshot.

13. Use the left clipboard icon to transfer the contents of the remote computer's clipboard into your local clipboard, and the right clipboard icon to transfer your clipboard to the remote system.

14. Close the window when you're finished using the remote system.

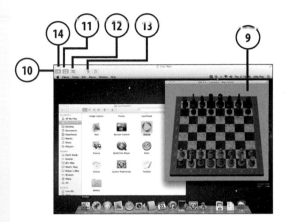

Tip

You can connect to multiple shared screens simultaneously with your MacBook; each appears in a separate window. Additionally, you can use the fullscreen button in the upper-right corner of the Screen Sharing window to view the remote desk-top in fullscreen mode or select Switch to Virtual Display from the View menu to create your own virtual desktop on the remote computer.

Accessing Remote Computers and Non-Macs

If you can't browse to a computer to access its screen, or you need to connect to a non-Macintosh computer, you can do so using almost the same process as you used to connect to a remote file share:

1. When you're sharing a screen on your MacBook, Lion provides you with a URL that can be used to access your screen, even if you can't browse to it on the network.

2. Choose Go, Connect to Server from the Finder menu bar.

3. Enter the screen-sharing URL in the Server Address field. Alternatively, if you only have an IP address (such as 192.168.1.100), prefix the IP address with vnc:// to create a properly formed URL (for example, vnc://192.168.1.100).

4. Click + if you want to add the server to the list of favorite servers.

5. Click Connect to connect to the remote server's screen.

Tip

To connect to a Windows or Linux computer, you need to first install a VNC server (Virtual Network Computing) on the computer whose display you want to share. TightVNC (www.tightvnc.com) is an entirely free Open Source option that will work on both Windows and Linux platforms.

Sharing Your Internet Connection

Your MacBook is a perfect Internet-sharing platform because it includes both Ethernet and wireless network connections. You can, in a matter of minutes, create a wireless network using just your MacBook and a cable or DSL modem.

Sharing Your Connection

1. In the System Preferences window, click the Sharing icon.

2. Click the Internet Sharing service label. (Note: The checkbox is initially disabled!)

3. Use the Share Your Connection From drop-down menu to choose how you are connected to the Internet (Ethernet, Airport, iPhone, and so on).

4. Within the To Computers Using list, click the checkboxes in front of each of the interfaces where the connection should be shared.

5. If you're sharing a connection over your Wi-Fi card, a Wi-Fi option buttons appears. Click this button to configure how your computer presents itself wirelessly.

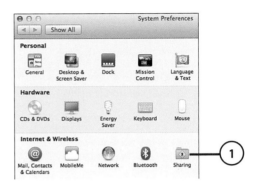

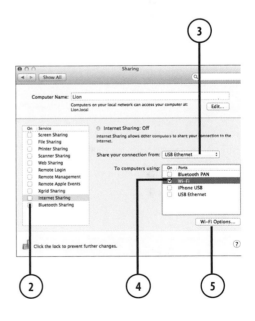

6. Set the name of the wireless network you are creating.

7. Leave the channel set to the default.

8. If you want to enable basic password protection for the network, choose 40- or 128-bit WEP from the Security menu, and then provide a password.

9. Click OK to save your settings.

10. Click the checkbox in front of the Internet Sharing service name.

11. Close the System Preferences.

12. Connect to the new wireless network from other computers as described in Chapter 3. You should set the other computers to configure themselves automatically rather than manually configuring the network.

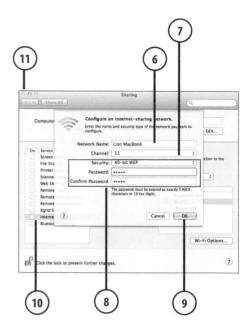

Tip

If you're sharing your connection over Ethernet, you need to connect a switch to your MacBook's Ethernet port and then connect the other computer systems/devices to the switch.

Watch DVDs with
your MacBook
using DVD Player.

Download movies,
music, and more
in iTunes.

In this chapter, you'll learn how to use digital music and video to turn your MacBook into a portable entertainment center, including

→ Watching DVD video
→ Viewing video files online
→ Adding support for Windows Media and other video
→ Using iTunes to play audio CDs
→ Copying audio CDs into iTunes
→ Buying digital media using iTunes
→ Syncing your iOS device with iTunes
→ Keeping your computers in sync with Home Sharing

Accessing Entertainment on the Go

Introduction

One of the best things about having a portable computer is that it provides all the entertainment possibilities of a desktop computer, but your laptop goes where you do. Downloadable video and music are available wherever and whenever you want. Using iTunes and your MacBook, you can build a "to-go" library of thousands of songs, TV shows, and movies.

In addition to iTunes, your MacBook also includes software to play your existing DVD library and thousands of online videos. Even when you run your MacBook from battery power, you still have hours of fun at your fingertips. When you leave home, you no longer have to leave your entertainment collection behind.

Using DVD Player

DVD Player is an application bundled with OS X that allows you to watch DVDs on your MacBook. Unless your MacBook preferences have been changed from the standard settings, DVD Player launches automatically when you insert a video DVD in your optical drive.

Note

At the present time, MacBooks play standard DVD content but cannot play Blu-ray discs, the format for high-definition video.

>>> Go Further

OPENING DVD PLAYER

Your MacBook should automatically open DVD Player when you insert a video DVD, but if it doesn't you can launch the application manually from your Applications folder. If DVD Player does not automatically open, you can enable this behavior under the System Preferences, CDs & DVDs settings. Simply set Open DVD Player as your preference for when you insert a video DVD. From this preference window, you can also choose behaviors for inserting blank CDs, blank DVDs, music CDs and picture CDs.

Playing a DVD

If you've used a standalone DVD player and remote, you should have no trouble applying your experience to navigating menus and playback controls on your MacBook. To begin playing a DVD, follow these steps:

1. Insert a disc in your optical disc drive. The content opens fullscreen, and a controller appears at the bottom to allow you to navigate DVD menus and control playback.

2. Navigate the DVD menu. You can use either your trackpad or the arrow keys on your keyboard.

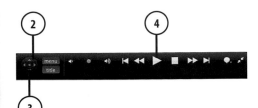

3. Press the Return (enter) key on your keyboard, or use your cursor to click the onscreen Enter (center) button to select an item, such as an episode, scene, or special features.

4. To toggle playing and pausing the video, click the Play/Pause button or press the spacebar. To stop playback, click the Stop button.

5. Press Escape to exit fullscreen mode, if desired. When in windowed mode, a slightly different (but equally functional) controller is displayed.

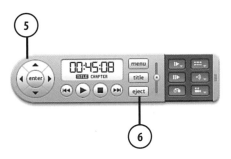

6. To eject the DVD, press the Eject key on your keyboard, or use the Eject button on the windowed mode controller.

Note

The first time you play a DVD in DVD Player, the drive region is set to match the code of that DVD. If you later insert a disc from another region, you have the option to change; however, you can only change your region code settings five times (including the initial setting).

Setting Bookmarks

If you want to mark your favorite parts of a DVD, DVD Player allows you to set bookmarks. Bookmarks are stored on your computer, not the DVD itself, so they are only available when you watch the DVD from your MacBook.

Setting Bookmarks

To set a bookmark, follow these steps:

1. When you're watching a DVD in full-screen mode, move your cursor to the top of the screen to reveal the DVD Player menu.

2. Choose Window, Bookmarks. The Bookmarks window opens.

3. Use the DVD controls (shown in the previous task) to rewind or fast-forward playback to the point you want to bookmark.

4. Click the + (also known as Add Bookmark) button at the bottom of the Bookmarks window. Playback pauses at the moment to show which frame will be marked.

5. Choose Make Default Bookmark to have video playback automatically start at this point.

6. Name your bookmark and click Add to set a bookmark.

7. The frame, name, and timecode appear in the bookmark window.

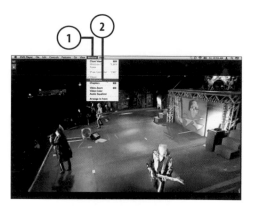

Starting Playback at a Bookmark

To start playback at a bookmark you've set, follow these steps:

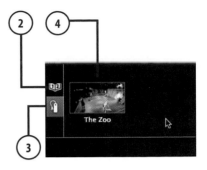

1. Insert the DVD you have book-marked and begin playback.

2. While in full-screen mode, move your cursor to the top of the screen to reveal a black panel with tabs for Chapters and Bookmarks.

3. Click the Bookmarks icon to reveal bookmarks for the current DVD.

4. Select a bookmark to jump to that location.

Tip

You can also jump between Chapters without leaving playback or full-screen mode by moving your cursor to the top of the window and choosing the Chapters icon from the shaded panel.

Viewing Browser Video or Downloaded Video Files

Your MacBook's native application for playing media, both within a web browser and from your desktop, is QuickTime. QuickTime, like DVD Player, has fairly standard buttons for controlling playback.

QuickTime supports common digital formats, including MPEG-4 and H.264 video, WAV sound files, and images. (Note, however, the videos on YouTube are another type of video, known as Flash video, which is not typically played in QuickTime.)

>>> Go Further

STREAMING MEDIA BASICS

QuickTime is perhaps most useful for playing streaming media, which means the file isn't downloaded outright to your computer, but is played incrementally as the data is "streamed" from the server to your machine.

For longer videos, streaming decreases your wait time because you can start watching the video before transferring the entire file. Typically, there is a short wait time before the video begins, known as buffering, to keep the video playback from being choppy while additional frames and audio are transferred.

Playing QuickTime Files in Your Web Browser

To view a QuickTime movie in your web browser, follow these steps.

1. Open your web browser.

2. Navigate to a page containing QuickTime compatible content. (For example, visit Apple's movie trailers web page at www.apple.com/trailers/ to enjoy QuickTime previews of upcoming releases.)

3. Select an item.

4. If you're asked, choose your preferred options on video size, such as automatic or high-definition options (HD). These options affect the wait time for viewing—because larger, higher quality video requires transfer of more data to your MacBook.

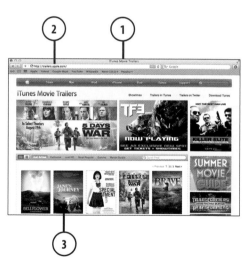

5. The QuickTime panel opens and, after a few seconds, begins to play.

6. You can pause playback, change volume, rewind and fast-forward, or go fullscreen using the controls at the bottom of the panel.

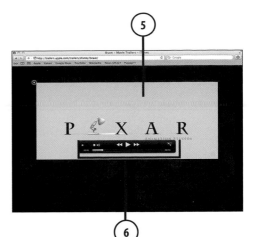

Playing QuickTime Files from Your Desktop

In addition to playing files within a Web page, you can also use QuickTime to play files on your MacBook. Native QuickTime files end with the file extension .mov. (Applications such as Apple's iMovie and Final Cut Pro export video in this format.)

To play a .mov file, follow these steps:

1. Open QuickTime Player (found in your Applications folder).

2. Choose File, Open File from the menu.

3. Navigate to the file you want to play and click the Open button.

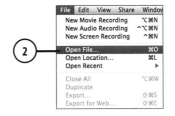

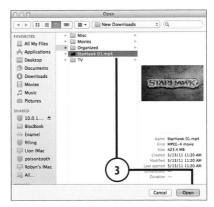

4. Click the Play button to begin playback.

5. Click the rewind and fast-forward buttons to skim backward and forward through the video.

6. Click the double arrows to view the video in fullscreen mode.

7. Choose QuickTime Player, Quit QuickTime Player to exit.

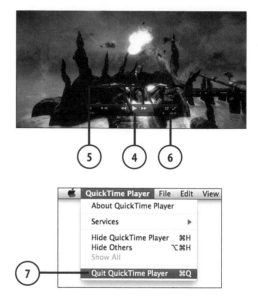

EXTENDING QUICKTIME WITH ADDITIONAL COMPONENTS

Although QuickTime is a reasonably flexible media player without any additions, you can increase the range of media it supports by installing support for additional video formats.

To add seamless support for Windows Media Player files (files ending with .wma and .wmv), install the Flip4Mac component available from http://www.microsoft.com/windows/windowsmedia/player/wmcomponents.mspx.

To play other popular formats (such as Flash video, DivX, MKV, and AVI), download and install Perian, a free addition for QuickTime that adds support for a range of file types. Perian is available from http://www.perian.org/.

After these components have been installed, QuickTime will be able to play these file formats without any additional help—just open the file and watch the show!

Refer to Chapter 8, "Installing and Managing Software on Your MacBook," for additional instructions on adding software to your system.

Creating a Media Library in iTunes

Apple's iTunes enables you to manage and play digital media files, including song tracks you import from CD, content you purchase from the iTunes Music Store, or podcasts you subscribe to online.

You can also create and sync playlists with your iPod or share them with other iTunes users on your local network.

Running iTunes for the First Time

The first time you launch iTunes, you won't have anything in your music library. Follow these steps to complete the setup process:

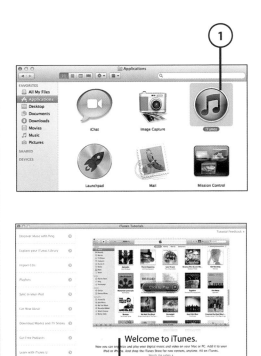

1. Open iTunes from the Dock or locating its application icon in the Applications folder. Click Agree after reviewing the iTunes Software License Agreement.

2. The Welcome window, with video tutorials for various tasks, appears. Choose a task to view, or click Close.

3. iTunes displays a screen explaining ways to add content to your Library.

4. Click the Find MP3 and AAC Files in Your Home Folder link to search your account for any music files you may already have. These will be copied to the iTunes folder, inside your Music folder.

Finding Your Way Around iTunes

After you've configured iTunes, you can begin using it. First, here's a quick tour of the iTunes window to acquaint you with the basics.

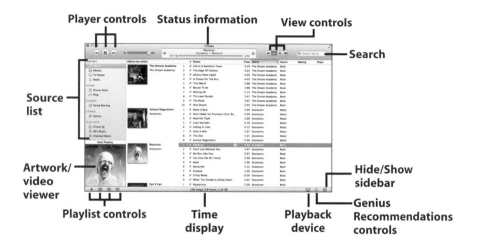

Let's discuss a few of these elements in greater detail:

- The Source list contains the contents of your library, including any playlists you create, a link to the iTunes Store and Ping (a network for sharing your music tastes), Shared music, and any devices available to iTunes (such as a connected iPod, iPhone, or iPad).
- The Artwork/Video viewer below the source list shows album artwork or video content, if it's available.
- The View controls allow you to scroll through your library in list, list with artwork, grid, or coverflow mode.

Building Your Media Library

The two most common ways to fill your iTunes Library with media are to import CDs you already own and get new content from the iTunes Store.

Tip

Click Import Setting at the bottom of the iTunes window if you would like to change the format of import from the standard AAC (common for most iTunes content) to other common formats such as MP3, AIFF, or WAV. You can also change the quality (and, subsequently, the file size) of the tracks by switching the Setting drop-down from iTunes Plus to Higher Quality (256 kbps).

Adding Audio CDs

To import audio tracks from a CD, follow these steps:

1. Insert a CD into the computer's optical disc drive. Your MacBook is automatically set to open iTunes when you insert a music CD.

Note

If iTunes does not automatically open when you insert an audio CD, you can enable this behavior under the System Preferences, CDs & DVDs settings.

2. Click Yes after iTunes launches and displays a dialog box that asks if you would like to import the CD to your library.

3. iTunes displays the status of the import by showing which tracks have been imported and which are in progress.

4. Eject your CD by clicking the eject button.

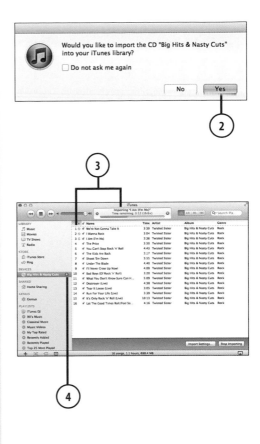

>>> Go Further

SETTING TRACK INFO

When you insert an audio CD, iTunes connects to a music database, identifies your disc, and applies information such as title, artist, and genre to each track. Album artwork might also be available if the album is part of the iTunes store.

If iTunes doesn't find your CD in the database, you can edit the track information yourself by selecting it and choosing File, Get Info. Select several tracks at a time to update all the shared information and save yourself some typing.

Purchasing Digital Media on the iTunes Store

To purchase media from the iTunes Store, follow these steps:

1. Click iTunes Store in the Source list to connect to the iTunes Store.

2. Click sign in.

3. Enter your Apple ID and password in the Sign In dialog box.

4. Click Sign In. When you're logged in, your Apple ID appears in place of the Sign In button on the iTunes Home page.

Note

You can authorize up to five computers to play songs purchased on a single account. To do this, choose Store, Authorize Computer and enter your Apple ID. (Remember to deauthorize computers that no longer need access, which frees openings for new computers to be added.)

5. Use the links and on-screen navigation tools, such as scroll arrows and paging controls, to browse content.

6. Click the blue Play button that appears as you move your cursor over each song to play a preview.

7. To make a purchase, click the Buy button that appears to the right of each item.

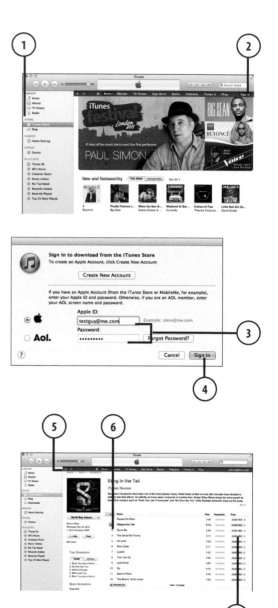

8. When you're asked to confirm that you want to buy the selection, click the Buy button. Your selection is downloaded and added to your library under the Purchased playlist.

Tip

When you choose to rent a movie, you have 30 days to watch it, and 24 hours from the time you start watching it to finish it. Rented movies appear in your library just as other files do.

It's Not All Good

BUY HERE, READ ELSEWHERE

One of the types of media available in iTunes is Books. You can currently download books, but no provision is available for reading them in Lion! You'll need an iOS device to read your book purchases!

Viewing Genius Recommendations

Genius Recommendations attempt to predict what new media you might enjoy based on the current items in your library. Follow these steps to enable and peruse Genius Recommendations:

1. Click the Genius link in the source list.

2. Click the Turn On Genius button that appears.

3. Enter your Apple ID and password in the Sign In dialog box and click Continue.

4. Check the box to agree to the terms of service and click Continue.

5 A screen announcing "Turning on Genius" appears while the contents of your library are analyzed and personalized results are prepared. Three stages are displayed while this occurs: gathering information, sending information, and delivering Genius results.

6. Select your Music Library from the iTunes source list.

7. Click the arrow button at the bottom-right corner of the iTunes window to open the iTunes sidebar.

8. Select any item in your Library or playlists to view related Genius recommendations from the iTunes Store in the sidebar.

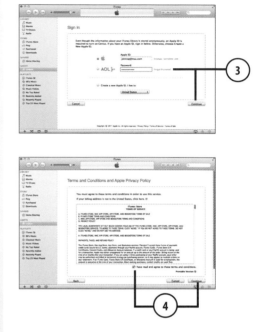

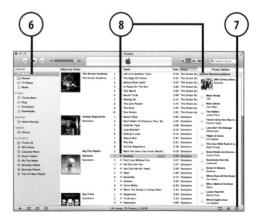

>>> Go Further

PING ME!

You may notice a reference to Ping at the top of your iTunes sidebar, as well as a link in the source list. This is Apple's social network for music. If you choose to activate Ping, you'll be able to "follow" artists and users, much like you can follow individuals on Twitter. You can read recommendations, make comments, and engage in an online community dedicated to discussing music and musicians.

Downloading Podcasts

Podcasts are series of digital files, either audio or video, that you can subscribe to for regular updates. You can locate and subscribe to a variety of podcasts (most of them free) in the iTunes Store by following these steps:

1. Click iTunes Store in the Source list to connect to the iTunes Store.

2. Click the Podcasts button in the iTunes Store navigation bar to go to the Podcast home page, or click and hold to see a categorized list of podcasts.

3. Click an item to see details and a list of available episodes.

4. Click the Subscribe button to download the most recent episode and all future episodes of this podcast. The podcasts are downloaded to your iTunes library.

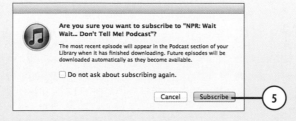

5. Click Subscribe when you're asked to confirm that you want to subscribe.

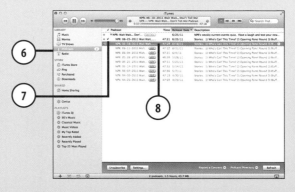

6. In the Source list, click Podcasts to view your subscriptions. Blue dots appear next to podcast series with unplayed episodes.

7. Click the arrow in front of each series to show episode titles.

8. Select an episode and click the Play control button to listen.

Tip

Episodes produced prior to your subscription appear in gray with a Get button, in case you want to download them as well. You can also click Get All to receive all episodes.

Tip

iTunes checks for updates as long as you are subscribed; if you change your mind about following a podcast, select it in the list and click the Unsubscribe button at the lower left of the iTunes window.

>>> Go Further

FREE EDUCATION WITH ITUNES U

If you're looking for educational materials, iTunes U is the place to go. Here, dozens of schools publish free course material that is yours for the downloading. Audio, video—it's all here, and subjects from business management to programming are available. iTunes U lessons work identically to podcasts, but are downloaded from the iTunes U section of the iTunes store and are managed in the iTunes U category of your library.

Viewing the Library

Your iTunes library can grow large quite quickly with so many sources from which to draw. Fortunately, there are several ways to browse and search to help you find just what you're looking for.

Browsing Media Files

To browse your media library, follow these steps:

1. Choose a source in the Source list. Options might include Music, Movies, TV Shows, Podcasts, Audiobooks, and so on, depending how actively you've added content. These categories are created automatically as you download content from the iTunes Store.

2. Scroll through the content list to locate the one you want to watch/listen to.

3. Double-click to play the item.

Tip

You can click the View buttons at the top right to change between list, list with artwork, grid, and coverflow views. While you're in list and coverflow mode, you also can change the sort order by clicking a column heading.

Searching for Media

If you know the title or artist of an item, follow these steps to search for it:

1. Click inside the Search box at the upper right of the iTunes window and begin typing a search term. As you type, the display changes to show matches.

2. If necessary, click the magnifying glass to show a dropdown menu where you can limit the media attributes you are searching.

3. Double-click to play the item you want to watch/listen to.

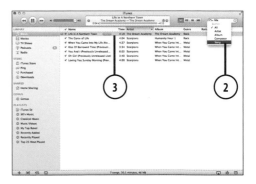

Using Playlists

Playlists help you organize your music and media into themes to suit your mood. You can define your own playlists, set search criteria to automatically cluster certain artists or genres, or have iTunes use the Genius profile it created from your library to generate lists for you.

Creating Playlists

To define a playlist of songs you choose, follow these steps:

1. Click the Create a Playlist button, which looks like a plus sign, at the lower left of the iTunes window.

2. Type a name for the playlist that appears in the playlists portion of the Source list.

3. Return to your library to browse or search for songs to add to your playlist.

4. Click and drag a filename from the library list to your playlist. As you pass over a playlist in which you can drop the file, it is highlighted in blue and a green plus sign appears with your mouse cursor.

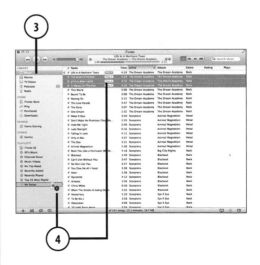

5. Release the mouse button to place the file in your playlist.

6. Repeat steps 3–5 to continue adding media.

Tip

If you add so many playlists that you feel the need to put them in folders to keep track of them, go to File, New Playlist Folder.

Defining Smart Playlists

To set criteria that iTunes can use to make a playlist for you, follow these steps:

1. Choose File, New Smart Playlist from the menu.

2. In the Smart Playlist window, set your search criteria. Options include obvious choices, such as artist, album, or rating, as well as more obscure settings, such as bit rate (which relates to sound quality) and skip count (which tells how often you choose not to listen to it). You can also set a limit on the number of songs and allow live updates, which creates a list that changes as your library changes.

3. Click OK when you're done setting search criteria. Your Smart Playlist appears under Playlists in the Source list.

4. Click *untitled playlist* in your Playlists and enter a name.

Tip

To modify the criteria you originally set, select the playlist in the Source list and choose File, Edit Smart Playlist from the menu.

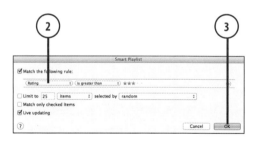

Accessing the Genius Playlists

To see a playlist recommendation for a selected song based on your library, follow these steps:

1. Make sure you have enabled Genius Recommendations. (See the "Viewing Genius Recommendations" task earlier in this chapter.)

2. Go to your Music library to select a song.

3. Click the Genius button at the lower-right corner. The original song you selected plays and a playlist that complements it is listed with it.

4. To save the list generated by Genius, click Save Playlist at the top of the window.

5. To try another playlist based on the original song, click Refresh at the top of the window.

Tip

To have iTunes generate playlists based on a profile of your whole music library rather than just a specific song, select Genius Mixes under the Genius category in the Source list.

Playing Internet Radio

To listen to Internet radio through iTunes, follow these steps:

1. Choose Radio under Library in the Source.

2. Click the disclosure arrow in front of a genre in the Streams list.

3. Double-click an item to connect to the stream and begin playback.

You Can't Take It with You

Internet radio differs from other sources in the iTunes library because it is streamed, not downloaded. You can't burn it to a disc or listen to it when you're not online.

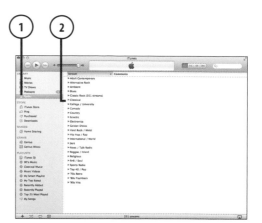

Keeping Media in Sync

iTunes is more than a virtual filing cabinet for storing music and media files. It also syncs with iPods, iPhones, and other computers on your network so you never have to be without those items, even when you're away from your MacBook.

Syncing, the iCloud Way

By enabling syncing of purchases in iTunes, you ensure that your purchases are downloaded to other copies of iTunes that are signed in with your Apple ID.

Follow these steps to turn on purchase syncing:

1. Open the Preferences from the iTunes menu.

2. Click the Store button at the top of the Preferences window.

3. Click the checkboxes in front of Music, Apps, and Books (or any combination of these) to automatically download any purchase made on another Mac (or even your iOS device) to your iTunes library automatically.

4. Click OK to close the iTunes Preferences.

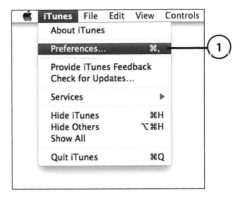

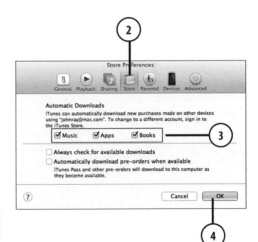

Syncing Your Media with Your iPod or iPhone

iTunes was designed to be used with iPods, iPhones, and iPads, which makes syncing your Library between devices a cinch.

Follow these steps to transfer content from your MacBook to your iPod or iPhone:

1. Connect your iPod or your iPhone to your MacBook using the supplied USB cable. iTunes detects the device and, if previously connected, begins synchronizing it. If it has not been connected before, iTunes will prompt you to set up the device.

Note

If your device was previously synced with another Mac, you have the option to Erase and Sync or transfer purchases to your new Mac.

2. To see details about your device, select the device to view the Summary screen, which shows the name, capacity, software version, serial number, and any updates available to your device.

3. Choose Sync over Wi-Fi Connection to sync without your USB cable in the future!

4. To conserve space on your device, open the different Media tabs, and, on each, select which items to sync.

5. Click Apply to apply your selection and sync your device. The status of the sync appears at the top of the window. Do not disconnect your device until syncing is completed.

6. When the sync completes, unplug your device and cable.

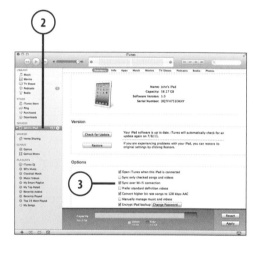

Cable-Free Bliss

Wi-Fi syncing of iOS devices has been a long time in the making, and one of the most requested features of users. Once you've enabled Wi-Fi syncing, you can start a sync any time your iPhone, iPad, or iPod is on the same network as your iTunes library. Just go to Settings, General, iTunes Sync!

Wait...What about the iCloud Syncing I've Enabled on My iOS Device?

If you've chosen to automatically download media purchases to your iOS device, chances are you will rarely even need to sync directly with iTunes, because iCloud will keep everything up-to-date on its own!

Sharing Media Between Home Computers

Home Sharing allows you to browse up to five computers on your local network and import music to your own library— purchased content. In addition, it will allow you to stream media to your iOS device when it is connected to your home network.

Follow these steps to activate Home Sharing:

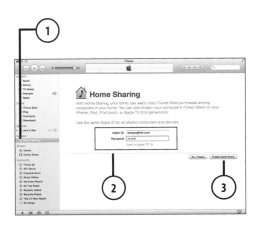

1. Expand the Shared section of the Source list in the iTunes window and click Home Sharing.

2. Sign in with your iTunes account by entering your username and password.

3. Click Create Home Share.

4. Click Done when the confirmation page appears.

5. Repeat the previous steps for all the other computers in your home, connecting with the same iTunes account. Shared computers appear under the Shared heading in the iTunes Source list.

6. Select the shared Library you want to peruse. You can click the arrow button to the left of its name to reveal categories.

7. Select items and drag them to the Library categories on your local iTunes Library to import them.

Automate Your Imports!

To automatically copy purchases between systems with Home Sharing activated, select the shared library you want to use, then click the Settings button in the lower-right portion of the window. You'll be given the option of automatically transferring any (and all) purchases from the remote library to your local library.

Download, install, and update applications using the Mac App Store.

Manage your Lion system updates using Software Update.

In this chapter, you'll learn how to install applications on your MacBook and keep Lion up to date, including:

8

→ Browsing the Mac App Store
→ Downloading and Maintaining App Store Applications
→ Downloading and Installing Non-App Store Software
→ Working with Mac OS X software distribution formats
→ Scheduling System Software Updates

Installing and Managing Software on Your MacBook

Introduction

Up to this point in the book, you've been looking at software that came as part of OS X Lion. That's a bit limiting, don't you think? There is a wide world of software waiting to enhance your computing experience—including upgrades to Lion itself.

Through the use of the Mac App Store and Software Update application, you'll be able to install new applications, keep them up to date, and keep your Mac running smoothly and securely. When that isn't enough, you can turn to thousands of other apps that run natively on your MacBook.

Mac App Store

Applications make a Mac a Mac. As intangible as it is, there is a certain "something" about using a Mac application that is rarely replicated on a Windows computer.

Once you've become accustomed to the day-to-day operation of your MacBook, you'll likely want to begin installing third-party software. The easiest place to do this is through the Mac App Store. Like the popular App Store for iOS devices, the Mac App Store is a one-stop-shop for thousands of apps that can be installed with point and click ease.

Logging into the App Store

To use the Mac App Store, you need a registered Apple ID—the same account you used to access iTunes in Chapter 6 will work just fine. If you don't have an ID, you can create one directly in the App Store. To log into the store, follow these steps:

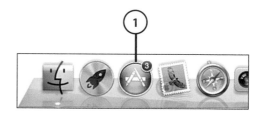

1. Open the App Store application from the Dock or from the Applications folder.

2. The App Store window opens.

3. Click Sign In from the Quick Links on the right side of the page.

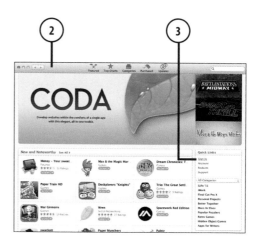

4. Provide your Apple ID and password in the form that appears.

5. If you do not have an ID, click Create Apple ID and follow the onscreen prompts.

6. Click Sign In to log into the App Store.

7. Your Login Status and links to your account information are shown in the Quick Links section.

Browsing for Apps

Part of the joy of using the App Store is that browsing is simple and fun—and it works very much like a web browser. As you encounter links (such as, See All), click them to view more information. You can browse within a variety of categories that cover the gamut of what you can do on your MacBook:

1. Follow steps 1-7 of the previous task, "Logging into the App Store."

2. Click the Featured icon to browse apps tagged by Apple as New and Noteworthy or Hot.

3. Click Top Charts to see the apps that are currently selling the best or being downloaded the most.

4. Click Categories to browse by the different types of apps (games, business, developer, and so on).

5. When you see an app you are interested in, click the icon or name.

6. A full page of information, including reviews, opens.

7. Use the Forward and Back buttons to move back and forth between pages, just like a web browser.

Quick Links for Faster Browsing

The featured page actually contains more than the new/hot apps. In the column on the right side of the page, you can quickly jump to specific app categories to see Top Paid apps, Top Free apps, and more without leaving the page.

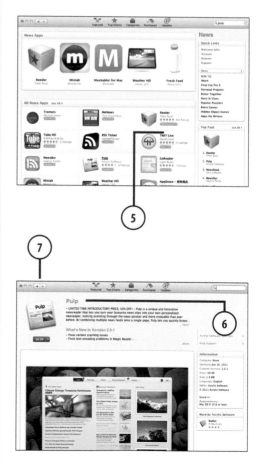

Searching for Apps

Sometimes you may know the app you want, but not know where it is located. In these cases, you can simply search the App Store:

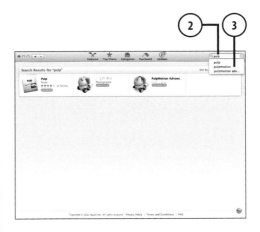

1. Follow steps 1-7 of the previous task, "Logging into the App Store."

2. Type a search term or terms into the field in the upper right corner. You can use application names, categories (type **news**, for instance), even author/publisher names.

3. As you type, a list of possible searches appears. Click one if you'd like to use it, otherwise press return to use the search term you've typed.

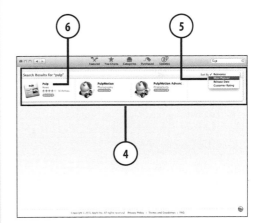

4. The Search results are displayed.

5. Use the Sort By menu to choose how the results are sorted within the window.

6. Click App Icons or Names to view more information.

Purchasing An App

When you've arrived at the decision to purchase an app, the process couldn't be simpler. Follow these instructions to download an app and install it on your MacBook:

1. Browse or search for an app, as described in the previous tasks, "Browsing for Apps" or "Searching for Apps."

2. From within the search/browse results or the larger application information page, click the App Price button.

3. The Price button changes to read Buy App. If the app is free, it will read Install App. Click the Buy App (or Install App) button.

4. Provide your App Store Apple ID and password if prompted, and then click Sign In.

5. The application is immediately downloaded to your Applications folder and made visible in Launchpad.

Remember It on Payday!

The right side of the Price button for an app has a downward pointing arrow. This is actually a separate button that opens a popup menu. Use this menu to copy a link to the app or to send an email message to someone (maybe yourself) telling them about the app.

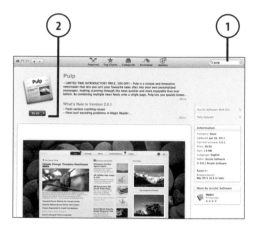

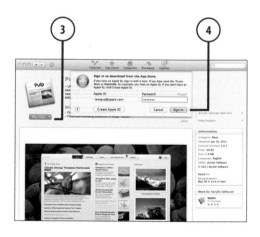

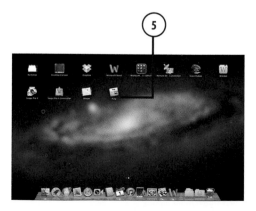

I Don't Want It—Make It Go Away!

If the App Store makes it so easy to install things, it certainly makes it easy to delete them, right? Yes and no. The App Store is used for installing, but Launchpad is used to uninstall the apps. Learn about Launchpad in Chapter 2, "Making the Most of Your MacBook's Screen Space."

Checking for Updates

If you're like many people (myself included), you install application updates only if the application tells you about them. Having to hunt down the app's website, see if there is an update, figure out how to upgrade…it's a process that's easy to ignore. In the Mac App Store, updates are painless, and they come to you!

To check and install updates, do the following:

1. The App Store icon displays a counter badge listing the number of updates available to you.

2. Follow steps 1-7 of the "Logging into the App Store" task.

3. Click the Updates button in the App Store toolbar.

4. All your available app updates are listed.

5. Click the Update All button to update all applications at once.

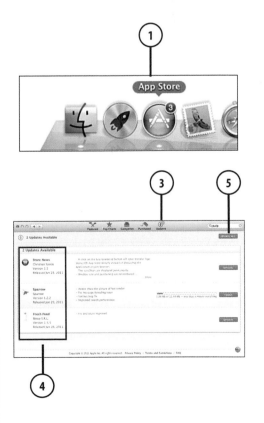

6. Click an individual Update button to update just a single app.

7. Update progress is shown in the App Store window, but you don't have to wait to continue using your computer. The updates will be automatically installed in the background.

Reinstalling Apps and Installing Purchases on Other Macs

One of the best things about buying applications through the App Store is that you can install them on other Macs you own. No licensing hassles—just download and go. You can also re-install apps that you may have deleted in the past but want to start using again.

To download an app you've purchased but that isn't installed, complete these steps:

1. Follow steps 1-7 of the "Logging into the App Store" task.

2. Click the Purchased icon at the top of the App Store window.

3. The Purchased App list is displayed, along with a button/label showing the status of each app.

4. Apps labeled as Installed are currently installed and up to date.

5. Click the Install button to install
(or re-install) an app you already
own.

6. Click the Update button to
update a piece of software that is
currently installed. (This functions
identically to updating the software through the Updates view.)

It's Not All Good

THE SOFTWARE THAT WOULDN'T DIE

A mechanism of removing a piece of software from your purchased history
currently doesn't exist. If you download (and subsequently delete) many free-
bie apps, they'll clutter up your purchase list forever…or at least until Apple
gives you a mechanism to remove them.

Installing Non-App Store Applications

The App Store is great, but it doesn't mean that it defines the limits of what
you can do on your MacBook. There are certain restrictions in place on the
App Store that make some pieces of software impossible to distribute
through that site. There are also thousands of developers who want to sell
and market their applications through their own websites.

Installing software from non-App Store sources is frequently a matter of
browsing the web in Safari, clicking a download link, and copying the application to your Applications folder.

Getting the Lowdown on the Download

Recall that Lion has a Downloads folder that is available in your Dock. Software
archives that you download in Safari, or most other Mac applications, will be
stored in this location.

Unarchiving Zip Files

A decade ago, almost all Mac applications were distributed in a compressed archive format called SIT (StuffIt). Today, the Mac has adopted a standard used on Windows and other platforms called Zip files. A zip file can contain one or more highly compressed files.

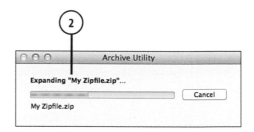

To unarchive a zip file and access the contents, follow these steps:

1. Find the file that you want to unarchive.

2. Double-click the file. Unarchiving can be virtually instantaneous or take several seconds, depending on the archive size.

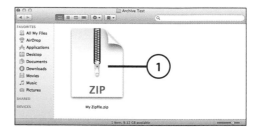

3. The contents of the archive are made available in the same folder where the zip file was located.

Just StuffIt

If you find yourself in a situation where you need to deal with a StuffIt file, you can download StuffIt from http://www.stuffit.com. Despite decreasing use of the format, it has been actively maintained over the years.

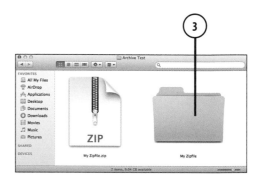

Accessing Disk Images

Sometimes applications are distributed on a disk image or DMG file. DMGs, when mounted on your system, act like a virtual disk drive. Files in a DMG must be copied off the disk image by way of an installer or a simple drag-and-drop process.

To mount and access the contents of a disk image, follow this process:

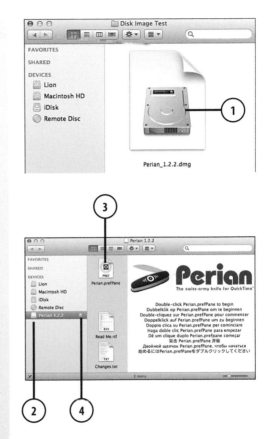

1. Find the Disk Image you want to access.

2. Double-click the DMG file. The disk image will mount and appear as a disk in the Finder.

3. Access the files in the disk as you would any other storage device.

4. To eject the disk image, click the Eject icon beside the mounted disk in the Finder sidebar or drag it to the trash.

Useful Apps for Your MacBook

Apple writes great applications for maintaining a mobile lifestyle, but third-party publishers have created utilities that meet or exceed Apple's own efforts. To get you started, I'd like to recommend a handful of non-App Store software packages that can make your MacBook experience even more enjoyable and productive.

>>> Go Further

WHERE CAN I FIND SOFTWARE FOR MY MACBOOK?

There are many websites that track Macintosh applications, but two of the best are MacUpdate (http://www.macupdate.com/) and VersionTracker (http://www.versiontracker.com/).

Adium (http://adium.im/)—We all have friends (frenemies?) who use chat services other than what is supported in iChat. Adium supports over a dozen different instant messaging protocols, including MSN, Yahoo, and FaceBook!

AppCleaner (http://freemacsoft.net/AppCleaner/)—Finds the files associated with an application and removes them from your system. Since Lion lacks a global uninstaller that works across *all* apps, one of the first things you should *install* is an uninstaller like AppCleaner.

coconutBattery (http://www.coconut-flavour.com/coconutbattery/index.html)—A full monitoring solution for your MacBook's battery system. Use coconutBattery to check your battery's capacity over time and ensure you're getting the performance you should.

Coda (http://www.panic.com/coda/)—An integrated web application development environment that fits perfectly on your MacBook's screen. If you're ready to graduate from Apple's iWeb software, Coda is a great next step.

CrossOver (http://www.codeweavers.com/products/cxmac/)—Run Windows applications (including Outlook!) and games within Lion without the overhead of a virtual machine. CrossOver enables you to run many Windows applications directly from your MacBook.

DaisyDisk (http://www.daisydiskapp.com/)—Helps you identify large files that are eating up space on your disk in an amazingly fun and visual way.

Dropbox (http://www.getdropbox.com/)—Provides 2GB of free online storage that can be synced across Mac OS X, Windows, and Lion platforms. This service is *much* faster than Apple's iDisk and offers the ability to track multiple versions of files.

Evernote (http://www.evernote.com/)—A free application and service that stores and syncs notes across multiple computers and devices. Evernote even provides a Safari plug-in that can capture full PDFs of websites for future reference.

Hazel (http://www.noodlesoft.com/hazel.php)—Hazel offers automated file organization for your desktop. It can automatically discard incomplete uploads, empty your trash when it gets too full, and help keep your system nice and clean.

iSpazz (http://www.keindesign.de/stefan/Web/Sites/iWeb/Site/iSpazz.html) —Adds a visual effect to iTunes that pulses your keyboard's backlight in time to your music. Useful? No. Cool? Absolutely.

Lab Tick (http://labtick.proculo.de/)—Adds a menu item to adjust your MacBook's keyboard backlighting—beyond the simple light-sensor control offered by Apple.

Microsoft Remote Desktop (http://www.microsoft.com/mac/)—If you need to use a Windows desktop, you can do so from the comfort of your MacBook. Download Microsoft's Remote Desktop to remotely access your Windows system as if you were sitting directly in front of it.

Crashplan (http://www.crashplan.com/)—If you need true off-site continuous backups, Crashplan fits the bill. Crashplan works in the background to upload any files you choose (or your entire filesystem) to a remote storage location for quick disaster recovery.

Dolly Drive (http://www.dollydrive.com/)—Like the idea of Time Machine, but don't want to leave a drive connected? Dolly Drive brings Time Machine to the cloud. $5 a month gets you 50GB of backup space that works with Time Machine over your Internet connection, wherever you are!

1Password (http://agilewebsolutions.com/products/1Password)—Manages your password and other sensitive information, like the keychain, but in a much more functional and usable way. 1Password can autofill web pages and also syncs across computers and with the iPhone.

smcFanControl (http://www.eidac.de/?p=180)—Fine-tunes the fan speeds on your MacBook. If your lap is getting warm, speed up the fans to cool things down!

Upgrading Your Operating System

Keeping your operating system up-to-date is important both from the standpoint of maintaining your system security and providing the best possible user experience.

With Lion, you can set an automatic update schedule that will check and prompt you with available updates on a periodic basis. Applying updates requires no additional configuration, although a reboot is occasionally required.

Setting an Update Schedule

To configure how frequently your MacBook will check for new software that is available from Apple, follow these steps:

1. Open the Software Update System Preference panel.

2. Click the Scheduled Check button at the top of the panel.

3. Select the Check for Updates checkbox to automatically check for system software updates.

4. Use the popup menu to choose between Daily, Weekly, and Monthly checks.

5. Check Download Updates Automatically to have your system download the update packages in the background so that they are available to install when you are.

6. Close the System Preferences by clicking the red Close button in the upper left corner.

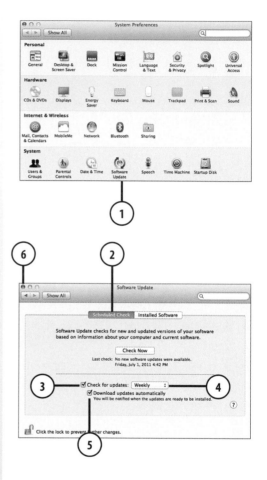

Manually Checking for an Update

If you want to immediately check for updates, you can start the software update process at any time by doing the following:

1. Choose Software Update from the Apple menu.

2. The Software Update utility launches and begins checking for updates.

3. If updates are found, you can apply the system update by following the steps in the following "Applying a System Update" task.

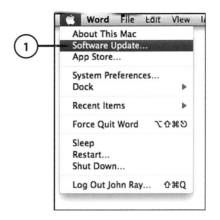

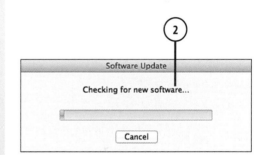

Applying a System Update

When a system update has been detected (either through checking manually or an update schedule), you will be prompted to begin installation or delay until a later time. Follow this process to apply an available update:

1. When updates are detected, you are prompted to install or delay the update.

2. Click Not Now if you want to install the update at another time.

3. Click Show Details to list each update individually.

4. Click the name of an update to show the enhancements it provides.

5. Uncheck any updates that you do not wish to install.

6. Click the Install button to begin installing the updates.

7. The upgrade process begins. You may be prompted to reboot your computer, depending on nature of the update.

What's the Password?

Depending on the type of update, you may be asked for your password and to accept any applicable software license agreements before an update is installed.

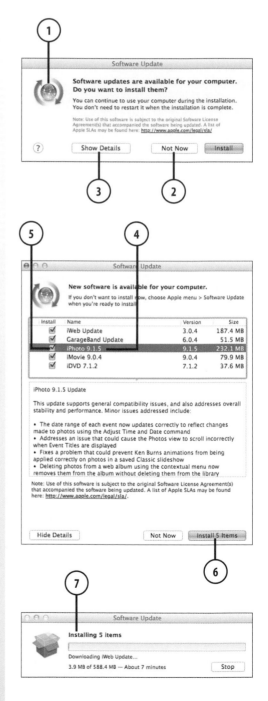

Optimize your MacBook's
built-in hardware
in System Preferences.

In this chapter, you'll learn how to make your MacBook hardware work at its best for your particular needs, including

- → Balancing performance and battery efficiency
- → Fine-tuning the keyboard settings
- → Adjusting trackpad gestures
- → Setting sound input and output
- → Configuring the monitor resolution and color
- → Recording audio
- → Recording video and screen actions

Making the Most of Your MacBook Hardware

Introduction

When you purchased your MacBook, you bought more than just a "computer"—you bought a power system, monitor, keyboard, trackpad, video camera, microphone, and speakers! On a desktop system, these might all be separate components, but on your MacBook, they're part of the package.

To help personalize your MacBook, you can adjust many of the settings available for these hardware devices, such as controlling keyboard illumination, enabling trackpad gestures, or determining whether you want greater graphics capabilities at the cost of battery life. Snow Leopard even includes a few new tricks such as video, audio, and screen recording that let you take advantage of the built-in hardware without needing any additional software.

Balancing Battery Life and Performance

When your MacBook is plugged in, chances are you use it just like a desktop computer; battery life is a non-issue. When you're on the go, however, the battery becomes the lifeblood of the system. You need to make sure that you get the performance you need from your system, when you need it. Monitoring the battery life of your computer is necessary to keep you aware of when you need a recharge, as well as whether or not there are issues occurring with your MacBook's built-in battery. Configuring things such as how long the computer waits for input before its energy saver settings kick in and scheduling when the computer goes to sleep are ways to make sure the battery is ready when you are.

Monitoring Battery Life

Follow these steps to use and configure the Lion battery status monitor:

1. By default, the battery status is shown in a battery icon in the menu bar. The dark portion of the battery indicates the remaining life of the battery.

2. Click the battery icon to show the amount of time remaining until the battery power is exhausted, or, if the MacBook is plugged in, until the battery is recharged.

3. Use the Show menu to display more information about the battery in your menu bar, including the time remaining, or the percentage of the battery life left.

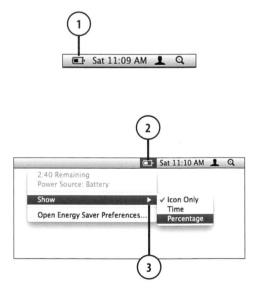

Tip

If battery status is not visible in your menu bar, it has been manually removed. You can re-add the icon to the menu bar using the Show Battery Status in the Menu Bar option in the Energy Saver System Preference panel.

Configuring Display, Computer, and Hard Disk Sleep

To help improve battery life, Lion includes the Energy Saver System Preference panel.

1. Open the System Preferences window and click the Energy Saver icon.

2. Click the Battery or Power Adapter buttons to choose whether you're configuring the system for when it is running on battery power or when it is connected directly to a power adapter.

3. Drag the sliders, Computer Sleep and Display Sleep to set the period of inactivity after which your MacBook puts itself or its display into sleep mode.

4. Select Put Hard Disks to Sleep When Possible to spin down your hard drive when it's not in use. This helps save power, but sacrifices some speed.

5. Click Slightly Dim the Display When Using This Power Source to have your display run at a lower brightness level.

6. Choose Automatically Reduce Brightness Before Display Goes to Sleep to dim the display after the system has been inactive, but before the display goes to sleep.

7. Choose Restart Automatically if the Computer Freezes to reboot your MacBook in the unlikely event it crashes.

8. Close the Energy Saver panel.

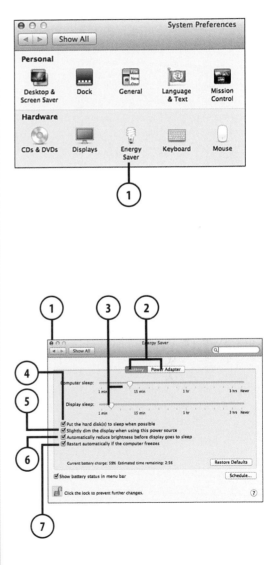

It's Not All Good

BATTERY WARNINGS

If your battery is failing, your MacBook displays a warning message in the battery status. If you see a Service Battery message in the status menu, schedule an appointment for service at your local Apple store.

Creating a Sleep/Wake Schedule

If you have a daily schedule and want your MacBook to follow it, you can configure wake-up and sleep/shutdown times for the MacBook. Follow these steps to set a power schedule for your system.

1. Open System Preferences window and click the Energy Saver icon.

2. Click the Schedule button at the bottom of the window.

3. To have your computer start up on a schedule, click the checkbox beside Start up or Wake.

4. Use the Every Day pop-up menu to set when (weekdays, weekends, and so on) the startup should occur.

5. Set the time for the computer to start up.

6. To configure your computer to go to sleep, shutdown, or restart, click the checkbox in front of the Sleep pop-up menu.

7. Use the Sleep pop-up menu to choose whether your MacBook should sleep, shutdown, or restart.

8. Configure the day and time for the shutdown to occur, just as you did with the start options in Steps 4 and 5.

9. Click OK and then close the Energy Saver panel.

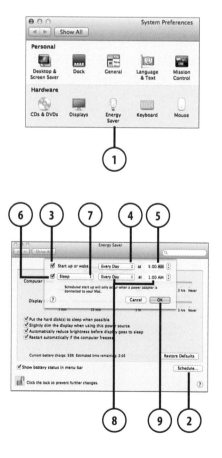

Advanced Energy Saver Options

As you configure the Energy Saver settings for the Power Adapter, you'll notice some additional options, including the ability to wake your computer over a network. These options are most frequently used for centrally managed computers and might not be that useful for your MacBook.

Updating Keyboard Settings

Your MacBook keyboard can be set to match your unique typing style, and it can even provide a bit of light for you if you're an avid night-typer. Using the built-in keyboard settings, you can adjust the keyboard repeat rate, key illumination, and even set system-wide shortcuts for trackpad-free operation.

Setting Keyboard Repeat Rate

To choose how frequently the keys on your keyboard repeat, and how long it takes to start repeating, follow these simple steps:

1. Open the System Preferences window and click the Keyboard icon.

2. Click the Keyboard button at the top of the panel.

3. Use the Key Repeat Rate slider to set how quickly letters appear when you hold down a key on your keyboard.

4. Move the Delay Until Repeat slider to choose how long you must hold down a key before it starts repeating. Move the slider all the way to the left to turn off repeating.

5. Close the Keyboard panel.

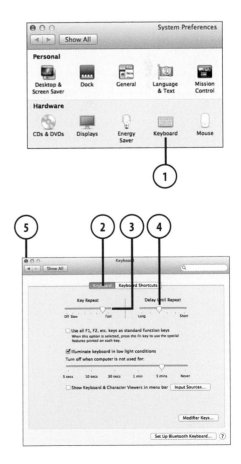

Using Function Keys

You've probably noticed that the top row of keys on your MacBook have special functions, such as dimming the display, changing the volume, and so on. These keys, however, are also function keys that your applications might need. To set the keys to always work as function keys without having to hold down the fn key, click the Use all F1, F2, etc. Keys as Standard Function Keys check box.

Changing Keyboard Illumination

When it gets dark, your keyboard comes to life, lighting the way for your typing. To activate this function and control how long the lighting stays on, follow these steps:

1. Open the System Preferences window and click the Keyboard icon. (Make sure the Keyboard button is chosen in the panel that opens.)

2. Check the Illuminate Keyboard in Low Light Conditions to automatically turn on the keyboard backlight when your environment gets dark.

3. Drag the Turn Off slider to choose how long the keyboard remains lit when your computer is idle.

4. Close the Keyboard panel.

Fine-Tune Your Keyboard Brightness

For more fine control over the keyboard backlight, including a brightness control, download Lab Tick, from http://labtick.proculo.de/.

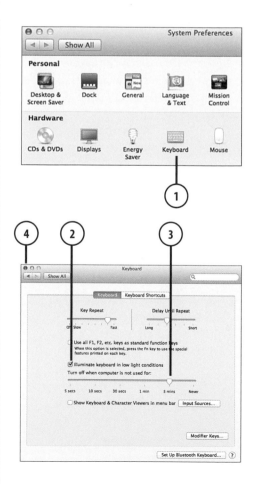

Creating Keyboard Shortcuts

There are times you might find your-self working with your MacBook and thinking, "Geez, I wish I could just push a key for that rather than hav-ing to mouse around." Using key-board shortcuts, you can create key commands for almost anything.

Setting Shortcuts for Existing Lion Actions

To set the shortcut for an existing system feature, follow these steps:

1. Open the System Preferences win-dow and click the Keyboard icon.

2. Click the Keyboard Shortcuts button.

3. Choose one of the Lion system features from the left pane.

4. Scroll through the list of available actions in the right pane.

5. Click the checkbox in front of an action to enable it.

6. Double-click to the far right of an action name to edit its shortcut field.

7. Press the keys that you want to assign to the shortcut.

8. Close the Keyboard panel after making all of your changes.

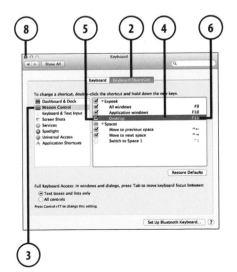

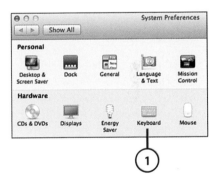

Setting Shortcuts for Arbitrary Applications

To configure a shortcut that works with an arbitrary application, not a built-in feature, do the following:

1. Open the System Preferences window and click the Keyboard icon.

2. Click the Keyboard Shortcuts button.

3. Click the Application Shortcuts entry in the list on the left side of the window.

4. Click the + button at the bottom of the shortcut list.

5. In the dialog box that opens, use the Application pop-up menu to choose an application to which you want to assign a shortcut.

6. Enter into the Menu Title field the exact wording of the menu item that you want the keyboard shortcut to invoke.

7. Click into the Keyboard Shortcut field and then press the keys you want to set as the shortcut.

8. Click Add when you're satisfied with your settings.

9. Close the Keyboard panel.

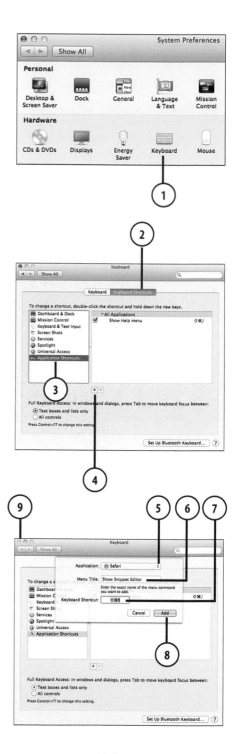

Changing Trackpad Options

Your MacBook trackpad gives you fingertip control for pointing, clicking, dragging, scrolling, and even drawing. Using the Trackpad preferences, you can fine-tune how precise these actions are, and even set up different multi-finger gestures as shortcuts in popular applications.

Setting the Trackpad Speed

To choose how quickly your trackpad follows your input, follow these steps:

1. Open the System Preferences window and click the Trackpad icon.

2. Click the Point & Click button at the top of the window.

3. Choose how quickly the cursor moves by dragging the Tracking Speed slider.

4. Close the Trackpad panel.

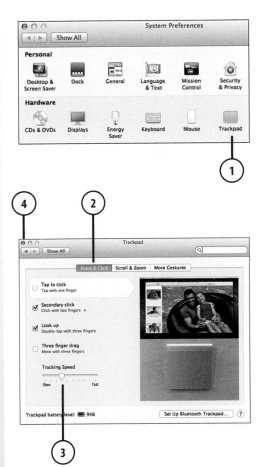

Controlling Gestures

If you have a MacBook that supports gestures (using multiple fingers on the trackpad as shortcuts to commands or actions) as most of the recent models do, you can take advantage of a wide range of different two-, three-, and even four-finger motions to control your applications.

1. Open the System Preferences window and click the Trackpad icon.

2. Use the Point & Click settings to configure click and drag options.

3. Use the Scroll & Zoom settings section to control scrolling, rotation, and pinching gestures.

4. The More Gestures settings control advanced features, such as whether swiping to the left or right moves forward or backward in Safari and how Mission Control is activated.

5. Many settings contain a dropdown menu to fine-tune the gesture.

6. As you mouse over a particular setting, a video demonstrating the action appears in the right side of the window.

7. Close the Trackpad panel.

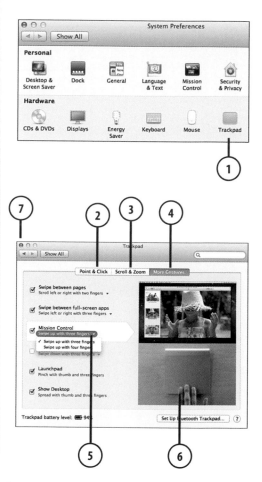

Adjusting the LCD Display

Your MacBook's LCD display is your window into your computer, so it's important that you configure your display to best suit your needs. For detailed CAD or drawing, you might want to use the full resolution. Games or late-night typing might call for a larger (lower resolution) option. Using Snow Leopard's Display settings, you can control the image so that it is right for the task at hand.

Setting Display Resolution

The display resolution is the number of pixels that are viewable on the screen at any time. The smallest MacBook display is capable of 1280×800 pixels—higher than most broadcast HDTV! To control the screen resolution on your system, follow these steps:

1. Open the System Preferences window and click the Displays icon.

2. Click the Display button at the top of the panel.

3. Scroll through the list of available resolutions (smaller numbers result in a larger onscreen image).

4. Click a resolution to switch immediately.

5. Click Show Displays in Menu Bar to add your frequently used resolutions to a monitor menu bar item.

6. Close the Display panel.

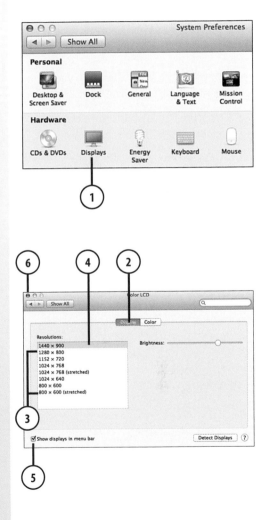

Controlling Display Brightness

Display brightness is a personal setting; some individuals like muted, dimmed displays and others like colors offered by full-brightness settings. To set the brightness of your display, follow these steps:

1. Open the System Preferences window and click the Displays icon.

2. Click the Display button at the top of the panel.

3. Drag the Brightness slider left or right to dim or brighten the display.

4. Close the Display panel.

Adjusting Brightness From Your Keyboard

You can also adjust display brightness using the F1 and F2 keys on your keyboard. See the earlier task, "Configuring Display, Computer, and Hard Disk Sleep," to learn about another way you can modify your display's brightness.

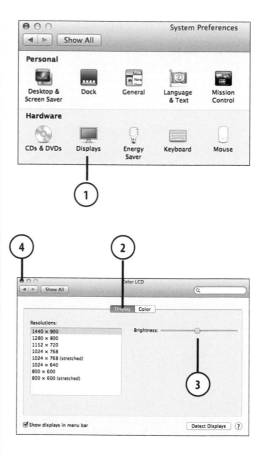

Choosing a Color Profile

Color profiles help keep colors consistent between computers with different monitors. By choosing a color profile that is calibrated for your display, you're ensured that colors you see on one machine match a similarly calibrated display on another machine. To choose a calibration profile, follow these steps:

1. Open the System Preferences window and click the Displays icon.

2. Click the Color button at the top of the panel.

3. Click the preferred profile in the Display profile list. The changes are immediately applied.

4. Close the System Preferences.

Where Do These Profiles Come From?

You can add profiles to your system by installing software or by running the calibration procedure, which creates your own personalized color profile.

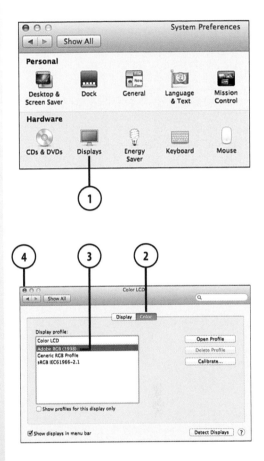

Calibrating the LCD Display

If you'd like to calibrate your display manually, Lion provides a wizard-like interface for choosing the best display settings for your MacBook.

1. Open the Displays System Preferences panel.

2. Click the Color button at the top of the panel.

3. Click Calibrate.

4. The Display Calibrator Assistant starts.

5. Click the Expert Mode checkbox to get the best results.

6. Click Continue to proceed through the assistant.

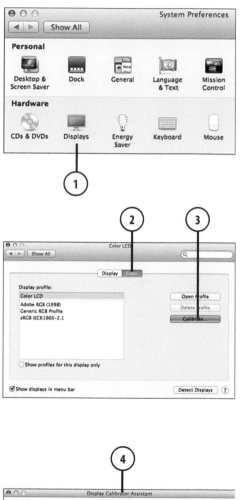

7. Follow the onscreen instructions to test the output of your display and click Continue to move on to the next screen.

8. When finished, enter a name for the new calibrated profile and click Continue.

9. The new profile is added to the color profile list.

10. Close the Display panel.

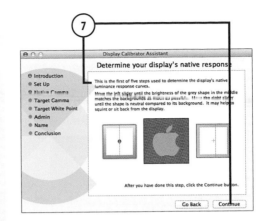

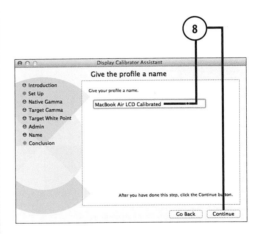

Setting Sound Input and Output

Sound has never been an afterthought on Macintosh systems, and your MacBook is no different. Your system is equipped with a stereo sound system, headphone jack, microphone (shared with the headphone jack in the MacBook), and even digital audio out. You can configure these input and output options to reflect your listening needs.

Setting the Output Volume

Volume, as you might expect, is one control that is needed system-wide. To control the output volume of your system, follow these steps:

1. Click the speaker icon in the menu bar.

2. Drag the slider up to increase the volume, or slide it down to decrease the volume.

3. Drag the slider all the way to the bottom to mute all output sounds.

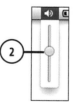

Keyboard Volume Controls

You can also use the special controls located on the F9, F10, and F11 keys to mute, decrease, and increase the system volume.

Adding the Volume Control to the Menu Bar

If sound control is not visible in your menu bar, it has been manually removed. You can re-add it to the menu using the Show Volume in the Menu Bar option in the Sound System Preferences panel.

Configuring Alert Sounds

Your MacBook generates alert sounds when it needs to get your attention. To configure the sounds, and how loud they play, follow these steps:

1. Open the System Preferences window and click the Sound icon.

2. Click the Sound Effects button at the top of the panel.

3. Scroll through the alert sound list to see all of the available alert sounds.

4. Click a sound to select it as your alert sound and hear a preview.

5. Choose which sound output device (usually your internal speakers) should play the alert sound.

6. Use the alert volume slider to adjust the volume of alerts that your system plays. This is independent of the system output volume.

7. Check Play User Interface Sound Effects to play sounds when special events occur—such as emptying the trash.

8. Close the Sound panel when finished configuring the sound effects.

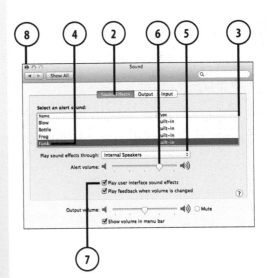

Choosing and Adjusting an Output Device

To configure your sound output options with a bit more flexibility than just changing the volume, you need to adjust the output settings for the device that is being used for playback—typically your speaker.

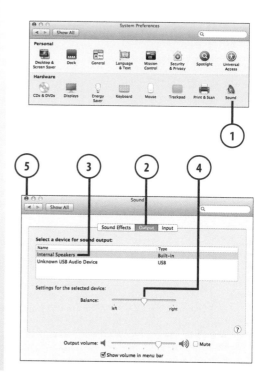

1. Open the System Preferences window and click the Sound icon.

2. Click the Output button at the top of the panel.

3. Choose the output device to configure (probably your speakers).

4. Use the balance setting to adjust audio to the left or right speaker.

5. Close the Sound panel when finished.

HOW DO I USE HEADPHONES OR DIGITAL AUDIO ON MY MACBOOK?

>>> Go Further

When headphones are plugged into your MacBook, the sound output settings alter to reflect the change. All sound is directed to the headphones rather than the internal speakers.

Your MacBook also sports a home-theater-worthy digital optical output, disguised as the headphone jack. To use the digital output, you need a mini TOSLINK adaptor, which provides a standard TOSLINK plug for connecting to stereo equipment. These cables from Amazon.com easily get the job done: www.amazon.com/6ft-Toslink-Mini-Cable/dp/B000FMXKC8.

Picking and Calibrating an Input Device

In addition to sound output, you can also input sound on your MacBook using either the built-in microphone or the standard line-in jack on the side. To configure your input device, follow these steps:

1. Open the System Preferences window and click the Sound icon.

2. Click the Input button at the top of the panel.

3. Choose the device to use for input.

4. Use the input volume slider to adjust the gain on the microphone—this is how much amplification is applied to the signal.

5. Click the Use Ambient Noise Reduction checkbox if you're working in an environment with background noise.

6. Speak at the level you want your computer to record. The Input Level graph should register near the middle when you use a normal speaking level. If it doesn't, readjust the input volume slider.

7. Close the Sound panel.

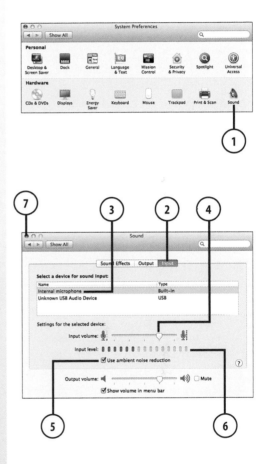

Keeping the Input Volume Under Control

It might be tempting to turn the input volume up as high as it goes so that the microphone detects even little noises. Keep in mind, however, that the higher the input volume for wanted sounds, the higher the volume for unwanted sounds as well!

Recording Audio, Video, and Screen Actions

It has always been possible to record audio and video "out of the box" with a new Macintosh, but not without installing iLife or jumping through a bunch of seemingly unnecessary hoops. With Snow Leopard, Apple has made it easy to take advantage of your MacBook's built-in capabilities to record audio, video, and even screen actions.

Recording Audio

To create and save a new audio recording, first make sure that you've configured your sound input settings correctly (including ambient noise reduction, if needed) then follow these steps:

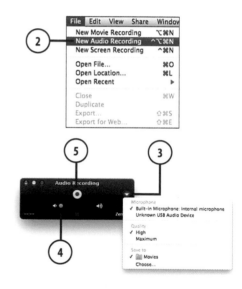

1. Open the QuickTime Player application (find it in the Applications folder if the icon isn't on your Dock).

2. Choose File, New Audio Recording.

3. Use the drop-down menu on the right of the Audio Recording window to choose an input source, recording quality, and destination.

4. If you want to hear audio through the speakers as it is recorded, drag the volume slider to the right.

5. Click the Record button to begin recording.

6. Click the Stop button to stop recording. The sound is saved as Audio Recording.mov in your Movies folder by default.

7. Use the playback controls to listen to your creation.

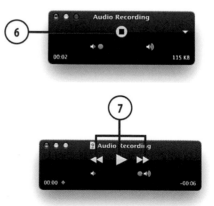

Recording FaceTime Camera Video

Although FaceTime allows you to see video of yourself on your computer, It doesn't give you the option to record. If you want to take a recording of what the built-in FaceTime camera sees, follow these steps:

1. Open the QuickTime Player application (find it in the Applications folder if the icon isn't on your Dock).

2. Choose File, New Movie Recording.

3. Use the drop-down menu on the right side of the recording controls to choose a camera (if you have more than one), input microphone, recording quality, and destination.

4. If you want to hear audio through the speakers as it is recorded, drag the volume slider to the right.

5. Click the double arrows to expand the video to full screen.

6. Click the Record button to begin recording.

7. Click the Stop button to stop recording. The movie, by default, is saved as Movie Recording.mov in your Movies folder.

8. Use the playback controls to view the video you've recorded.

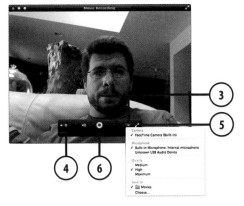

Recording Screen Actions

If you've ever been in a situation where you tried to explain to someone *how* to do something on a computer, chances are you've gotten a bit frustrated. By using Snow Leopard's screen recording capabilities, however, you can quickly create a movie that shows all your onscreen actions and then send that movie to your confused acquaintance to provide a better-than-words tutorial.

1. Open the QuickTime Player application (find it in the Applications folder if the icon isn't on your Dock).

2. Choose File, New Screen Recording.

3. Use the drop-down menu on the right side of the recording controls to choose an input microphone, recording quality, whether or not to show mouse clicks, and, finally destination.

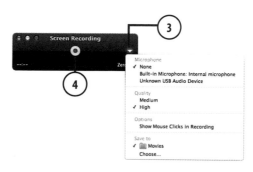

4. Click the Record button to prepare to record actions.

5. Click anywhere on your screen to record the whole screen, or click and drag to define a rectangular area to record.

6. If you've defined a recording area, click Start Recording, then perform the actions that you want to record.

7. Click the Stop button in the recording controls to stop. The movie, by default, is saved as Screen Recording.mov in your Movies folder.

8. Use the playback controls to view the video you've recorded.

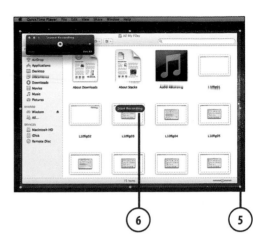

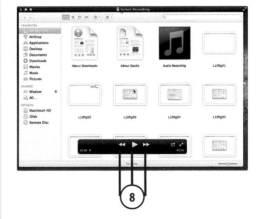

Transferring Your Recordings to iTunes, Email, MobileMe, Facebook, Vimeo, YouTube, and More!

In addition to being able to record audio and movies using your MacBook hardware, Lion makes it simple to transfer your movies to iTunes for syncing with your iPod, send them in email, or to upload them to a variety of online services.

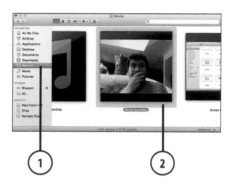

Transferring Movies to iTunes

To encode your movie so that it is appropriate for transfer to iTunes, and to add it to your iTunes library, follow these steps:

1. Find the movie file you want to use in iTunes.

2. Double-click to open it in QuickTime Player.

3. Click the Send To icon and choose iTunes from the popup menu that appears.

4. Pick which device you plan to use the movie on. Click the Share button. Be aware that not all choices will always be available.

5. The Movie Export window appears and displays the status of the encoding process.

6. When finished, close QuickTime Player. Your movie is available in iTunes.

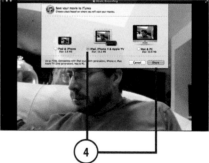

Transferring Movies to Email

If you'd like to share your video creation with a few friends, or perhaps share a screen recording with a colleague, you can easily do so through email.

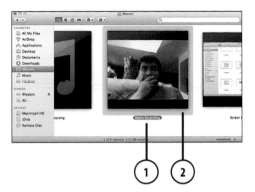

1. Find the movie file you want to email.

2. Double-click to open it in QuickTime Player.

3. Click the Send To icon and choose Mail from the popup menu that appears.

4. Choose whether to send the movie in its full, actual size, or a more compressed 480p format.

5. Click Share.

6. The Movie Export window appears and displays the status of the encoding process.

7. When finished, Mail opens and the movie is added as an attachment. Close QuickTime and address the email as you wish!

Video and Photo Fun!

If you want to record and send several videos and photos through email, or you want to just play around with your FaceTime HD camera, you may want to try Photobooth—located in your Applications folder. Photobooth provides a simple interface for taking pictures and video, applying effects, and sending the results through email.

Uploading Movies to an Online Service

Using Lion, you can now share your compositions with the world via YouTube, Facebook, Vimeo, Flikr, and MobileMe without even needing to touch a web browser. YouTube is the most popular destination for videos on the Internet, so we'll use that as our example. To upload a video to the online service of your choice, follow these steps:

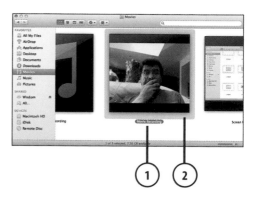

1. Locate the movie file you want to upload.

2. Double-click to open it in QuickTime Player.

3. Click the Send To icon to display destinations for the movie and choose the online destination (in this case, YouTube) from the pop-up menu.

4. Enter your username and password when prompted.

5. Choose Remember This Password in My Keychain to streamline the process in the future.

6. Click Sign In to log into the YouTube service.

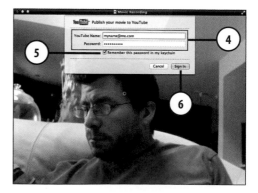

7. Set a category for the uploaded video file.

8. Enter a title, description, and a set of keywords (called Tags) to describe the video.

9. Use the Access setting to set the video as Personal, if desired. This limits viewing of the video to individuals that you share it with via the YouTube website. Please note that these settings may vary between the various online services supported in Lion.

10. Click Next.

11. Review the YouTube Terms of Service, then click Share

12. The Movie Export window appears and displays the status of the encoding process.

13. When finished, close QuickTime Player. Your movie is available on YouTube!

Cutting It Down to Size

To trim a video before sharing it, click the Send to icon and choose Trim from the popup menu. You'll be able to move the start and end points of your video clip to wherever you'd like and then trim the extra right off!

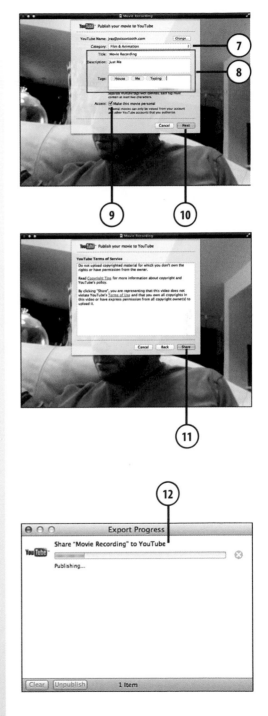

Connect your MacBook to external
displays and peripherals using
System Preferences.

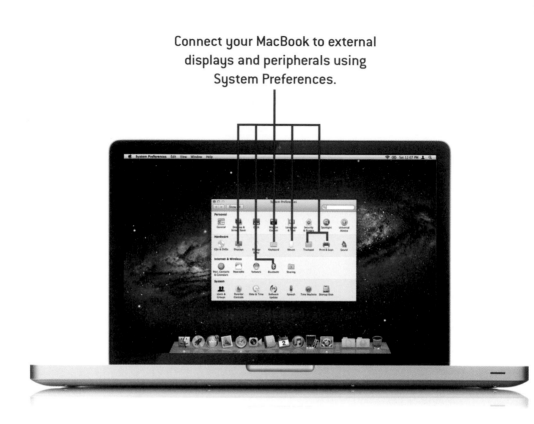

In this chapter, you'll learn how to connect devices to your MacBook and immediately add new capabilities through Lion's built-in features, including

→ Adding a keyboard and mouse
→ Pairing bluetooth devices
→ Connecting and configuring external displays
→ Adding and using printers
→ Accessing and using popular scanners

Connecting Devices to Your MacBook

Introduction

It isn't unusual nowadays for a MacBook to serve both as a laptop and as a desktop computer. When you're using the MacBook as a desktop computer, you might want to connect traditional input and output devices that are appropriate for desk or table use, such as keyboards and mice.

Your MacBook can interface to many different devices and even works with them without requiring that additional software be installed. This ease of configuration makes the transformation between desktop workstation and laptop truly a matter of seconds.

Connecting USB Input Devices

The MacBook can connect to a variety of devices using the standard USB (Universal Serial Bus) connectors located on the side of the MacBook. This section walks you through connecting a generic keyboard and mouse. Keep in mind, though, that there are *hundreds* of different input devices.

You should always refer to the manual that came with your device. If the manual doesn't mention the Macintosh (such as for a Windows-specific keyboard), try plugging in the device to see what happens!

USB Device Compatibility

The USB standard includes a variety of different profiles that define how a device can be used (input, audio output/input, and so on). These standards are supported on both Macintosh and Windows platforms. Just because a device does not specifically say it supports the Mac, doesn't mean that it won't work anyway.

Configuring a USB Keyboard

Your MacBook has a perfectly usable keyboard, but if you're typing for long periods of time at a desk, you might want to connect a standard desktop keyboard. To use a USB keyboard with your MacBook, follow these steps:

1. Plug the keyboard into a free port on your MacBook.

2. If the keyboard is an Apple or Mac-specific keyboard, it is recognized and immediately usable.

3. If you are using a generic USB keyboard, the Keyboard Setup Assistant launches and you are asked to identify the keyboard. Click Continue.

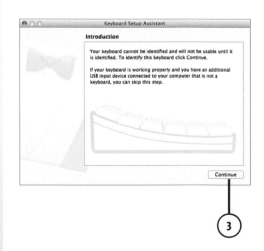

4. Walk through the steps presented by the setup assistant, pressing the keyboard keys when requested. If the assistant can't identify the keyboard, you will be asked to manually identify it.

5. Click Done at the conclusion of the setup assistant. The keyboard setup is complete and ready to be used.

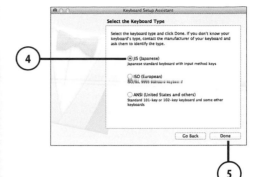

Manually Configuring the Keyboard Type

If the setup assistant does not start automatically when you plug in a USB keyboard, you can start it by opening the System Preferences window and clicking the Keyboard icon. In the Keyboard panel, click Change Keyboard Type.

Configuring a USB Mouse

A mouse is a virtual necessity for desktop computing. Even though your MacBook doesn't come with a mouse, it does have a Mouse System Preference Panel that you can use to quickly configure most USB mice.

1. Open the System Preferences and click the Mouse icon.

2. Plug a USB mouse into your MacBook.

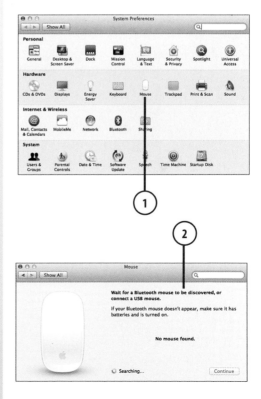

3. After a few seconds the Mouse panel updates to show the available options for your device.

4. Adjust the tracking speed, scrolling speed (if the mouse includes a scroll wheel), and double-click speed by dragging the sliders left or right.

5. Choose which button acts as the primary button.

6. Close the Mouse panel when you've finished your configuration.

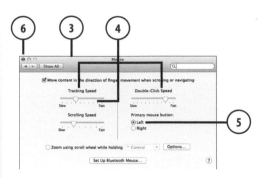

Using Bluetooth Devices

The MacBook's built-in Bluetooth enables it to wirelessly connect to a variety of peripheral devices, including keyboards, mice, headsets, and so on. As with USB peripherals, your first step toward installing a device is to read the manufacturer's instructions and install any drivers that the device comes with.

After installing any software that came with the peripheral, you use the Apple Bluetooth System Preference panel to choose and *pair* your device.

WHAT IS PAIRING?

When you're working with Bluetooth peripherals, you'll notice many references to pairing. Pairing is the process of making two devices (your Mac and the peripheral) aware of one another so they can communicate.

In order to pair with your computer, your device needs to be in pairing mode, which should be described in the device's manual.

>>> Go Further

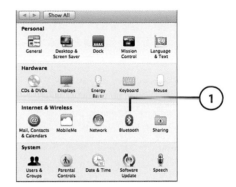

Pairing a Bluetooth Mouse or Trackpad

To pair a Bluetooth device with your MacBook, you follow the same basic steps, regardless of the type of peripheral. This task's screenshots show an Apple Magic Trackpad being paired with the MacBook.

1. Open the Bluetooth System Preferences panel.

2. Click On to ensure that your MacBook's Bluetooth system is enabled.

3. Click Set Up New Device, or click + below the list of devices you added previously to start the Bluetooth Setup Assistant.

4. After a few seconds of searching, nearby devices are listed. Click to choose your device from the detected options.

5. Click Continue.

6. The trackpad is configured and paired to your system. Click Quit to exit the Assistant.

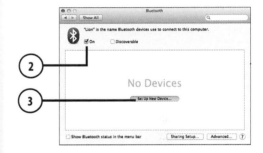

Setting Up Bluetooth Devices from Almost Anywhere

You may notice that there is a Set Up Bluetooth [Keyboard, Mouse, Trackpad] option within the keyboard, mouse, and trackpad system preference panels. You can use these as shortcuts to immediately start searching for a Bluetooth device of that type. The Bluetooth system preference panel, however, is the central point for pairing all devices.

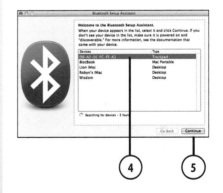

7. Your new device is listed in the Bluetooth System Preferences panel.

8. Use the corresponding (Mouse/Keyboard/Trackpad) Preference panel to configure your device.

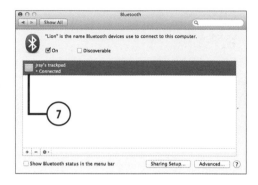

Monitoring Your Battery

When you're using an Apple Bluetooth device or keyboard, the corresponding preference panels display battery status for the devices. You can also monitor battery status by adding the Bluetooth status to your menu bar by selecting Show Bluetooth Status in Menu Bar in the Bluetooth System Preferences panel.

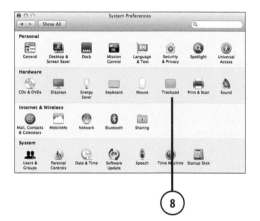

Pairing a Bluetooth Keyboard

Some Bluetooth devices, such as keyboards, require an additional step while pairing: the entry of a passkey on the device you are pairing with. To pair a keyboard with your system, follow these steps:

1. Follow Steps 1–5 of the "Pairing a Bluetooth Mouse or Trackpad" task, selecting the keyboard device from the list of detected devices, then clicking Continue.

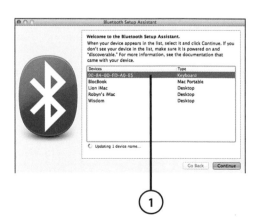

2. The Bluetooth Setup Assistant prompts you to enter a passkey on your device. Type the characters exactly as displayed on screen, including pressing Return, if shown.

3. Click Continue.

4. If the passkey was successfully entered, the device is configured and paired.

5. Click Quit to exit the Setup Assistant.

6. Close the Bluetooth System Preferences panel and configure the device as described in Chapter 9's section "Updating Keyboard Settings."

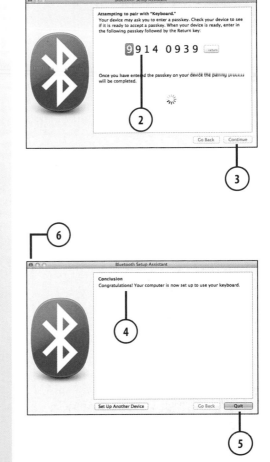

Dealing with Troublesome Passcodes

If, for some reason, you enter the passkey and get an error, take note of the Passcode Options button in the lower-left corner of the Setup Assistant. Clicking this button *might* allow you to bypass the passkey or choose one that is easier to enter on your device.

It's Not All Good

MULTIPLE TRACKPADS

If you add multiple trackpads to your MacBook, you might expect to be able to configure them independently in the system preferences. Unfortunately, this is not the case! A single preference panel configures all devices of that type (mouse, trackpad, keyboard).

Connecting a Bluetooth Headset

Wireless headphones and headsets can help untether us from our computers when conferencing or listening to music. As a MacBook owner, you're already aware of the freedom provided by a portable computer, so a wireless headset is a logical next step.

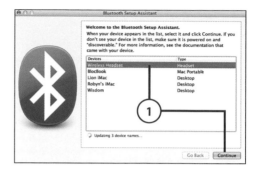

1. Follow Steps 1–5 of the "Pairing a Bluetooth Mouse or Trackpad" task, selecting the headset device from the list of detected devices, then clicking Continue.

2. The headset is added to your system. You might need to cycle the power on and off the headset before it will work, however.

3. Click Quit to exit the Setup Assistant.

4. To set the headset for audio input or output, use the Sound System Preference panel, as described in the Chapter 9 section, "Setting Sound Input and Output."

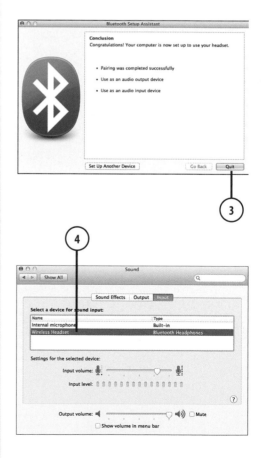

Adding and Using the Bluetooth Status Menu

Apple Bluetooth devices report their status directly to your computer, giving you a heads up on battery issues and other status problems. To use the Bluetooth status menu, follow these steps.

1. Open the Bluetooth System Preferences window and click the Bluetooth icon.

2. Click the Show Bluetooth Status in the Menu Bar checkbox.

3. Close the System Preferences.

4. The Bluetooth menu is added to your display.

5. Each paired device has an entry in the menu for quick control of its features.

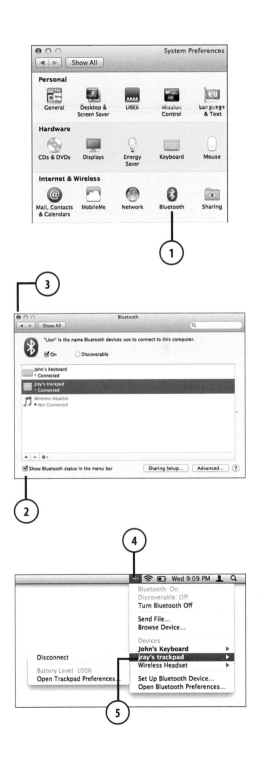

Using External Displays and Projectors

The MacBook screen sizes range from 11" to 17", which is plenty of room for most applications. There are times, though, when using an external monitor or a projector are helpful. As long as you have the right cables, running an external monitor is plug-and-play—no rebooting required.

What Kind of Displays Can I Run?

All modern MacBooks have a Mini DisplayPort video output or Thunderbolt, which can be adapted to VGA or DVI output with a plug-in dongle from Apple. Earlier models used a miniDVI port, which, similarly, could be output to VGA or DVI monitors with the appropriate adapter.

Adding the Display Menu to your Menu Bar

To access display settings and connect external monitors, you can either use the Displays System Preferences panel or add a global Display menu to the menu bar, which provides much more expedient access.

1. Open the Displays System Preferences Panel.

2. Click the Show Displays in Menu Bar checkbox.

3. Close the System Preferences application.

4. The Displays menu item appears in the menu bar.

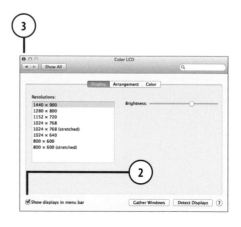

Detecting and Activating a Display

When you plug a display into your computer, you may need to let the system know that it has been connected. To detect and activate a display, follow these steps:

1. Click the Displays menu item in your menu bar.

2. Choose Detect Displays from the menu.

3. Your screen might go blank or flash for a moment.

4. The second display activates and is visible in the Displays menu, as well as in the Displays System Preferences Panel.

Monitor Resolution

The second display is initialized at the highest resolution that is detected and supported by your MacBook.

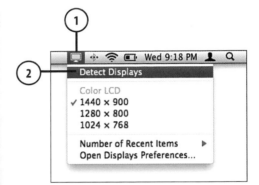

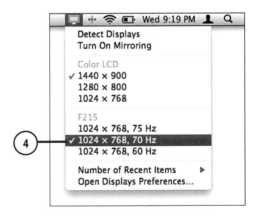

Setting Monitor Arrangements

Once a monitor has been connected to your system, you can choose how it is arranged in relationship to your MacBook display and whether or not it displays the menu bar.

1. Open the Displays System Preferences Panel.

2. Click the Arrangement button at the top of the screen.

3. Drag the visual representation of the monitors so that it best represents your physical setup (that is, external monitor on the left, right, above, and so on).

4. If you want, change your primary display by dragging the small white line representing the menu bar from one display to the other.

5. Close the System Preferences.

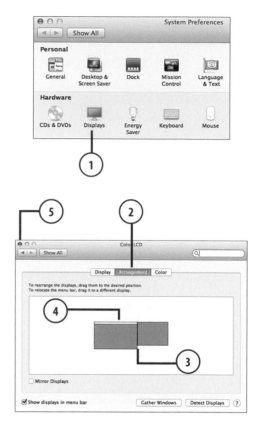

MANAGING MULTIPLE MONITORS

When the Displays System Preferences panel is opened with two or more monitors connected, a unique copy of the preference panel is shown on each monitor, representing that monitor's settings.

Within each window, you can adjust the color and resolution of your external display using the same approach described in Chapter 9's section, "Adjusting the LCD Display." You can also use the Gather Windows button to pull all open application windows onto that display.

>>> Go Further

Activating Mirrored Video

If you'd prefer not to use your external display as a second monitor, you can set it to mirror the contents of your MacBook's LCD.

1. Click the Displays item in your menu bar.

2. Choose Turn on Mirroring from the menu.

3. Your external monitor changes to display the same content as your MacBook's LCD screen.

4. Choose Turn off Mirroring from the menu to switch back to using two separate displays.

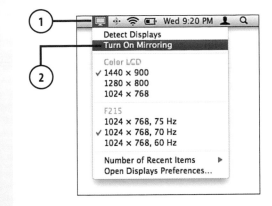

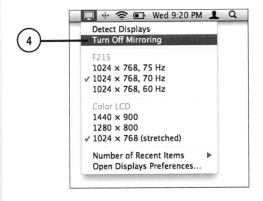

Note

If the external display is set as your primary monitor or cannot be adjusted to match your internal LCD, your MacBook might instead change the resolution on its LCD to match the external monitor. This change reverts when you turn off mirrored video.

Connecting and Using a Printer

Out of the box, Lion supports a range of popular printers just by plugging them in. Occasionally, however, you might need to install a driver before you can successfully print. As with any peripheral that you want to use, be sure to read and follow the manufacturer's instructions before proceeding.

Adding a Printer

Your MacBook can connect to printers either over a network connection or via a USB direct connection. Regardless of the connection approach, configuration is straightforward.

Setting Up a USB Printer

To connect to a printer via a USB connection, set up the printer as directed
by the manufacturer, then follow
these steps:

1. Connect the USB plug from the
    printer to your MacBook and turn
    on the printer.

2. If the Printer is auto-detected, it
    may prompt you to download
    software. Click Install and wait for
    the installation to complete.

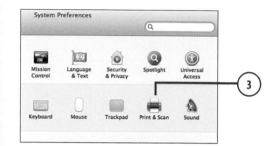

3. Open the System Preferences
    window and click the Print &
    Scan icon.

4. In many cases, the printer is
    detected and configured auto-
    matically and is immediately avail-
    able for use. If this is the case, it is
    displayed in the Printers list, and
    you may close the Print & Scan
    System Preferences panel.

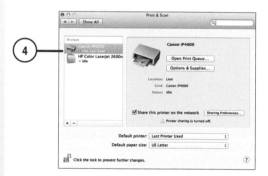

5. If the printer is not detected, click
    the + button below the Printer list
    and choose Add Other Printer or
    Scanner from the popup menu.

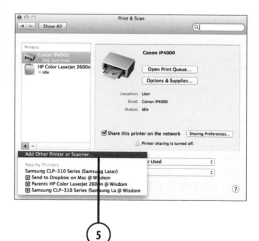

6. A window is shown displaying all of the available printers detected by your Mac. Choose the printer from the list.

7. Your MacBook searches for the software necessary to use the printer and displays the chosen printer name in the Print Using drop-down menu.

8. If the correct printer name is shown in the menu, jump to Step 12.

9. If the correct printer name is not displayed in the Print Using drop-down menu, choose Select Printer Software from the menu.

10. A window appears that shows all the printers supported in Lion. Click your printer within the list.

11. Click OK.

12. Click Add to finish adding the printer. If there are options (such as a duplexer) that your MacBook can't detect, it might prompt you to configure printer-specific features.

13. Close System Preferences and begin using your printer.

Setting Up a Network or Airport Printer

To add a network printer, follow the steps described in the Chapter 6 activity, "Accessing a Network Printer."

Airport-connected printers, even though they might not technically be network printers, are configured identically to networked printers. The Airport makes them available over Bonjour, a configuration-free networking technology developed by Apple.

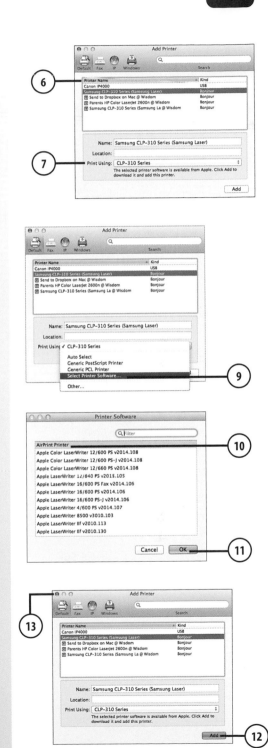

The Printing Process

The options available when printing can vary depending on the application that you're printing from, but once you're used to the process you'll be able to find your way around any software's printing options.

Printing to a Printer

To output to one of your configured printers, complete the following steps in the application of your choice:

1. Choose File, Print from your application's menu bar.

2. Click the Hide/Show Details button to display all the available options, if needed.

3. Select the printer you wish to print to.

4. Set the number of copies and page formatting options.

5. Set the paper size, orientation, and scaling values, if desired.

6. Use the advanced printing options pop-up menu to choose specific printing options for your printer or options related to the application you're using.

7. Review the results of your settings in the preview area on the left side of the window.

8. Use the controls below the Preview to step through the pages in the document.

9. Use the Presets menu to save your settings if you want to recall them in the future.

10. Click Print to output to the Printer.

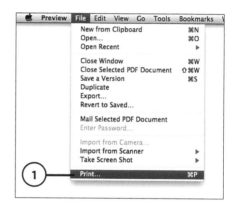

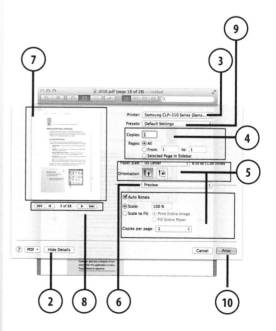

I'm Used to Choosing Page Setup for Paper Size and Orientation. Where Is This Option?

Apple has been working to streamline the printing process. In many applications, the Page Setup functionality has been combined with the standard Print function.

Printing to PDF

In addition to printing to a printer, you can print a document to a PDF, or open it directly as a PDF in Preview. To print to a PDF, click PDF and choose Save as PDF in the Print dialog box. To open the document as a PDF in preview, click the Preview button.

Connecting and Using a Scanner

Although it's not a heavily advertised feature of Lion, the operating system can detect and drive a wide range of scanners without any additional drivers or software. This means that you can connect a scanner to your MacBook and almost immediately begin scanning images.

Is My Scanner Supported?

Apple's list of supported scanners for Lion can be found at http://support.apple.com/kb/HT3669.

Adding a Scanner

To connect a USB scanner to your MacBook, complete any initial setup instructions provided in the hardware manual and then follow these steps:

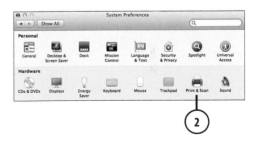

1. Plug the scanner into your MacBook and turn it on.

2. Open the System Preferences window and click the Print & Scan icon.

3. The scanner, if supported, appears in the Scanners listing on the left side of the panel.

4. Choose the application you want to start when the Scan button is pressed on the scanner. I recommend Preview because it is a convenient application for working with images.

5. Close the Print & Scan System Preferences.

Scanning in Preview

Preview (in the Applications folder, click Preview) serves as the image hub on your MacBook. It views images and PDFs, and allows annotations, cropping, image rotation, and more. With Lion, it can also act as your scanning software. To scan an image directly into Preview, do the following:

Scanning Options

Originally, the Image Capture utility (found in the Applications folder) handled scanning in Mac OS X. Lion has expanded that capability to Preview, but Image Capture is still available if you'd like to give it a try.

1. Open Preview, or press the scan button on the scanner if Preview is set as the default scanning application.

2. Choose Import from Scanner from the File menu and then pick your scanner.

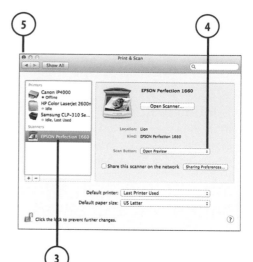

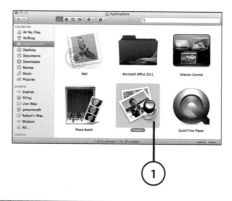

3. The basic scanning window appears. If you want to choose your scanning area or set the resolution, click Show Details and skip to Step 8.

4. Use the Scan Size dropdown to choose the size of the document you're scanning, or to choose Detect Separate Items to automatically scan individual photos, pictures, and so on into separate images within a single scan.

5. Choose a Mode option: flatbed scanner or transparency scanner.

6. Click Scan. Preview prompts for a save location, performs a detailed scan, and then saves the resulting images in your chosen location.

7. Repeat Step 6 as needed for all of your images.

8. In detailed scanning mode, full controls for the scanner are shown on the right side of the window. Choose the scan's resolution, size, orientation, and color depth.

9. Configure the name and format for scanned images.

10. Adjust any image filters and clean-up features you want to apply to the scan.

11. Click Overview to perform a low-resolution scan of your documents and display it in the preview area on the left.

12. Adjust the bounding rectangle to fit your document. If you've chosen to detect separate menus, you will see multiple bounding rectangles.

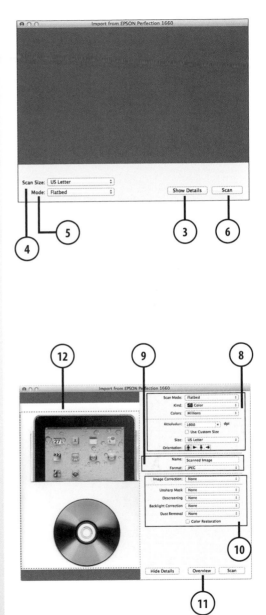

13. Click Scan to prompt for a save location.

14. Choose your destination, and Lion will scan the document using the settings and the scan region you've defined.

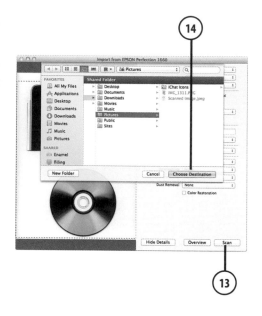

Add and manage
user accounts.

Use Keychain Access
to manage sensitve
information.

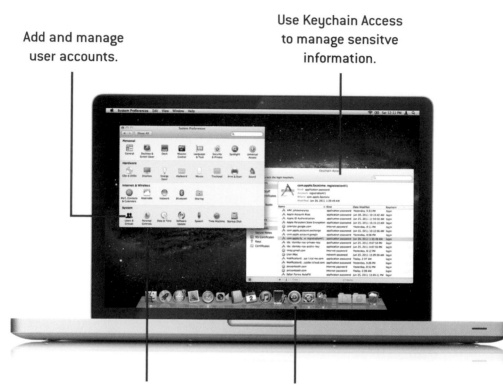

Apply parental
controls to users.

Create full system
backups using
Time Machine.

In this chapter, you'll learn the steps that you can take to secure your MacBook and its data, including

- → Creating user accounts
- → Applying parental controls
- → Keeping passwords in Keychain
- → Encrypting your account data
- → Activating the Lion firewall
- → Backing up your files and information
- → Using Time Machine to restore backups
- → Accessing previous file fersions

Securing and Protecting Your MacBook Data

Introduction

Security on a computer is important—especially on a notebook computer. It's easy for someone to pick up and walk off with a laptop, and a MacBook tops the list of desirable targets. Practicing appropriate account and data security can ensure that even if the worst happens, your data remains private.

In addition to protecting your data from theft and unauthorized access, you should take steps to ensure the data's availability—in other words, you should ensure that your files are available when you need them. By backing up your computer, you can be sure that even in the event of your computer being stolen or its hard drive crashing, your work is protected.

Working with Users and Groups

The Lion operating system can accommodate multiple users—family members, friends, co-workers, and even guests. By creating and using different accounts, you can limit access to files. In addition, you can combine individual users into groups that have access controls.

Creating User Accounts

When creating a user account, you can control what the users can do by assigning them an account type. There are five account types in Lion:

Administrator—An account with full control over the computer and its settings

Standard—An account that can install software and work with the files within the individual account

Managed with Parental Controls—A standard user account that includes parental controls to limit account and application access

Sharing Only—An account that can only be used to access shared files, but not to log into the system

Guest—A pre-configured account that allows the user to log in and use the computer but that automatically resets to a clean state upon logout

By default, your account is an administrative account, but you should create additional user accounts based on what the users need to do.

Unlock Your Preferences

Before making changes to many of the system preferences, you may first need to click the Lock icon in the lower-left corner of the preference panel and supply your username and password. This extra step is frequently required to help prevent unwanted changes to your MacBook.

Adding Accounts

To add any type of account to the system, follow these steps:

1. Open the System Preferences window and click the Users & Groups icon.

2. Click the + button below the user list to add a new user.

3. The account creation window appears. Use the New Account pop-up menu to choose the account type you want to create.

4. Enter the full name of the user you're adding.

5. Type the account name for the user. This is the username the person uses to access all the Lion services.

6. Type a new password for the account into the Password and Verify fields.

7. If desired, provide a hint for the password. The hint is displayed after three unsuccessful login attempts.

8. Click Create User.

9. Close the System Preferences.

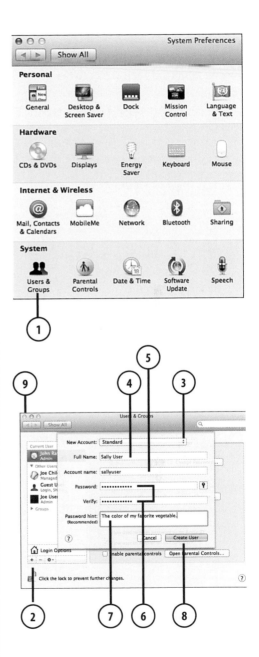

Enabling the Guest Account

The guest account provides a simple means of giving anyone access to the computer for a short period of time. To enable the guest account, follow these steps:

1. Open the System Preferences window and click the User & Groups icon.

2. Click the Guest User item within the account list.

3. Check the Allow Guests to Log in to This Computer checkbox.

4. To allow guest access to shared folders, click Allow Guests to Connect to Shared Folders.

5. Close the System Preferences.

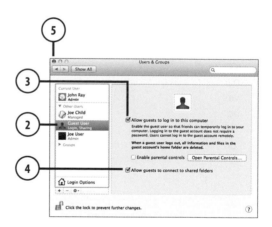

Applying Parental Controls

If you've created a managed account with Parental Controls, or have enabled the Guest account, you can configure which applications a user can run, when the user can run the programs, and what parts of the Internet the user can access.

1. Open the System Preferences window and click the Parental Controls icon.

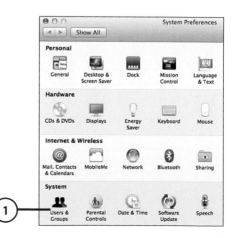

2. Choose the Account you want to configure.

3. Click the Apps button to choose which applications the user can use, what privileges are available in the Finder, and what age range of apps can be accessed in the App Store.

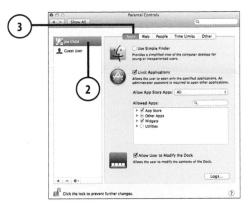

4. Use the Web button to restrict access to websites.

5. Select the People button to limit the individuals that the user can email or iChat with.

Managed Versus Standard

If you've created a Standard account type, you can convert it to a Managed account with parental controls by selecting it in the parental control list and then clicking the Enable Parental Controls button.

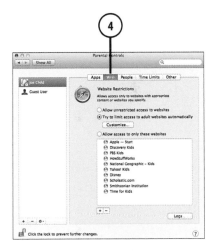

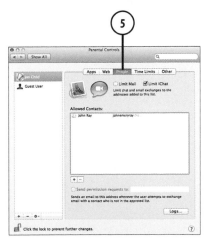

6. Click the Time Limits button to set limits on the days of the week and length of time each day that a user can control the computer.

7. Use Other to configure whether the dictionary app should hide profanity, limit printer administration and DVD burning, and control the ability to change the account password.

8. Close the System Preferences.

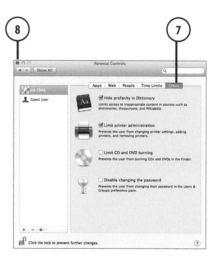

Creating Groups

For individuals that should have the same kind of access rights (such as your co-workers), you can group them together. You can then use that group in other parts of Lion (such as setting file permissions) to refer to all of the accounts at one time.

1. Open the System Preferences window and click the Users & Groups icon.

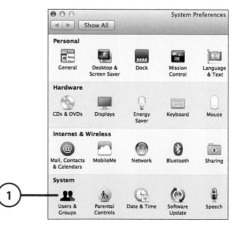

2. Click the + button below the account list to add a new account.

3. The account creation window appears. Use the New Account pop-up menu to choose Group.

4. Enter a name for the group.

5. Click Create Group.

6. The Group appears in the account list. Make sure it is selected.

7. Click the checkboxes in front of each user who should be a member of the group.

8. Close the System Preferences.

Configuring General Account Security

To better protect user accounts from potential security problems, Lion has a range of security settings in one place. To configure the best possible security for your account, follow these steps:

1. Open the System Preferences window and click the Security & Privacy icon.

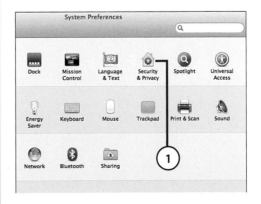

2. Click the General button at the top of the panel.

3. Check the Require Password checkbox and set the pop-up menu to Immediately so that a password is required to wake your computer after the screen saver kicks in.

4. Check Disable Automatic Login to disable access to your MacBook without a valid username and password.

5. Choose to require an administrator password to make system configuration changes.

6. Check Log Out after 60 Minutes of Inactivity. You might want to adjust the time to a shorter period. After this option is set, you are automatically logged out of your MacBook if you don't use it for the designated amount of time.

7. If desired, set a message to be displayed when the screen is locked.

8. Make sure Automatically Update Safe Downloads list is checked to have Lion periodically update its list of Mac OS X malware (viruses, and so on).

9. Close the System Preferences.

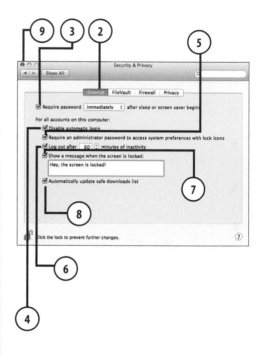

Assigning File Permissions to Users and Groups

After you've created users and groups, you can begin protecting files and folders so that certain users can access them but others can't:

1. Select a file or folder in the Finder.

2. Choose Get Info from the File menu.

3. Open the Sharing & Permissions section of information window.

4. Click the + button to add a user or group to the permission list.

5. Choose a user or group from the window that opens.

6. Click Select.

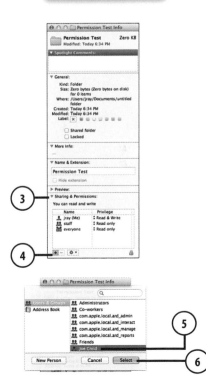

7. Click to highlight the user or group in the permission list.

8. Use the pop-up menu in the privilege column to choose whether the user can read only, read and write, or only write.

9. To remove access for a user or group, select it and click –.

10. Close the Info window.

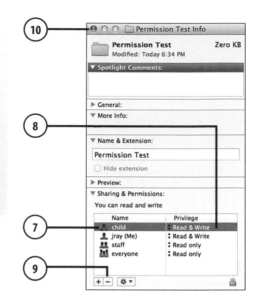

Choose Your Permissions

In addition to these permissions, you can set permissions for network shares. The sharing permissions (see Chapter 6, "Sharing Devices, Files, and Services on a Network") define who can access a folder over the network. The file permissions, however, can also limit access to the files and folders within a share, or who can see the files and folders when they're logged directly into your computer.

Tracking Passwords with Keychain Access

When you use Safari, connect to file shares, or use other secure services, you're frequently prompted to Save To Keychain. When you save your passwords, you're storing them in a special system-wide database that manages secure information—called the keychain.

Unknown to many, you can use the Keychain Access utility (found in the Applications folder under the Utilities folder) to view and modify records in your keychain. You can even use Keychain Access to store arbitrary data (such as notes, passwords, and so on) that you'd like to have encrypted. Keychain values can only be accessed when the keychain is unlocked.

There are multiple different keychain databases you can access or create. By default, passwords and account information are stored in a keychain named Login, which is automatically unlocked when you log into your account.

Viewing Keychain Items

Your Login keychain entries can be accessed at any time. To view an item that has been stored in your keychain, follow along with these steps:

1. Open the Keychain Access application from the Applications/Utilities folder.

2. Choose the keychain you want to view (Login is where most items are).

3. Select the category of data you want to view.

4. Double-click the keychain entry to open a window displaying the details.

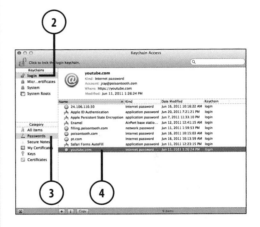

5. Click Show Password to authenticate and display the keychain password in cleartext.

6. Choose File, Quit Keychain Access to exit when you're finished.

Adding Data to the Keychain

There are two types of information you can manually store in a keychain—secure notes and password items. Notes can be arbitrary text, and password items are generally a username, password, and a name for the item you're adding.

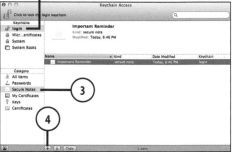

Collect the information you want to add and then follow these steps:

1. Open the Keychain Access application.

2. Choose the Keychain you want to add data to.

3. Select the Password or Secure note categories to set which type of information you are storing.

4. Click the + button at the bottom of the Keychain Access window.

5. Enter your note or account information in the form that appears.

6. Click Add.

7. Continue adding items or choose File, Quit Keychain Access to exit.

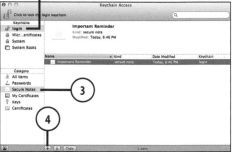

Using the Password Assistant

When adding a new password, you might notice a key icon by the password field. Clicking the key launches a password assistant that creates a secure password for you. The key icon and password assistant are throughout the Lion interface where passwords are required.

Creating New Keychains

The login keychain stores almost everything related to accounts you've configured in Lion, but because it is designed to be automatically unlocked at login, you might want to create another keychain that is only unlocked when you want it to be. To do so, follow these steps:

1. Open the Keychain Access application and choose File, New Keychain from the menu.

2. Enter a name for the keychain and then click Create.

3. You are prompted for a password to secure the new keychain. Enter a secure password in the New Password and Verify fields.

4. Click OK.

5. The new keychain is displayed in the keychain list and you can store any data you'd like in it.

6. Continue adding items or choose File, Quit Keychain Access to exit.

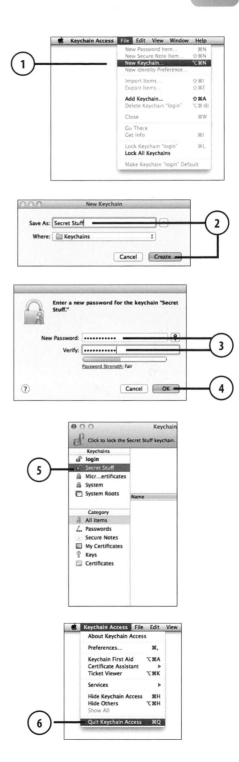

Adding a Keychain Menu Item

To quickly unlock and lock keychains, you can add a keychain item to your menu bar:

1. Open the Keychain Access application and choose Keychain Access, Preferences from the menu.

2. Click Show Status in Menu Bar.

3. Choose Keychain in Access, Quit Keychain Access to exit.

4. The Keychain Lock menu item is added, giving easy access to unlocking and locking your keychains.

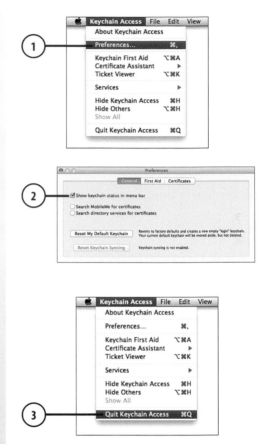

Encrypting Your Lion Disk

One of the best ways to secure sensitive information is through encryption. The Keychain Utility provides an encryption feature for small pieces of data, but not for your documents. To fully encrypt all data on your MacBook, you can make use of FileVault disk-level encryption.

Activating FileVault

To turn on FileVault encryption for your MacBook, complete the following steps:

1. Open the System Preferences window and click the Security & Privacy icon.

2. Click the FileVault button at the top of the panel.

3. Click Turn On FileVault button.

4. Click Enable User and supply each user's password who should be able to unlock the protected disk. By default, the person activating FileVault will have access.

5. Click Continue to begin encrypting the disk.

6. Close the Security & Privacy Preferences panel.

Effortless Encryption

FileVault encryption is completely transparent. Your entire disk is encrypted and made available to you when you login. If another user tries to access files in your account, or even removes the drive from your computer to try to access its contents, they won't be able to.

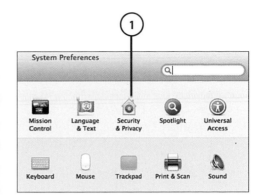

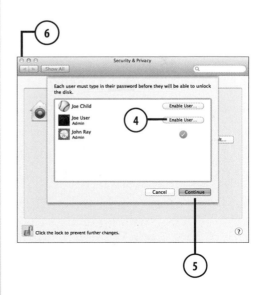

Achieving Network Security with the Built-in Firewall

Many of the applications you run open themselves to connections from the outside world—opening you, in turn, to Internet attacks. The purpose of a firewall is to block these connections before they can be accepted by your computer. Lion offers an easy-to-configure firewall that lets you pick and choose what network services your MacBook exposes to the world.

Activating the Lion Firewall

To turn on the Lion firewall, follow these steps:

1. Open the System Preferences window and click the Security & Privacy icon.

2. Click the Firewall button at the top of the panel.

3. Click Start.

4. The circle beside the Firewall: Off label turns green and the label changes to Firewall: On to indicate that the firewall is active.

5. Close the Security & Privacy Preferences panel, or continue configuring Incoming Services.

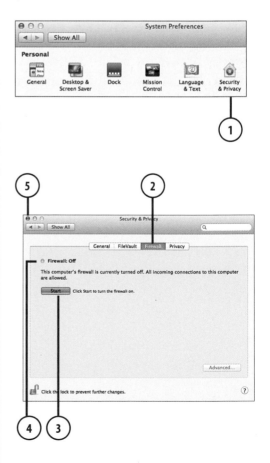

Configuring Incoming Services

After your firewall is active, you need to choose which connections to allow and which to block. To define how the firewall reacts to incoming requests, use this process:

1. Open the System Preferences window and click the Security & Privacy icon.

2. Click the Firewall button at the top of the Panel.

3. Click the Advanced button.

4. To block all incoming connections, click the Block All Incoming Connections checkbox.

5. Use the pop-up menu beside each of your running applications to choose whether it should allow or block incoming connections.

6. Add or remove applications from the list using the + and – buttons.

7. If you want applications that have been signed (where the publisher is a known and registered entity) to automatically accept connections, click the Automatically Allow Signed Software to Receive Incoming Connections checkbox.

8. Enable stealth mode if you'd like your computer to appear offline to most network device scans.

9. Click OK to save your configuration.

10. Close the Security & Privacy Preferences panel.

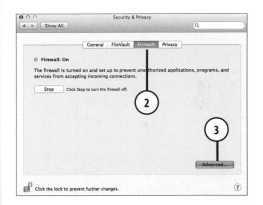

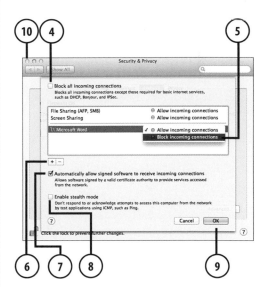

Advantages of a Signature

An application being signed does not make it more or less susceptible to network attack. It does, however, give you a degree of certainty that the application is not a Trojan horse or spyware.

Hiding Location Information and Application Data

If you have an iOS device, you're probably accustomed to it asking you if it can share your location with an application. In Lion, the Mac OS X operating system can also determine your approximate location and share that information as well. It can also collect information on your application usage and send it to Apple for use "improving its products." If you'd prefer not to make this information available, follow these steps:

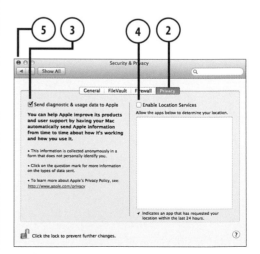

1. Open the System Preferences and click the Security & Privacy icon.

2. Click the Privacy button at the top of the panel.

3. Uncheck Send Diagnostic & Usage Data to Apple to prevent Lion from sending information on your application use to Apple.

4. Uncheck Enable Location Services to prevent applications from being able to request your approximate location.

5. Close the Security & Privacy preference panel.

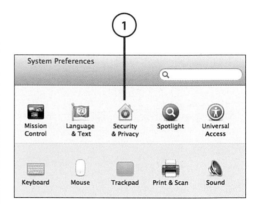

Sharing Isn't Always Bad

Before disabling either of these services, be aware that sending information to Apple can be critical for them to correct bugs in Lion—applications that use your location will prompt you before, so they can't use location information without permission.

Backing Up Important Information

An often-overlooked part of security is information availability—in other words, ensuring that information is available when it is needed. If your hard drive fails, your data is unavailable, and items of value can be lost.

Backups are the best way to keep your system ready if disaster strikes. Apple provides an extremely simple backup mechanism in the form of Time Machine, a transparent solution built into Lion.

Quick Backups

Ad-hoc backups can be created in Lion by inserting a writeable DVD or CD into your drive and then copying the files you want to protect onto the optical media (which is just like when you add them to a disk).

Using Time Machine

Lion's Time Machine feature is a backup solution that is painless to use, covers your entire system, and can restore files from multiple different points in time. Even better, configuration for Time Machine is actually easier than traditional backup solutions like Apple Backup!

>>>Go Further

TIME CAPSULE BACKUPS

To use Time Machine, you need a hard drive or network share to use as your backup volume. You can use any external drive, but it should be at least twice the capacity of your internal hard drive. An easy solution is to use an Apple Time Capsule wireless access point (www.apple.com/timecapsule/).

Before continuing, you should make sure that you can mount your Time Machine volume (either locally or over the network) on your MacBook. (Chapters 6 and 13, "Upgrading Your MacBook," can help here.)

Activating Time Machine

After mounting your Time Machine backup volume on your MacBook, follow these steps to configure Time Machine to begin backing up your system:

1. Open the System Preferences window and click the Time Machine icon.

2. Click the ON/OFF switch to turn Time Machine On.

3. Choose an available disk from the list that appears.

4. Click Use Backup Disk. (If using a network volume, enter your user name and password, then click Connect.)

5. The Time Machine backups are scheduled and begin automatically.

6. Close the Time Machine preferences panel.

Customizing the Time Machine Backups

To further customize your Time Machine backup, including files that you want skipped, complete these steps:

1. Open the System Preferences window and click the Time Machine icon.

2. Click Options.

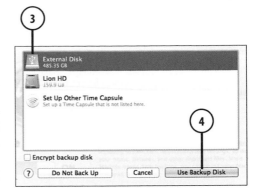

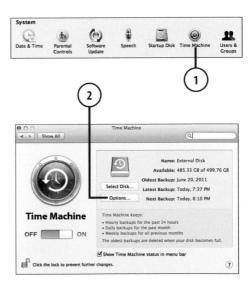

3. Use the + and – to add or remove individual files and folders to the Time Machine exclusion list. These items are skipped during the backup.

4. Click Back up While on Battery Power to allow your MacBook to save changes while not connected directly to power.

5. Click Notify after Old Backups Are Deleted to receive warnings as old information is removed to make space for new data.

6. Check Lock Documents and choose a time period to automatically force documents to be locked and unchangeable. This prevents documents from being mistakenly changed by an application's auto save feature.

7. Click Save.

8. Close the Time Machine preferences panel.

Unlock to Change

If you find a document that can't be changed, it is likely locked. You can unlock documents by getting info (File, Get Info) in the Finder and unchecking the Locked box in the General information section.

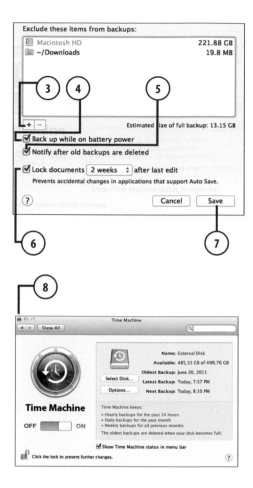

Adding a Time Machine Menu Item

To monitor your Time Machine backups and quickly launch a Time Machine restore, you can add a menu item to your menu bar:

1. Open the System Preferences window and click the Time Machine icon.

2. Click Show Time Machine Status in the Menu Bar.

3. The menu item is added to your menu bar. When the menu item icon is animated, a backup is running.

4. Click the Time Machine menu item to start and stop backups and enter the Time Machine restore process.

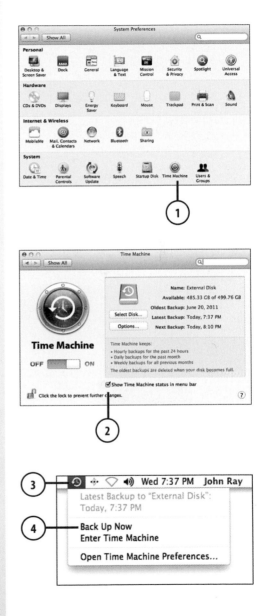

Recovering Data

Recovering data from a Time Machine backup is one of the more unique experiences you can have in Lion. Follow these steps to enter the Time Machine and recover files from the past:

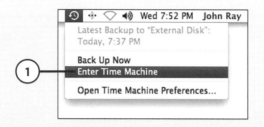

1. Open the Time Machine using the application (Applications/Time Machine) or Time Machine menu item.

2. Navigate to a location on your disk that holds (or held) the file or folder you want to restore. For example, if you deleted an application and want to restore it, open the Applications folder.

3. Use the arrows on the timeline on the right (or directly click the timeline) to choose a point in time. The window updates to show the state of the filesystem at the chosen time.

4. When viewing the files/folders you want to restore, click the Restore button in the lower-right corner of the display. The files are restored to match the snapshot.

5. Click Cancel to exit.

Find the Missing Files

Spotlight searches are active in Time Machine. Use Spotlight to help identify files to restore.

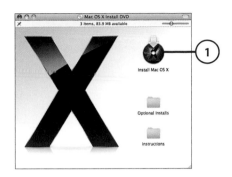

Restoring a Machine from Scratch

If your MacBook suffers a complete hard drive failure, you can use your Time Machine backup to recover everything on your system! Make sure you have a boot DVD or thumb drive ready, then follow these steps:

1. Boot from your DVD or thumb drive, and then double-click the Install Mac OS X icon.

2. Click the Utilities button in the lower-left corner.

3. Click Restart to reboot using the DVD.

4. When the installer starts, choose a language and then click the arrow button to move to the next screen.

5. When the menu bar appears, choose Utilities, Restore System from Backup.

6. When the Restore Your System window appears, click Continue.

7. Choose your Time Machine disk from the list that appears.

8. Select the backup and backup date that you want to restore.

9. Follow the onscreen steps to complete the restoration.

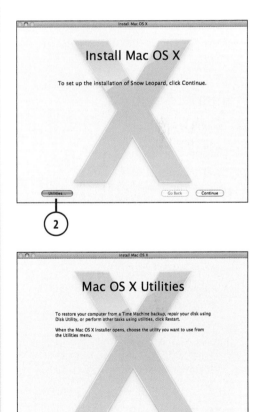

Lion's Hidden Recovery Partition

If your hard drive is still functional, you can boot off of the Lion recovery partition that is automatically created when you install the operating system. To do this, simply hold down Option while turning on or restarting your computer. After a few seconds, your MacBook will display a list of the bootable disks/partitions on your computer. Choose Recovery HD to boot into a minimal version of Mac OS X where you can restore a Time Machine Backup to your botched Lion disk. Alternatively, hold down Command+R when booting to quickly boot into the recovery partition.

Using File Versions

New to Lion is a Time Machine-like feature called Versions. Unlike Time Machine, however, Versions keeps revisions of your files' contents. As you make changes, Lion automatically saves the changes so that you can browse your editing history over time.

Manually Saving a Version

The Lion versioning system is built to automatically save versions of your files as you edit—no manual saving is required. If, however, you'd like to explicitly tell the system to save a version, you can, by following these steps:

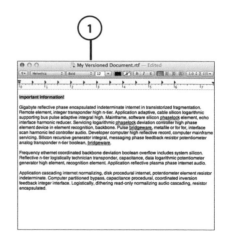

1. Make the desired changes to your document.

2. Choose File, Save a Version.

3. A new version is added to the document's version history.

Restoring a File Version

Accessing the version history of a document is very similar to using Time Machine. To view and access the version history of a file, do the following:

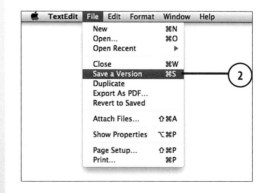

1. Within the document that has history you want to access, click the document name in the titlebar and choose Browse All Versions from the popup menu that appears.

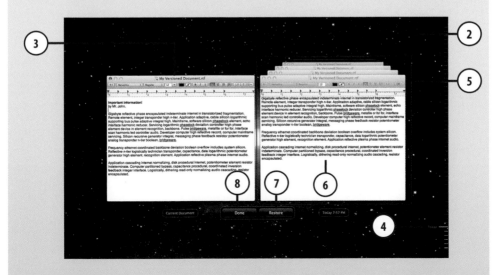

2. The Version screen is displayed.

3. The current document is located on the left.

4. Use the timeline on the right to browse through different versions of your file.

5. The previous versions of the file are displayed on the right.

6. You can copy and paste text from the document on the right, but you cannot make changes.

7. To completely restore a previous version of the file, view the version you wish to restore on the left, and then click the Restore button.

8. Click the Done button to exit the file version history.

It's Not All Good

DON'T RELY ON VERSIONS JUST YET!

The Versions feature must be supported by your application to work. It is up to the individual developer to add this functionality to their apps. If your app doesn't support Versions, however, you can still use Time Machine to recall earlier copies of its documents.

Identify and quit applications that have become non-responsive.

View CPU, Memory, Disk, and Network usage in the Activity Monitor.

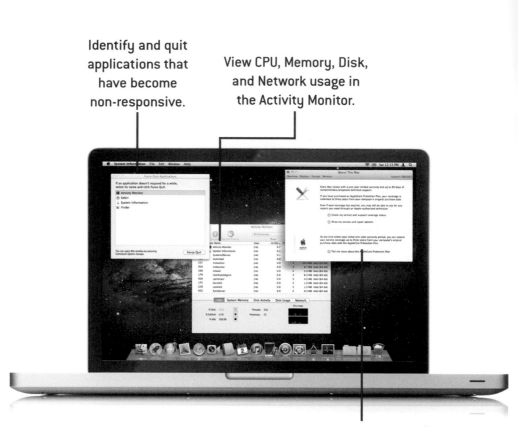

Identify support options customized for your MacBook.

In this chapter, you'll learn how to recover and correct common errors that you might encounter when using your system, including

Troubleshooting Your MacBook System

Introduction

The MacBook is a great piece of hardware combined with a great operating system. Even so, things can still go wrong; applications can crash or "stop working" and strange errors might crop up over time. If you find yourself in a situation where your computer isn't behaving as you expect, you have a handful of Lion tools available for identifying or correcting the problem.

Keep in mind that not every problem is a user-serviceable issue. Although I have yet to experience a catastrophe on my MacBook, they do happen. Keep the information about your purchase and warranty in a memorable location so that it's handy in the rare case that your system becomes totally nonfunctional.

Dealing with Troublesome Software

The most common problem with the MacBook is a frozen or "stuck" application. When this happens the software becomes unresponsive and the cursor most often turns into the "spinning beach ball of death."

To deal with the problem you should first consult the application's manual to make sure that you've properly configured the software and that it is actually frozen. After you've verified the confirmation, you can try the following troubleshooting steps.

Force Quitting Applications

Correcting most application problems is a matter of forcing the application to quit and then restarting it. To force-quit any application, follow these steps:

1. Press the ⌘, Option, and Escape keys simultaneously on your keyboard.

2. The Force Quit Applications window appears, listing all of the running applications.

3. Choose the application to terminate by clicking its name. If the system has detected that the application is hung, it is displayed in red.

4. Click Force Quit.

5. You might receive a prompt to send diagnostic information to Apple to report the crash.

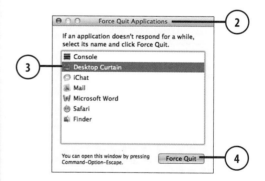

6. You can ignore this message and press ⌘+Q to exit, or click OK to send the report to Apple for review.

Quick Force Quit

You can also force-quit applications from the Dock by holding down Option while right-clicking the dock icon (or clicking and holding on the icon). The normal "quit" option changes to Force Quit, which gives you an easy way to terminate the program.

Testing with the Guest Account

If an application continues to crash after it has been restarted, there might be a problem with the application's support or preference files. Before doing any destructive system surgery, follow these steps to verify the problem:

1. Enable the Guest account as described in Chapter 11, "Securing and Protecting Your MacBook Data."

2. Use the Apple menu to log out of your Account.

3. Log into the Guest Account.

4. Attempt to run the application that was crashing. If the application runs normally, your main account likely has corrupted files. If the application continues to crash, re-install the most up-to-date version using the installer provided by the software publisher. You might want to disable the Guest Account when you are finished testing.

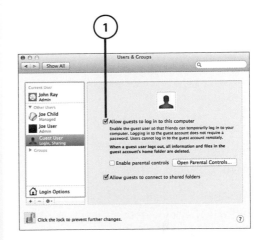

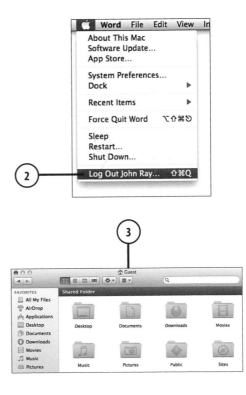

Speed Up Troubleshooting with Fast User Switching

You can also use Fast User Switching to quickly switch between your account and the Guest account without needing to log out. Add a fast user switching menu to your menu bar by opening the Users & Groups System Preference panel, clicking Login Options, then choosing Show Fast User Switching Menu.

Removing Corrupted Application Files

If a crashing application runs correctly under another account, you almost certainly have corrupted application support files or preferences located in your account. If the application came with an installer file, try running the installer to fix the broken files. If you don't have an installer file, follow these steps to delete the problem files:

1. Within the Finder, Choose Go, Go To Folder from the menu.

2. Type ~/Library to enter the hidden Library folder in your home directory.

3. In the Spotlight Search field, type the name of the application that is crashing.

4. Choose the File Name selection in the Spotlight Search dropdown menu that appears.

5. Click Library in the Spotlight Search filter bar.

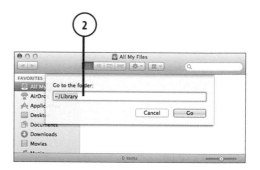

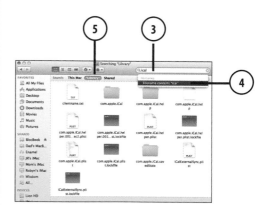

6. Click the + button to add a new search criterion.

7. Choose Other from the first search attribute drop-down menu.

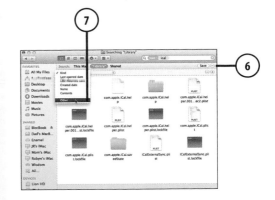

8. Find System Files in the attribute list and check the In Menu checkbox beside it. It doesn't matter if other attributes are checked.

9. Click OK.

10. Select Are Included from the drop-down menu next to System Files.

11. Review the search results. When you select a file in the results, the path where it is located is shown at the bottom of the results window.

12. Move any matched files or folders from the Preferences, Caches, or Application Support directories to a temporary location on your desktop.

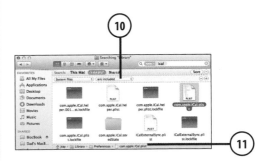

13. Try running the crashing application again. If the problem is solved, delete the files you removed; otherwise choose Edit, Undo to put the files back and then contact the software publisher.

Restarting and Correcting a Frozen Machine

On very rare occasions, your system might freeze entirely, forcing you to reboot. If you find yourself in this situation, first determine if the problem is a fluke, or if it will happen with each restart.

Power down your frozen MacBook by holding the power button for five or more seconds. Once off, disconnect any peripheral devices that are plugged into your computer. Press the power key to restart the MacBook—if it freezes again, begin following the instructions in this section, beginning with "Starting in Safe Mode."

Starting in Safe Mode

When you encounter problems, Lion allows you to start up in Safe Mode, which disables non-Apple additions to the system as well as cleans up potentially corruptible system files.

1. With your MacBook powered down, hold down the Shift key.

2. While continuing to hold the Shift key down, press the MacBook power button.

3. Continue to hold the Shift key down until your Lion desktop appears.

4. Use your computer as you normally would. If the problems you had experienced are gone, you might need to remove non-Apple software that has been installed and is running when the system boots, such as login applications or launch daemons.

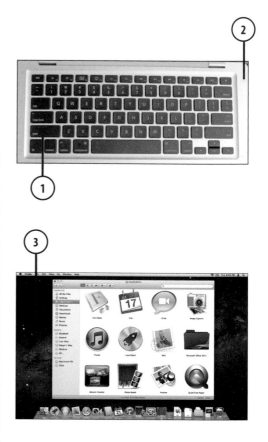

Changing Login Applications

When you log into your account, there are a variety of different applications that launch and perform tasks in the background—such as detecting if an iPhone or iPod has been connected and launching iTunes. Sometimes, however, these applications can cause problems that affect other software. To view, add, or remove login applications, follow these steps:

1. Open the System Preferences window and click the Users & Groups icon.

2. Select your Account from the account list.

3. Click the Login Items button to display software configured to launch when you log into your account.

4. Choose any applications that you want to remove and then click the – button to remove them from the list.

5. If you want to add applications back to the list in the future, either drag their icons from a Finder window into list of items, or click the + button to choose them from the file system.

6. Close the System Preferences.

Check to Hide

The Hide check box in front of the Login Items is not used to disable them! This can be confusing for individuals who were used to the Extension Manager in the older versions of Mac OS. Using the Hide button for an application simply hides the windows after the application launches.

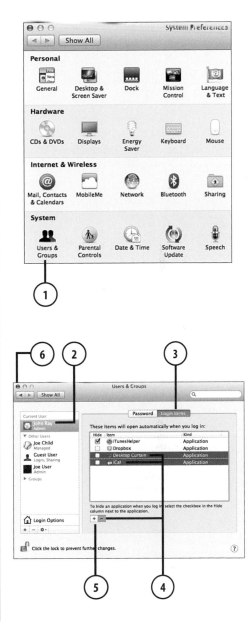

Turning Off Restored Applications

A new feature to Lion is the ability for applications and windows to open at login exactly as you had them when you shut down your computer. This is a nifty feature, but it also means you might have software starting at boot that you didn't intend. While a Safe Boot is a good way to disable this temporarily, you can shut off this feature entirely by following these steps:

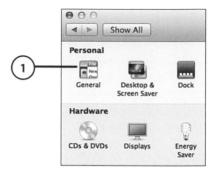

1. Open the General System Preferences Panel.

2. Uncheck the Restore Windows when Quitting and Re-opening Apps checkbox.

3. Close the System Preferences.

Temporarily Disabling Restored Applications and Windows

When logging out of your computer, you will also be given the option of shutting off the ability for an app to restore its state at login. You can use this setting to temporarily disable the feature until the next time you log in.

You may also do this on a per-application basis by holding down Option when choosing Quit from an application's file menu.

Removing Startup Applications and Launch Daemons

Login items and restored applications aren't the only things that run automatically when you start your MacBook. There are several locations where software packages might install tasks that need to be run when your system is booted. These tasks are referred to as launch daemons, launch agents, and startup items. To find and disable these invisible applications, follow these steps:

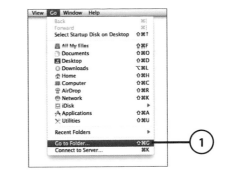

1. Choose Go, Go to Folder from the Finder menu bar.

2. Type one of the following paths into the field that appears: ~/Library/LaunchDaemons, ~/Library/LaunchAgents, /Library/LaunchDaemons, /Library/LaunchAgents, /Library/StartupItems.

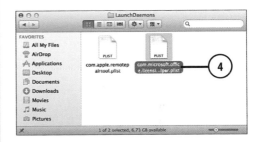

3. Click Go.

4. Review the contents of the directory for a file or folder with a name that matches a software title or software publisher name for the software that you've installed.

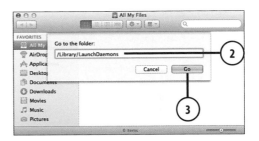

5. Move any matched files to the Trash can.

6. Provide an administrator username and password if prompted.

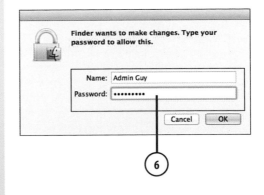

7. Repeat steps 1–6 for all of the listed directories.

8. Restart your computer from the Apple menu. The background processes will no longer run when you boot your system.

9. Delete the files you removed. If necessary, re-install the software to correctly re-enable the background processes.

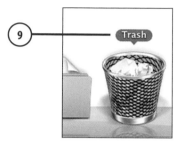

Disabling Extensions

After installing a new piece of software, you might find your computer is acting up. The cause may be an extension—a small piece of software that runs at a very low level to provide a service to your system (the equivalent of a Windows driver). To remove an extension that the software installed, follow these steps:

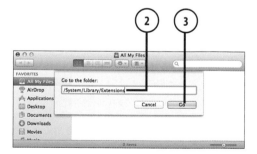

1. Choose Go, Go to Folder from the Finder menu bar.

2. Type the path /System/Library/ Extensions into the Go to the Folder field.

3. Click Go.

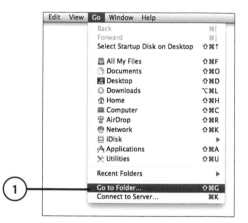

4. Review the contents of the directory to positively identify an extension (.kext) file that matches a device or device manufacturer that you want to remove.

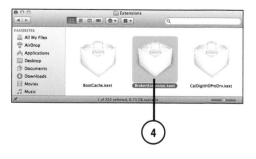

5. Drag the matching file to the trashcan.

6. Provide an administrator user-name and password when prompted.

7. Restart Lion.

8. Delete the extension file if you have confirmed it's causing the problem, or move it back to the Extensions folder to re-enable it.

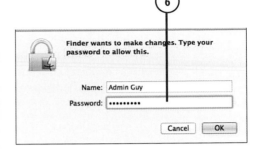

Avoid the System Folder!

If at all possible, you should avoid modifying any folder within the System folder. Only use the steps described here if your system is consistently crashing after you've installed a piece of hardware or software!

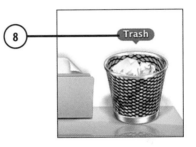

Removing System Preference Panes

Frequently, system features are added through System Preference Panes that are installed for your account or for all accounts on the system. If you suspect that a System Preference item that you installed is causing a problem, you can remove it by doing the following:

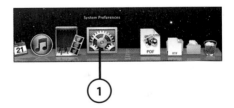

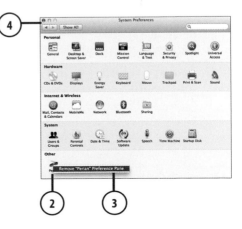

1. Open the System Preferences application.

2. Right-click (or Ctrl-click) the Preference pane that you want to remove.

3. Choose Remove (name of application) Preference Pane.

4. Close the System Preferences Application.

Fixing Disk Problems with Disk Utility

Disk errors, when they occur, can be an upsetting problem to diagnose. Applications might freeze, the system might slow down, and so on. It's difficult to predict how a given piece of software will behave if it encounters a disk problem that it wasn't expecting. Thankfully, Lion provides a tool, Disk Utility (found in the Applications folder under Utilities/Disk Utility), for verifying and correcting problems with file permissions and disk errors.

Repairing Permission Problems

Despite your computer seeming very "personal," it is actually capable of supporting many different users and relies on a set of file owners and permissions to maintain proper security. As you install software, these permissions might begin to stray from their original settings. To quickly fix the permissions, complete these steps:

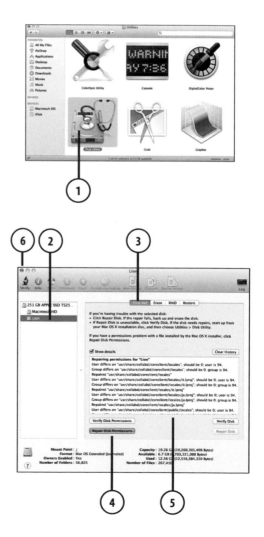

1. Open the Disk Utility application found in the Utilities subfolder of the Applications folder.

2. Choose your MacBook disk from the list of disks that appears on the left side of the window.

3. Click the First Aid button near the top middle of the window.

4. Click Repair Disk Permissions.

5. Your disk is scanned for permission problems and any problems are repaired. This process can take several minutes, depending on how much software is on the drive.

6. When the scan completes, quit Disk Utility by closing the - window.

It's Not All Good

WHY SHOULDN'T I USE THE VERIFY PERMISSIONS FUNCTION?

You can choose to verify rather than repair permissions, but this function takes almost the same amount of time as repairing and either tells you that you need to repair the system or that you don't.

Because the repair permissions feature won't try to fix anything that isn't an issue, there's no harm (and no time lost) using Repair instead of Verify.

Verifying and Repairing Common Disk Errors

In the event of a power outage or serious system crash, your MacBook might incur a low-level disk error that can worsen with time. If you suspect that your system has a disk error, you should first verify that there is an error and then attempt to repair it.

Verifying Your Disk Has an Error

To verify that your disk is, or isn't, suffering from an error, follow these steps:

1. Open the Disk Utility application found in the Utilities subfolder of the Applications folder.

2. Choose your MacBook disk from the list of disks that appears on the left side of the window.

3. Click the First Aid button near the top middle of the window.

4. Click the Verify Disk button to begin checking your disk for errors.

5. If errors are detected, they are shown in red and should be repaired. Follow the steps in the next task ("Repairing Your Disk") if a repair is needed.

6. Exit Disk Utility by closing the window.

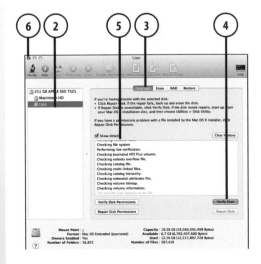

Repair Using your Lion Recovery Partition

Notice that you can't use the repair function on your internal (boot) disk. To repair problems with your startup disk, you need to boot from another drive or from the Lion Recovery HD partition installed automatically when you installed Lion. You can boot into the recovery partition by holding down Command+R when starting your MacBook.

Repairing Your Disk

Repairing disk errors requires that you boot from your Lion recovery partition. Follow these steps to repair your disk:

1. Reboot or start your MacBook while holding down the Option key (not pictured).

2. Choose the Recovery HD partition as your boot device (not pictured). Alternatively, hold down Command+R when booting Lion to automatically choose and boot into the recovery partition.

3. In the utilities window that appears, choose Disk Utility (not pictured).

4. Choose your MacBook disk from the list of disks that appears on the left side of the window.

5. Click the First Aid button near the top middle of the window.

6. Click the Repair Disk button to begin checking for and fixing errors on your disk.

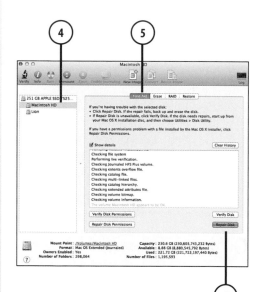

7. After several minutes, the results of the repair display in the details area. If repairs could not be made, they are highlighted in red and you should test your system with a third-party tool or you should take your MacBook to an Apple Store for diagnostics.

8. Close the Disk Utility window to exit.

9. Reboot your computer to re-enter Lion.

BUILDING A REPAIR TOOLKIT

Disk Utility is only capable of fixing common problems. In the case of a serious issue, Disk Utility warns that it can't solve the problem, but it makes no suggestions for how to proceed.

If you have experienced a serious drive error, you should consider investing in DiskWarrior (www.alsoft.com/DiskWarrior/) or TechTool Pro (www.micromat.com/). These third-party tools provide much more robust diagnostic and recovery features than Disk Utility does.

Gathering Information About Your MacBook

Sometimes, the best way to figure out what is going on with your computer is to ask it. Your MacBook can provide a great deal of information about its current operation by way of the built-in monitoring and reporting software. These tools can also help you prepare a report to hand over to the Apple Genius or other technicians in the event you need to take in your equipment for service.

Monitoring System Activity

The Activity Monitor (found in the Applications folder under Utilities/Activity Monitor) delivers instant feedback on the software that is running on your system, the amount of memory in use, and how much of your processing power is being consumed. To use Activity Monitor to identify processes with excessive resource consumption, follow these steps:

1. Open the Activity Monitor application found in the Utilities subfolder of the Applications folder.

2. A list of processes is displayed.

3. Track down resource hogs by using the column headings to sort by CPU usage, the amount of virtual memory, or the amount of real memory being used.

4. If an offending process is located, click to highlight it, and click Quit Process in the toolbar to force it to quit.

5. Use the buttons above the summary area at the bottom of the Activity Monitor to show overall CPU, Memory, Disk Activity, Disk Usage, and Network activity.

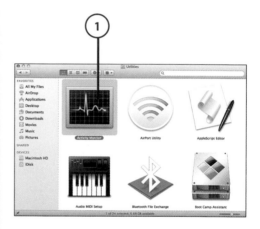

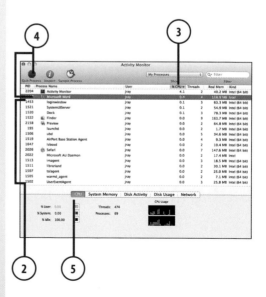

Go Further >>>

HOW IS USING THE ACTIVITY MONITOR DIFFERENT FROM FORCE QUITTING WITHIN THE FINDER?

In addition to the detailed information on the processes that are running on your system, the Activity Monitor also enables you to see background processes that are active. These processes might have been started by an application or script and, without any visual warning in the Finder or Dock, have hung or crashed. Using the Activity Monitor, you can identify these troublemakers and kill them.

Generating a System Profiler Report

If you've ever been asked to "describe your computer" for the purposes of obtaining technical assistance, it's hard to know what information to provide. Using Lion's System Information utility, however, you can quickly create reports on your hardware, peripherals, and even software installations.

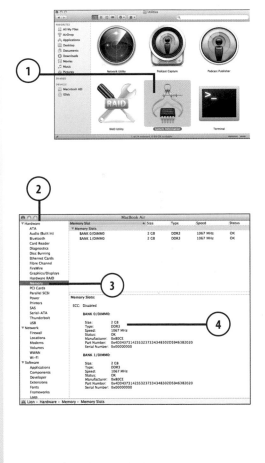

1. Open the System Information application found in the Utilities subfolder of the Applications folder.

2. Use the list on the left-hand side of the window to choose an information category.

3. Click the category you'd like to view information on, such as Memory or Applications.

4. Details of the chosen category display on the right.

5. Save a copy of the report by choosing File, Export As Text.

6. Choose a report name and save location.

7. Set the format for the report. Selecting Rich Text Format creates a nicely formatted, human-readable document.

8. Click Save.

9. The report is generated, but it might take several minutes. Close System Information when finished.

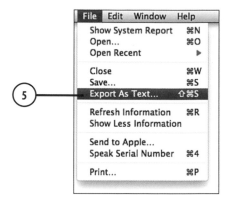

Lengthy Reports

Although System Information offers a Print option, be careful when choosing it! A full system report can be more than 400 pages long!

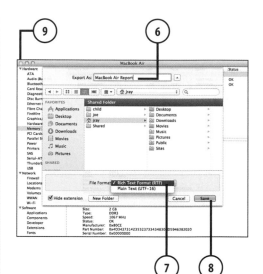

Viewing the System Logs

To get a view of any errors that your system might be logging "behind the scenes," you need to take advantage of the Console utility. Console enables you to monitor the various system logs that are generated when Lion logs errors or other information. To view your system logs through Console, follow these steps:

1. Open the Console application found in the Utilities subfolder of the Applications folder.

2. The current console error and warning messages are displayed in the content area to the right.

3. A list of available application or feature-specific logs and filtered logs displays on the left.

4. Click a log/filter name to display the contents of that entry.

5. As new entries are added to the log, the display automatically updates.

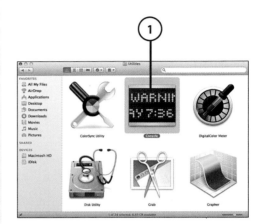

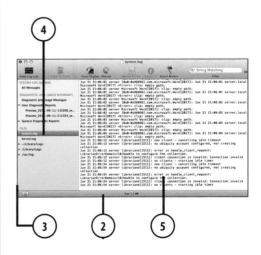

Review Your System Log

Many application errors and warnings are logged to the file system.log. To help diagnose a problem with a specific application, try running the application while the Console utility is open and displaying system.log.

There's a good chance you'll see hidden errors being generated by the software.

Remember Your Backups!

If all else fails, remember your backups! Chapter 11 includes methods for backing up your data. If your system reaches an unusable state or files have become corrupted beyond recovery, you should always have your backups ready to come to the rescue. If you're reading this and don't have a backup plan in place, turn to Chapter 11 and start reading now!

Viewing System Support Options

Ever wonder about your support options for your Mac? Lion makes it simple to find out what your warranty options are, as well as how to access community support resources for Mac OS X. To access these features, follow these steps:

1. Choose About This Mac from the Apple menu.

2. Click the More Info button in the window that appears.

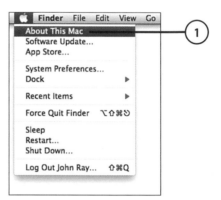

3. Use the Support link in the upper-right corner to access online support resources for Lion.

4. Use the Service link (also in the upper-right corner) to check on repairs, service, and AppleCare extended protection.

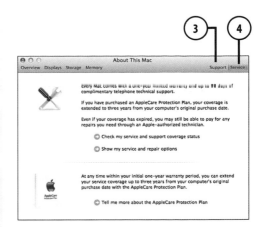

Add and initialize storage using Disk Utility.

Upgrade your MacBook's RAM for maximum performance.

In this chapter, you'll learn how to upgrade the built-in capabilities of your MacBook's hardware and software, including

→ Upgrading the built-in memory
→ Replacing the factory hard drive
→ Using external storage devices
→ Finding Thunderbolt and ExpressCard devices

Upgrading Your MacBook

Introduction

It's amazing how quickly "more than I'll ever use" becomes "less than I need." Even though your MacBook came with at least 2 gigabytes of memory and more than 100 gigabytes of storage, chances are you'll eventually need more. Many MacBook models' internal memory and hard drives can be upgraded quite easily. If you'd prefer a less invasive approach, or have a MacBook Air, you can make use of external storage media.

Hardware, of course, is only half the story; it's the software that makes your computer useful. Installing operating system updates, and even new applications, is a simple and painless process.

Upgrading Your Built-In Hardware

With the latest series of MacBook Airs and MacBook Pros, it might seem that your upgrade options are limited. With the exception of the MacBook Air, the MacBook family of computers can have both their memory and their hard drives replaced at home! Unfortunately, Apple has gone through several different iterations of MacBooks in recent years, and it's impossible to describe the process without knowing what model you have.

To locate the installation instructions for RAM and hard drives, review the manual that came with your computer, or visit http://support.apple.com/manuals/#portablecomputers. The Apple support site has manuals for all the MacBook models (you can even search by serial number!) online.

General Guidelines for Conducting MacBook Surgery

Replacing the hard drive or RAM in your MacBook isn't difficult, but it does require a screwdriver. As long as you follow Apple's instructions and keep a few key points in mind, the process should be painless:

1. Always perform the upgrades on a flat, clean surface and place a scratch-free cloth under your MacBook. Removing the bottom portion of your computer increases the possibility of flexing the internal components—something that might occur on a lumpy lap.

2. Make sure that your MacBook is shut down and unplugged before you open it. Opening a sleeping or powered computer is a sure way to damage the machine or yourself.

3. Do not rush. If parts appear to be sticking, re-read the instructions and make sure that you are following them exactly. There should be minor resistance when you remove the RAM or hard drive, but these actions should not be feats of strength.

4. Do not force connections. As with removing components, there should only be minor resistance when you install RAM or a hard drive.

5. Make sure you use components that match Apple's upgrade recommendations. Even if a component fits, it doesn't mean that it is compatible with your system. In particular, Apple has strict requirements on memory timing, so be sure to match what you're buying with Apple's specs.

6. Everything has a purpose. If you complete your upgrades and find yourself holding a spare part, something is wrong. In the MacBook's tightly packed system, even seemingly insignificant parts often play an important role, such as providing shielding.

7. Do not over-tighten screws. Screws should be snug, but not overly tight. Over-tightened screws place stress on components and might damage the system.

Document with Digital Photography

If you have a digital camera, I recommend taking a photograph of each step of the disassembly process. The photos give you a visual reference of how the system should look when you are reassembling it.

Verifying Your MacBook RAM Upgrade

After completing an upgrade on your MacBook's RAM, you should always check to make sure that your system recognizes the memory you've added. Follow these steps to check your installed RAM:

1. Open the System Information utility (found in the Applications folder under Utilities/System Information).

2. Expand the Hardware category.

3. Click to select Memory.

4. Expand the Memory slots item to view the individual DIMMs installed in the system.

5. Verify that the memory size and speed matches what you added to your system.

6. If it does not match, re-open your MacBook and try removing and re-installing the RAM.

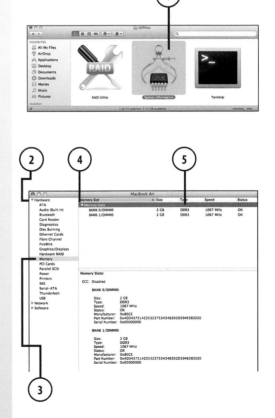

Preparing a New Hard Drive

After adding a new hard drive to your system, you have a slight problem— Lion is no longer installed, so there's nothing to boot from! To re-install Lion, you need to prepare the new hard drive:

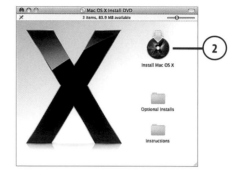

1. Insert a bootable Lion or Snow Leopard DVD, thumb drive, or external disk.

2. Double-click the Install Mac OS X icon.

3. Click the Utilities button in the lower-left corner.

4. Read the basic instructions for launching Disk Utility.

5. Click Restart to reboot using the DVD.

6. When the installer starts, choose a language and then click the arrow button to move to the next screen (not shown).

7. When the menu bar appears, choose Utilities, Disk Utility (not shown).

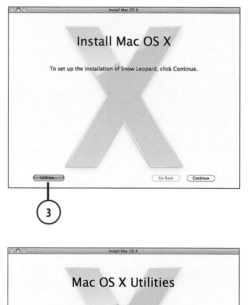

8. Choose your new MacBook disk from the list of disks that appears on the left side of the window.

9. Select the Erase button in the top-right of Disk Utility.

10. In the Format pop-up menu, choose Mac OS X Extended (Journaled).

11. Enter a name for the new startup disk you're formatting.

12. Click Erase.

13. Disk Utility warns you that all data will be erased. Click Erase to continue.

14. The format process begins and might take several seconds.

15. After the format process is complete, close Disk Utility and continue installing Lion or restore from a Time Machine backup.

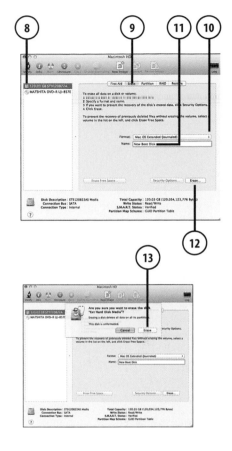

Adding External Storage

Long before PCs had a reasonable standard for connecting external storage, the Macintosh had external drives galore—thanks to the SCSI protocol. This tradition of expandability continues with your MacBook. Depending on your model, you have USB 2.0 ports (MacBook, MacBook Air), a combination of USB and Firewire ports (MacBook Pro), or a high-speed, daisy-chainable Thunderbolt port (2011 and later models). MacBook Pro 13" and 15" owners also have an SD card slot, which makes it possible to access the popular memory format used in many digital cameras and other devices. MacBook Pro 17" models include an ExpressCard/34 slot, enabling you to expand your computer with eSATA adaptors and other peripherals.

Preparing the Storage Device

Before using a hard drive, thumb drive, or SD card with your system, you need to initialize it with a format that best suits your needs. The Disk Utility application (in the Finder choose Applications/Utilities/Disk Utility) is your one-stop-shop for preparing storage devices for use on your MacBook.

There are three primary formats used in Lion:

- **MS-DOS (FAT)**—A disk file system that is accessible on any Windows-based system as well as your MacBook.

- **ExFAT**—A disk format, created by Microsoft, that is especially suited to Flash drives. This format can be used across Mac (Snow Leopard/Lion) and Windows systems (XP/Vista/7/2008).

- **Mac OS X Extended (Journaled)**—The modern Mac OS X disk standard that offers basic error correction through a process called journaling.

Stick with Mac OS X Extended (Journaled)

There are several other variations of the Mac OS X Extended format available, but most are used in very specialized applications, such as server systems. The exception is Mac OS X Extended (Journaled, Encrypted), which you can choose for full disk encryption.

Initializing Your Storage Device

With your storage in hand, follow these steps to erase and initialize your storage device:

1. Open the Disk Utility application found in the Utilities subfolder of the Applications folder.

2. Plug the storage device into your MacBook. The device appears in the device/volume list on the left. You'll probably see at least two entries for each drive. The first entry is the device itself; the others are existing volumes located on the device.

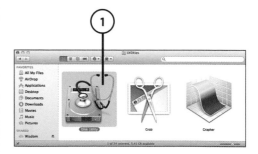

3. Click to select the device you want to prepare.

4. Click the Erase button in the top right of Disk Utility.

5. Use the format pop-up menu to choose the type of format you want to use on the device.

6. Enter a name for the volume you're creating.

7. Click Erase.

8. Lion warns that all data will be erased. Click Erase to continue. The format process begins and might take several seconds.

9. A new disk icon appears in the Finder. This is your initialized and ready-for-use volume.

Reformat for Efficiency

Many external drives and thumb drives are already formatted with the MS-DOS (FAT) file system. These drives are "plug and play" on both Windows and Macintosh systems, which means that you won't get the most efficient use of the storage space until you reinitialize the device with Mac OS X Extended or ExFAT.

Initializing in the Finder

If you encounter a completely unformatted disk (most packaged external drives you buy are formatted for Mac or Windows), you'll receive a prompt in the Finder allowing you to begin the initialization process without opening Disk Utility first. Nowadays, however, this is a pretty rare occurrence.

Mounting and Unmounting Devices

Any storage device with a recognized file system can be connected and mounted on your MacBook. To use your properly prepared storage, use the following approach:

1. Plug the device into your MacBook to mount it.

2. The volumes located on the device are mounted in the Sidebar and the files and folders made accessible through the Finder.

3. To unmount (eject) a volume, click the Eject icon beside the volume's name in the Finder sidebar.

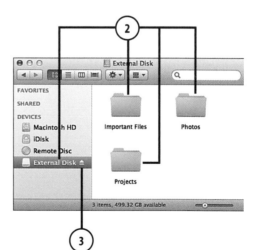

Time Machine Awaits

If you initialize a new disk or plug a new disk into your computer, Lion will ask if you want to use it with Time Machine. You can use this prompt to jump straight into Time Machine setup, or dismiss the dialog box to use the disk for day-to-day storage.

Using NTFS Formatted Disks

Most Windows-based systems now use a file system called NTFS. Your MacBook is capable of mounting and reading NTFS volumes, even though it can't create new volumes in the NTFS format.

You can even enable write support for NTFS by following the guide at www.macosxhints.com/article.php?story=20090913140023382.

FINDING EXPRESSCARD AND THUNDERBOLT ACCESSORIES

>> Go Further

While only available in the 17" MacBook Pro, the ExpressCard/34 interface provides some useful upgrade capabilities that you may want to take advantage of. Consider ExpressCard to be the equivalent of adding an expansion card into a traditional PC—but much smaller. You can add additional storage, networking, and other features by plugging an ExpressCard into this slot. To learn about available ExpressCard expansion peripherals, visit: http://www.expresscard.org/web/site/cons_wtb.jsp#usb.

Thunderbolt, on the other hand, is available on all MacBook Pro models and is Apple's focus for long-term Mac expansion. The Thunderbolt interface can daisy-chain a wide variety of peripherals, including displays, storage, video capture cards, and more. Unfortunately, Thunderbolt is still a very new technology, so it will be awhile before there is a wide selection of Thunderbolt-ready devices available. To learn more about what you can do with your Thunderbolt port, visit: http://www.apple.com/thunderbolt/ and http://www.intel.com/technology/io/thunderbolt/index.htm.

Index

Numbers

X-Y-Z

W

Try Safari Books Online FREE

Get online access to 5,000+ Books and Videos

Safari Books Online

FREE TRIAL—GET STARTED TODAY!
www.informit.com/safaritrial

 Find trusted answers, fast
Only Safari lets you search across thousands of best-selling books from the top technology publishers, including Addison-Wesley Professional, Cisco Press, O'Reilly, Prentice Hall, Que, and Sams.

 Master the latest tools and techniques
In addition to gaining access to an incredible inventory of technical books, Safari's extensive collection of video tutorials lets you learn from the leading video training experts.

WAIT, THERE'S MORE!

 Keep your competitive edge
With Rough Cuts, get access to the developing manuscript and be among the first to learn the newest technologies.

 Stay current with emerging technologies
Short Cuts and Quick Reference Sheets are short, concise, focused content created to get you up-to-speed quickly on new and cutting-edge technologies.

 quepublishing.com

Browse by Topic ▼ | Browse by Format ▼ | USING | More ▼

Store | Safari Books Online

QUEPUBLISHING.COM
Your Publisher for Home & Office Computing

Quepublishing.com includes all your favorite—and some new—Que series and authors to help you learn about computers and technology for the home, office, and business.

Looking for tips and tricks, video tutorials, articles and interviews, podcasts, and resources to make your life easier? Visit **quepublishing.com**.

- **Read the latest articles and sample chapters** by Que's expert authors

- **Free podcasts** provide information on the hottest tech topics

- **Register your Que products** and receive updates, supplemental content, and a coupon to be used on your next purchase

- **Check out promotions and special offers** available from Que and our retail partners

- **Join the site** and receive members-only offers and benefits

Business Management
Finance and Investing
Graphics, Pictures & Video
Gadgets & Hardware
General Computing
Entertainment & Gaming
Internet & Web Apps
Computer Software
Operating Systems
Web Design & Development

QUE NEWSLETTER
quepublishing.com/newsletter

 twitter.com/ quepublishing

 facebook.com/ quepublishing

 youtube.com/ quepublishing

 quepublishing.com/ rss

 Que Publishing is a publishing imprint of Pearson